EDITED BY
RAMON LOBATO
& JAMES MEESE
# GEOBLOCKING AND GLOBAL VIDEO CULTURE

Theory on Demand #18
Geoblocking and Global Video Culture

Editors: Ramon Lobato and James Meese
Copy-editing: Leonieke van Dipten

Editorial support: Miriam Rasch
Cover Design: Katja van Stiphout
DTP: Leonieke van Dipten
EPUB development: Leonieke van Dipten
Infographics: Sandra Hanchard

Printer: Print on Demand
Publisher: Institute of Network Cultures, Amsterdam, 2016
ISBN: 978-94-92302-03-8

Contact
Institute of Network Cultures Phone: +3120 5951865 Email: info@networkcultures.org
Web: http://www.networkcultures.org
This publication is available through various print on demand services. For more information, and a freely downloadable PDF: http://networkcultures.org/publications This
publication is licensed under the Creative Commons Attribution-NonCommercial-NoDe-
rivatives 4.0 International (CC BY-NC-SA 4.0).

institute of
network cultures

CONTENTS

PREFACE AND ACKNOWLEDGEMENTS

Geoblocking and Global Video Culture is the result of a collaborative research experiment we conducted with the contributors to this book. Our aim was to investigate how online blocking and circumvention are shaping access to digital video in different parts of the world, and explore what this means for screen culture today. Together, we set up a comparative research project around some common questions: What tools are people using to access blocked video content in different countries? What kinds of content are they watching? And what is the political context for these circumvention activities? The chapters collected here are the end result of this collaboration, and a corresponding call for papers. The first section of the book explores the dynamics, histories and possible futures of territorial rights control in various media industries, while the second section compares ground-level circumvention practices in nine countries – Australia, Brazil, China, Cuba, Iran, Malaysia, Sweden, Turkey, and the United States.

Given how fast things move in video culture, a book of this nature cannot be definitive. We wanted instead to produce a timely, transnational account of the geoblocking phenomenon, with a comparative dimension that could speak across diverse local experiences. Rather than dense academic prose, our contributors provide vivid snapshots of user practices and provocative reflections on the relationship between geoblocking, government censorship, circumvention, and copyright. We hope you enjoy the eclectic nature of the collection.

Of course, we could not have undertaken such a task without the support and assistance of numerous colleagues and friends. We would like to thank Leonieke van Dipten, Geert Lovink and Miriam Rasch at Institute of Network Cultures for their enthusiastic support of the project, Karen Horsley for production assistance, and Sandra Hanchard for the maps and data visualizations. We are also indebted to Philip Branch, Angela Daly, Evan Elkins, Scott Ewing, Dan Golding, Jennifer Holt, Grace Lee, Teresa Calabria, Rebecca Olive, Claudy Op Den Kamp, Hal Roberts, Nic Suzor, Leah Tang, Julian Thomas and Patrick Vonderau, among others, for their advice, support and feedback. Finally, we thank Swinburne University of Technology and the Australian Research Council Discovery programme for funding this project.

INTRODUCTION: THE NEW VIDEO GEOGRAPHY

RAMON LOBATO

This book is about the cultural geography of video streaming. It is about platforms – YouTube, iPlayer, DailyMotion, Netflix, Periscope, Youku – and how they manage their international audiences and shape them into markets. It is about governments, state institutions and public-service broadcasters, and the technologies they use to regulate video flows across national borders. It is about users and audiences, and how they negotiate diverse forms of access and restriction. Above all, it is about cultural circulation – how different kinds of content reach dispersed audiences through authorized and unauthorized channels.

As an entry point into these wider issues, contributors to this book focus on a specific technology of access control: geoblocking. Geoblocking, a spatially-aware filtering tech-nology that uses IP address databases to determine a user's location, has become a key mechanism for managing international video streaming traffic and maintaining separation of national media markets. The process is simple: when you visit a website, your IP address (e.g. 198.8.80.200) is run through a database to identify your ISP and geographic location, which is then matched against a blacklist or whitelist to establish access rights. If you are in an approved location, access is granted and the video automatically plays. Those outside the authorized zone will likely see a familiar error message – something like 'this video is not available in your region' – or perhaps an endlessly buffering screen.

Most major video platforms use geoblocking to filter international audiences. Geoblocking allows these platforms to customise their offerings according to territory, language, and advertising markets, and provides an automated mechanism to enforce territorial licensing arrangements with rights-holders. In this sense it is a form of access control enacted at the level of content and platform regulation, rather than network infrastructure.[1] But geoblocking has more subtle effects as well. Like search localisation and algorithmic recommendation, geoblocking is a 'soft' form of cultural regulation. Its widespread adoption is changing the nature of the open internet by locating users within national cyberspaces and customising content based on certain ideas about territorial markets.

Geoblocking and Global Video Culture takes these issues as the basis for a critical and eclectic discussion of the internet's changing cultural geography. Many contributors to this book are screen scholars, interested in the politics of media globalisation and how this translates into the digital environment. Other contributors approach the topic through legal analysis, cultural history, and spatial theory. Together, these essays offer a series of distinctive stories about a fast-changing and complex issue. Mixing macro-level insights with bottom-up accounts of everyday user experience, and moving from Europe to South

---

1   In this sense our approach can be distinguished from studies of the material infrastructure of the
      internet. For example, see: Lisa Parks and Nicole Starosielski, *Signal Traffic: Critical Studies of Media
      Infrastructures*, University of Illinois Press, 2015.

America to the Asia-Pacific, the various essays in this book provide provocative arguments about the cultural implications of the new video geography.

A major theme of the book is circumvention. As with many digital rights management technologies, geoblocking systems can be easily tricked. In recent years the appearance of user-friendly circumvention tools – including VPNs (virtual private networks), DNS (domain name system) proxies, web proxies, and location-masking browser extensions – has unleashed a wave of unauthorised cross-border media activity, allowing audiences to easily access streaming, news and sports services from other countries. As we shall soon see, these and other tools are used by a wide cross-section of users, and for remarkably different purposes. In exploring these various forms of blockage and circumvention, and the connections between them, our aim is to tell a different kind of story about internet blocking beyond the 'digital divide' paradigm.

Geoblocking circumvention is closely linked to other issues including internet governance, censorship, and cultural policy, because the same privacy tools that can be used to hack into iPlayer or Hulu are in other contexts used to get around state internet censorship. As researchers at Harvard University's Berkman Center for Internet and Society have documented, global circumvention – encompassing the use of commercial VPNs, activist-designed tools, simple web proxies and HTTP/SOCKS proxies – is an activity that involves tens of millions of internet users worldwide.[2] In Turkey, Iran, China and other nations where popular video and social networking platforms are regularly blocked by the state, circumvention is a mainstream practice.

One of our aims in *Geoblocking and Global Video Culture* is to explore linkages between these various blocking and circumvention practices – site-blocking, geoblocking, and the tactics people use to get around them. To this end, we have organized the book into two sections. The first section, 'Perspectives on Geoblocking', probes the historical, legal and cultural dimensions of geo-location and region control in media industries. These essays investigate a diverse array of platforms – from live-streaming apps and illegal streaming websites to the game consoles of the 1980s – and provide theoretical tools to understand the evolution of regional lock-out technologies in particular media sectors. The second section, 'Circumvention Case Studies', looks at these issues from the ground up, by analysing how users negotiate geoblocking and internet filtering controls in different countries. Here, our nine contributors – experts on informal media circulation that we have collaborated with over the course of a year-long research project – have written vivid first-hand accounts of ground-level circumvention practices in nine countries: China, Australia, Turkey, Sweden, Malaysia, Brazil, Iran, Cuba and the United States. Each of these countries has a different

---

2   Berkman Center researchers have produced a series of pioneering studies of internet filtering, censorship and circumvention. See: Ronald Deibert et al. (eds), *Access Denied: The Practice and Policy of Global Internet Filtering*, Cambridge, MA: MIT Press, 2008; Hal Roberts et al, *2010 Circumvention Tool Usage Report*, Cambridge, MA: Berkman Center for Internet and Society, 2010; Deibert et al (eds), *Access Controlled: The Shaping of Power, Rights, and Rule in Cyberspace*, Cambridge, MA: MIT Press, 2010; Deibert et al. (eds), *Access Contested: Security, Identity, and Resistance in Asian Cyberspace*, Cambridge, MA; MIT Press, 2012.

story to tell when it comes to geoblocking, and together these accounts provide a fascinating snapshot of global circumvention practice (broadly defined).

To provide a taste of what is to come, I will now introduce three cross-cutting issues that connect the various essays in this book. First, I discuss the experience of blockage as a foundational logic of the internet; second, the history of circumvention technologies and practices; and third, the relationship between political censorship and pleasurable consumption, as seen through the lens of geoblocking.

Blockage and Flow

One of our starting points when developing the idea for this book was the uncontroversial observation that, for many internet users, the experience of online video is characterised by blockage rather than flow. Governments (and ISPs) block internet sites for reasons related to public policy and political expediency. Media companies use geo-filtering to screen out undesirable audiences. Poor infrastructure and choked servers lead to delays, dropouts and buffering. The end result of these back-end blockages, from the perspective of the end-user, is that digital video culture becomes a set of unevenly distributed experiences with a peculiar geography of availability and unavailability. As Ira Wagman and Peter Urquhart observe, 'the fact remains that *where* you access the internet says a lot about *what kind* of internet you experience'.[3]

This is the messy reality of today's digital video ecology. Rather than free flow and instant access, the actually-existing experience from the user's perspective typically involves a series of partially-available platforms that shift and change according to one's location – a lumpy landscape of formal and informal services that sometimes work and sometimes do not, depending on where you are located. Consider the following examples:

- YouTube is available in 70 different country-specific versions, including dedicated platforms for countries such as Latvia and Yemen. But it is blocked in China, Iran, Pakistan and Syria, among other countries, and is intermittently unavailable in Thailand, Turkey, Bangladesh and Morocco.

- YouTube also has significantly restricted content in Germany because of a long-running copyright dispute with music collecting societies.

- The Netflix streaming catalog (as of 2016, unblocked everywhere but China) varies markedly between countries, with the availability of movies and TV content reflecting local licensing, copyright and censorship arrangements.

- Major streaming sites including BBC iPlayer and Hulu are available only in their coun-

---

3   Ira Wagman and Peter Urquhart, '"This content is not available in your region": Geoblocking culture in Canada', in Darren Wershle, Rosemary Coombe and Martin Zeilinger (eds), *Dynamic Fair Dealing: Creating Canadian Culture Online*, Toronto: University of Toronto Press, 2014, pp. 126.

try of origin (the United Kingdom and United States, respectively) and are geoblocked everywhere else.

- The catalogues of 'global' services such as Google Play, Amazon and iTunes vary widely between countries in terms of the content they offer and how much they charge for it, with 40%-50% price differentials between countries being a common occurrence.

- Wealthy countries have abundant local catch-up TV while poorer countries have little or none, and rely on piracy as a post-broadcast circulatory system.

As this list suggests, video services are fast and free in some countries but are unavailable or prohibitively expensive in others. These examples underscore the enduring importance of geography to digital video culture, reminding us that where we live – or at least where websites think we live – makes a big difference to how we experience the digital.

Jack Goldsmith and Tim Wu argue that internet history since the late 1990s can be described as a process of 'becoming bordered'. 'The result,' they write, 'is an internet that differs among nations and regions that are increasingly separated by walls of bandwidth, language, and filters'.[4] The end result is the fragmentation of the internet into a series of localised experiences and filtered environments. We are not just talking here about the infrastructural geography of networks, according to which some countries and demographics are blessed with cheap and fast connectivity while others live with dial-up, mobile-only, or no access at all. Instead, we are referring to an overlapping political-economic geography of content and service availability, shaped by market forces, licensing arrangements and state control, and which is premised on the availability of geo-location databases, geo-caching services (offered by content delivery networks such as Akamai), and location-aware credit card processing.

Geolocation technology dates back to the end of the 1990s when the first tech companies specialising in location detection, such as Infosplit, began to appear. Up to this point, most websites had only one interface for all global users. The more sophisticated corporate sites would customise their offerings based on user-entered information (*Please select your country/region*). But with the rise of geolocation databases and third-party location-detection services, it became practical to automate this process. Now location could be determined by IP address, with pages detecting your location then loading language- and territory-specific content to suit. The accuracy of these IP geolocation systems was sometimes questionable, as many readers will no doubt remember, and the present system still involves a messy patchwork of different databases that do not always play well together. But over time the kinks have been gradually ironed out to a point where IP geolocation works as intended most of the time.

---

4   Jack Goldsmith and Tim Wu, *Who Controls the Internet? Illusions of a Borderless World*, Oxford: Oxford University Press, 2006, p. viii.

To the delight of digital advertising companies, content could now be customised to local markets. Websites could now imagine, understand and process their customers in geographic market segments, down to their postcodes (Hulu, for example, boasts it 'can target [ads] by Nielsen DMA, State or zip code')[5]. For internet idealists with their dreams of global connectivity and universal access, this resurgence of physical geography has been problematic. One widely discussed consequence is that there is now no such thing as a universal internet – understood as a stable set of globally available cultural materials – because customisation means that content and experience change according to location.

This brings us to television, and to its ongoing metamorphosis into an online medium. As television becomes a streaming service, delivered over the internet rather than through the airwaves, it becomes location-aware (and location-blind) in new ways. IP geolocation now serves a primary role in determining what content is available where, reconfiguring the spatial 'footprints' and access-control functions familiar to us from the broadcast model (TV as a local/national medium transmitted over the airwaves) and through direct-broadcast satellite transmission (TV as a set of internationally available but locally decoded channels).[6] In other words, geoblocking becomes a kind of de facto global cultural policy, shaping the communication environment by making available certain kinds of materials, while restricting others.

One implication of this new TV landscape is that internet theory and broadcast history are brought closer together. Approaching the internet as a localised and unevenly available set of cultural experiences – as opposed to a global, universal superhighway – reminds us that the internet, like television, is always locally configured as well as globally networked. This diversity of institutional forms is noted by global television scholars, who emphasise that TV production cultures, advertising systems, and regulatory frameworks still vary significantly between countries. As Graeme Turner and Jinna Tay write in *Television Studies after TV*, 'Notwithstanding the internationalization of the media industries, these days the answer to the question 'What is television?' very much depends on where you are'.[7] Turner and Tay didn't have geoblocking in mind when they wrote that sentence, but they may as well have. Geoblocking reminds us that geography matters a great deal to television, and never moreso than in the internet age.

Control and Circumvention

A second cross-cutting theme in our book is circumvention – the tactics, tools and workarounds that people use to access blocked video sites. As our contributors elegantly describe, the geography of blockage and flow is provisional rather than absolute because

---

5   Derek Kompare, 'Adverstreaming: Hulu Plus', *Flow*, 24 Feb 2014, http://flowtv.org/2014/02/adverstreaming-hulu-plus/.

6   These issues have been explored through key works in video geography, to which we are indebted. See: Tom O'Regan, 'From Piracy to Sovereignty: International VCR Trends', *Continuum: The Australian Journal of Media & Culture*, 4.2 (1991): 112-135; Brett Christophers, *Envisioning Media Power: On Capital and Geographies of Television* Lanham: Lexington Books, 2009.

7   Graeme Turner and Jinna Tay, *Television Studies after TV: Understanding Television in the Post-Broadcast Era*, London: Routledge, 2009, p.8.

internet users have many ways to work around geographic restrictions. Indeed, IP address geoblocking is particularly easy to circumvent through basic software tools – including VPNs, DNS proxies, web proxies, and TOR – which can unlock geo-restricted content by rerouting data through an offshore IP address, making it appear as though the user is located in another country. In recent years a growing ecology of circumvention tools has emerged, including free ad-supported services (Hotspot Shield, Hola, Addtelly), subscription VPNs (Private internet Access, HotSpotNordVPN, TigerVPN), and DNS proxies designed explicitly for unlocking offshore content (Unblock-US, Getflix).

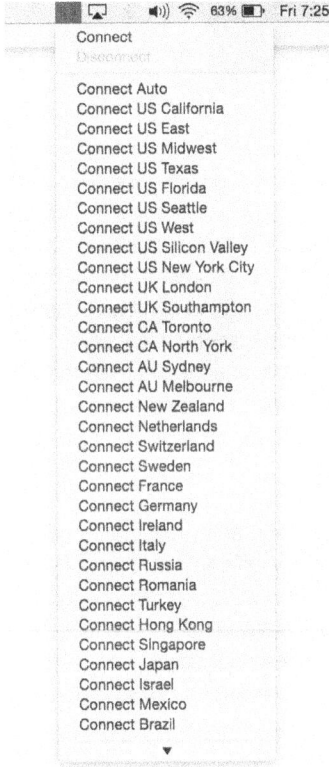

Figure 1. A VPN server selection menu

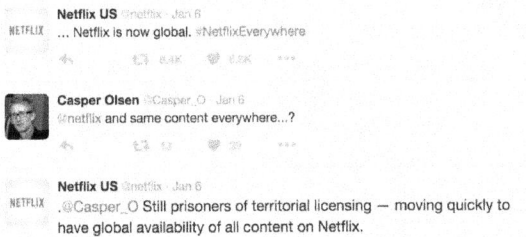

Figure 1b. A Twitter exchange following Netflix's global expansion on 6 January 2016

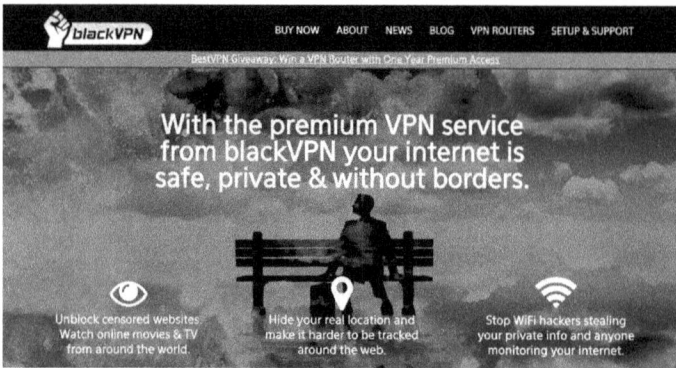

Figure 2. VPN marketing highlights unblocking functions

Circumvention is a complex topic, because most technologies used for geoblocking circumvention were not designed for this purpose and have other, licit functions. For example, VPNs are a popular security tool with privacy-conscious internet users who want extra protection when using public wifi networks. Others use VPNs for business-related networking or to dial into remote servers when working from home. There is nothing questionable about these activities, which are increasingly part of mainstream computer use. Indeed, many consumer groups advocate VPN adoption as a protection measure against hacking and identity theft. But VPNs are confounding objects for internet governance because they erode the link between IP address, location and identity. Allowing users to 'tunnel' outside national borders, they offer an ideal workaround for geoblocking, filtering and site-blocking, while presenting complex challenges for governments and media corporations.

Our point here is that there are different kinds of circumvention and proxying practices, associated with different kinds of internet use, and enabled by different kinds of software tools – and none of these things can be conflated in a straightforward manner. As Roberts, Zuckerman and Palfrey write, circumvention needs to be understood as 'a large topic that reaches deeply into a number of other large topics, including filtering, privacy, surveillance, and content neutrality'.[8] While the focus of this book is on geoblocking circumvention, many contributors in Section Two of the book also look at site-blocking circumvention, anonymization, and the links between these practices.

In China, Iran and Turkey, for example, circumvention tools are used widely because they open up access to YouTube, Twitter, and other blocked sites. Some of this activity is politically inflected but a lot of it is simply about social networking. In Australia, Sweden, and Brazil, in contrast, circumvention is more about access to first-release movies and TV, and to the expanded streaming catalogues available in the major markets. Some countries, such as Malaysia, display a mix of these two tendencies. In all cases, circumvention interfaces with anonymization and privacy, but not always in predictable ways.

---

8   Hal Roberts, Ethan Zuckerman, and John Palfrey, *2007 Circumvention Landscape Report: Methods, Uses, and Tools,* Cambridge, MA: The Berkman Center for Internet and Society, Harvard University, 2007, p. 9.

Thinking about circumvention from this perspective makes visible an array of everyday location-masking practices, from prosaic acts of access (Chinese teenagers using proxies to log into Facebook and YouTube, German tourists streaming Euro league matches) through to more overtly political resistances (as when Turkish activists share proxy settings in defiance of government internet censorship). So there is a nexus here between corporate media policies, censorship and circumvention, which are all linked through the use of informal software hacks. As our contributors show, this nexus is a rich site for theorising. In the small-scale tactics of internet circumvention we see larger stories unfolding about cultural regulation, networked activism, and cyber-identity.

There are also interesting possibilities here for media historiography, and for understanding the social shaping of network technologies. Each piece of circumvention software has its own fascinating and largely untold history: the VPN, for example, has been around for decades and was used primarily as a business networking tool until the early 2000s when it morphed into a personal computing product. Since then hundreds of small VPN companies have appeared and disappeared (by our count, there are at least 140 VPN brands in the market). In addition to these international VPNs, there are also 'local' VPNs running in some countries, notably Iran, which have Persian-language interfaces and local payment systems. There is much scepticism as to the bona fides of these companies, which are seen to be government-linked, but people use them anyway because they are functional and cheap. In this unusual state-supervised circumvention practice we see a strange mix of sanctioned and unauthorised, formal and informal, all blurring together.

Some popular VPNs, such as the British service Hide My Ass, have become major commercial enterprises. Founded in 2005 by a sixteen year old high-school student from Norfolk, Jack Cator, Hide My Ass has built itself into a mainstream privacy brand. Between its current VPN offering and its older web proxy service – which was tailor-made for kids to get around social media blocks on school computers – Hide My Ass claims to have had more than two million customers over the years, with 200,000 paying subscribers currently on the books, and almost 100 staff based in London, Kiev and Belgrade. This growth has paid off handsomely for Cator, who in 2015 cashed in and sold his business to the antivirus company AVG for £40 million.[9]

Browser plug-ins such as Unotelly and Hola Unblocker are another popular circumvention option. These proxy services are even easier to use than VPNs: just select a country or platform in the browser menu bar, and your IP address will be changed accordingly. Unlike VPNs, these are free services that do not require signup or subscription. But there is sometimes a hidden cost: the possibility for your IP address to be hijacked, as Hola users recently discovered when their bandwidth was loaned out to a third-party company for a botnet attack.[10]

---

9   Peter Shadbolt, 'How Misbehaving at School Made One Man a Millionaire', *BBC News*, 18 May 2015, http://www.bbc.com/news/business-32702501.

10   Ian Paul, 'Ultra-popular Hola VPN Extension Sold Your Bandwidth for use in a Botnet Attack', *PC World*, 29 May 2015, http://www.pcworld.com/article/2928340/ultra-popular-hola-vpn-extension-sold-your-bandwidth-for-use-in-a-botnet-attack.html.

Experiences such as this are common when it comes to free or ad-supported circumvention tools, especially apps, browsers extensions and web proxies with questionable business models that aren't immediately apparent to the end user. The number of free tools is always on the rise but the landscape is cluttered with commercial options of varying legitimacy and security, and the risk of virus and malware infection is ever-present.

Alongside these commercial products, there are other kinds of circumvention tools designed explicitly to get around government censorship. The peer-to-peer proxy service Lantern, for example, provides a popular way to evade national internet filtering. Lantern works by linking together users in filtered countries with a trusted international network of volunteers who share access to their IP addresses. A mix of start-up, NGO and private company, Lantern is ostensibly non-profit but somewhat opaque in its ambitions. It has been funded by the US State Department, reflecting the wider interest in circumvention technologies as tools of foreign policy.

As these examples suggest, internet circumvention is a space that brings together a strange mix of actors: activists, governments, entrepreneurs, criminals, geeks, pirates, school kids, and millions of ordinary people who wish to be conceal their identity or location temporarily. The chapters in this book trace out some of these unlikely connections in rich detail.

Censorship and Consumption

A third theme in this book is the relationship between market and state – or more specifically, the relationship between commercial technologies of access control and government site-blocking, surveillance and censorship. As we have seen already, from the user's perspective these two realities are closely intertwined: the geography of digital markets is overlaid with a political geography of unavailability. While technologically distinct, these two control systems need to be considered in tandem if we are to understand their cultural ramifications.

Geoblocking and government site-blocking occupy different ideological terrain. Geoblocking is typically discussed as an issue of access to markets and services. The paradigm here is consumer rights, rather than communication or citizenship. Key voices in the debate include early adopters, TV buffs and groups like the Electronic Frontier Foundation, all strident critics of geoblocking. In contrast, discussion of site-blocking tends to occur within a paradigm of internet freedom, and is typically linked to a discourse of free speech, political liberalism, communication rights and cyber-liberties.

Internet freedom is based on the idea that digital communication is inherently liberating and access control is inherently suspect. It tends to see the world through an ontology of free and unfree countries. A shortcoming of the internet freedom literature is that it has little to say about the everyday politics of pleasure and consumption. This realm, so familiar to media and culture critics, has been absent from the debate about internet filtering and censorship, which takes as its prototypical text not the quotidian experience of checking Facebook or watching a movie but the exceptional experience of political agitation, activism and resistance. Our book tries very deliberately to work across this gulf, foregrounding traces of the political in the everyday and vice versa. As the following chapters demonstrate, there is no clear distinction between pleasure and politics in internet use.

Does a Chinese VPN user need to be accessing an anti-government news site for their activities to be considered 'political'? If they are just accessing Facebook to catch up with friends, does that matter? Conversely, what larger political issues surround the seemingly innocuous acts of everyday consumption enabled by entertainment-related circumvention in the ostensibly 'free' West? What temporary political affiliations and alliances may be produced in the consumer VPN scene? These are some of the questions that arise when we think about consumption and censorship together.

Rather than distinguishing between free and unfree societies, we take as our departure point the understanding that internet access and cultural consumption in all nations are shaped by overlapping forms of power, including both state and market power. We keep an open mind to some of the larger ethical questions lurking behind the internet freedom debates, such as whether access in its own right is always unequivocally a good thing, and whether states have the right to regulate their national internet space.

We also pay attention to how ideas of internet censorship and consumption are articulated, valued and debated according to cultural context. As contributors to this book show, the problem of geoblocking plays out quite differently in different countries. With the possible exception of the United States – which, as Evan Elkins shows, is shielded from the drama of geo-restriction due to its massive media complex – each country has its own set of policies and priorities around the geoblocking issue. In Australia and Canada, for example, a consumer rights discourse prevails, in which the main issue is the timely and affordable provision of digital content. The debate here is framed around windowing and discrepant pricing policies, leading to delays and price hikes for 'peripheral' English-language markets. This is what Tama Leaver calls 'the tyranny of digital distance', or the lag between first release in the center and availability at the edges.[11]

In Europe, the politics of geoblocking are quite different. With its dense patchwork of languages, borders and diasporas, Europe has long been a hotbed of unauthorised cross-border media consumption: people watch satellite TV signals meant for other nations, buy multiply-subtitled DVDs, and make shopping trips to neighbouring countries where prices are cheaper. This is an enduring feature of European consumption, one that has diminished little with the establishment of a single currency. While much policy attention is now directed at the creation of an EU Digital Single Market – in which all 28 EU member countries would share common pricing and availability for digital goods – intra-European variances in price and availability naturally persist.

---

11   Tama Leaver, 'Watching "Battlestar Galactica" in Australia and the Tyranny of Digital Distance', *Media International Australia* 126 (2008), pp. 145-154.

Within the European integration project, geoblocking is starting to be seen by as an anti-competitive – indeed, anti-European – technological restriction on free trade. Andrus Ansip, the former Estonian prime minister and current European Commission vice-president, has been leading the charge. Since 2014, 'tackling geoblocking' has been an official policy priority of the European Commission. Its Digital Single Market policy reads like a *Lifehacker* post: 'Geo-blocking leaves many Europeans unable to use the online services available in other EU countries, or redirects them to a local store with different prices... Such discrimination cannot exist in a single market.'[12] Here we see the 'merely cultural' issue of geoblocking framed quite seriously as a threat to continental capitalism and its cherished values of free trade, consumer rights, and smart regulation.

The politics of blockage and flow are different again in China, where a fast-growing domestic media sector – including a massive digital media production ecology – is overlaid with a carefully managed state system of site blocks, filtering and slow-downs, designed to temper demand for offshore services (especially Facebook and Google) and direct this inward to the local, regulated alternatives. For China the geoblocking issue is not so much the unavailability of content; when it comes to Chinese-language media and services, everything you would need is now inside the Great Firewall. Instead, it is about how and why certain user groups feel the need to climb this wall. As Jinying Li's chapter in this book evocatively describes, 'wall crossing' desire is widespread but unevenly distributed among the middle classes, and linked in complex ways to internal governance.

All this represents a new challenge for digital media theory, because it requires us to rethink some of the paradigms of control and censorship that we have inherited from earlier periods. Geoblocking, broadly defined, is a problem for many internet users in many countries, but to different extents, and for different reasons. It affects rich and poor alike, but can be circumvented easily for those with money or know-how. It interacts in complex ways with other kinds of internet phenomena, such as peer-to-peer piracy.

For example, we can see that the geoblocking issue has relatively little in common with the paradigm of the 'digital divide' that shaped discussion of the first decades of global internet use. Initially organised around a binary of use and non-use, with use concentrated in the developed world and non-use in the peripheries – and later developing into a more complex theory about the mutually reinforcing dynamics of class, infrastructure, education and state investment – the spatial imaginary of the digital divide has limited relevance to the problem of geoblocking. Nor is geoblocking a simplistic story of internet freedom versus internet censorship, that Western liberal vision of a free West against a censorious Rest. The new video geography does not cleanly follow any of these imaginaries.

As the case studies in the second section of this book show, the rise of circumvention practices around the world may instead be linked instead to the emergence of a transnational class who are using circumvention software for a mix of reasons – not just for "resistance",

---

12   European Commission, 'Better Online Access to Digital Services', http://ec.europa.eu/priorities/digital-single-market/access/index_en.html.

nor exclusively for consumption. This requires a variegated model of both access and politics. As Sean Cubitt argues, the question of access in internet culture needs to be understood through multiple registers simultaneously:

> The network society affords various kinds of access: to the rich consumer, video-on-demand (VOD), and to the genuinely wealthy subscription or sale models which avoid the dull necessity of paying attention to ads. For the Chinese masses, the protection of the Golden Shield; for the wealthy, Virtual Private Networks (VPNs) which fasttrack past the firewall like express check-in at the airport. For the ordinary punter, a data feed from Bloomberg; for the wealthy subscriber, real-time data on every stock for sale on every market.[13]

It may be that VPNs, proxies, and other geo-evasion technologies provide a set of popular technical competencies that are, taken together, laying the foundations for a global geo-circumvention system. This system connects politics with pleasure; connects censorship with consumption; embraces cutting-edge technologies while drawing on longer prehistories of cross-border arbitrage; and brings activists, file-sharers, hackers and mainstream users into unlikely and uncomfortable contact with each other. The politics of circumvention are anything but straightforward, as our authors illustrate. But in their complexity they provide the coordinates for a different map of cultural power, and a new way to think about the geopolitics of internet control.

References

Christophers, Brett. *Envisioning Media Power: On Capital and Geographies of Television*, Lanham: Lexington Books, 2009.

Cubitt, Sean. 'Telecommunication Networks: Economy, Ecology, Rule', *Theory, Culture and Society* 31 (2014): 185-199.

Deibert, Ronald et al. (eds). *Access Controlled: The Shaping of Power, Rights, and Rule in Cyberspace*, Cambridge, MA: MIT Press, 2010.

Deibert, Ronald et al. (eds). *Access Contested: Security, Identity, and Resistance in Asian Cyberspace*, Cambridge, MA; MIT Press, 2012.

Deibert, Ronald et al. (eds). *Access Denied: The Practice and Policy of Global Internet Filtering*, Cambridge, MA: MIT Press, 2008.

European Commission, 'Better Online Access to Digital Services', n.d., http://ec.europa.eu/priorities/digital-single-market/access/index_en.htm.

Goldsmith, Jack and Tim Wu. *Who Controls the Internet? Illusions of a Borderless World*, Oxford: Oxford University Press, 2006.

Kompare, Derek. 'Adverstreaming: Hulu Plus', *Flow*, 24 Feb 2014, http://flowtv.org/2014/02/adverstreaming-hulu-plus/.

Leaver, Tama. 'Watching "Battlestar Galactica" in Australia and the Tyranny of Digital Distance', *Media International Australia*, 126 (2008): 145-154.

---

13 Sean Cubitt, 'Telecommunication Networks: Economy, Ecology, Rule', *Theory, Culture and Society* 31 (2014), p. 191.

O'Regan, Tom. 'From Piracy to Sovereignty: International VCR Trends', *Continuum: The Australian Journal of Media & Culture*, 4.2 (1991): 112-135.

Parks, Lisa and Nicole Starosielski. *Signal Traffic: Critical Studies of Media Infrastructures*, University of Illinois Press, 2015.

Paul, Ian. 'Ultra-popular Hola VPN Extension Sold Your Bandwidth for use in a Botnet Attack', *PC World*, 29 May 2015, http://www.pcworld.com/article/2928340/ultra-popular-hola-vpn-extension-sold-your-bandwidth-for-use-in-a-botnet-attack.html.

Roberts, Hal et al. *2010 Circumvention Tool Usage Report*, Cambridge, MA: Berkman Center for Internet and Society, 2010.

Roberts, Hal, Ethan Zuckerman, and John Palfrey, *2007 Circumvention Landscape Report: Methods, Uses, and Tools,* Cambridge, MA: The Berkman Center for Internet and Society, Harvard University, 2007.

Shadbolt, Peter. 'How Misbehaving at School Made One Man a Millionaire', *BBC News*, 18 May 2015, http://www.bbc.com/news/business-32702501.

Turner, Graeme and Jinna Tay. *Television Studies after TV: Understanding Television in the Post-Broadcast Era*, London: Routledge, 2009.

Wagman, Ira and Peter Urquhart. '"This content is not available in your region": Geoblocking culture in Canada', in Darren Wershle, Rosemary Coombe and Martin Zeilinger (eds), *Dynamic Fair Dealing: Creating Canadian Culture Online*, Toronto: University of Toronto Press, 2014, pp. 124-132.

PART I:
PERSPECTIVES ON GEOBLOCKING

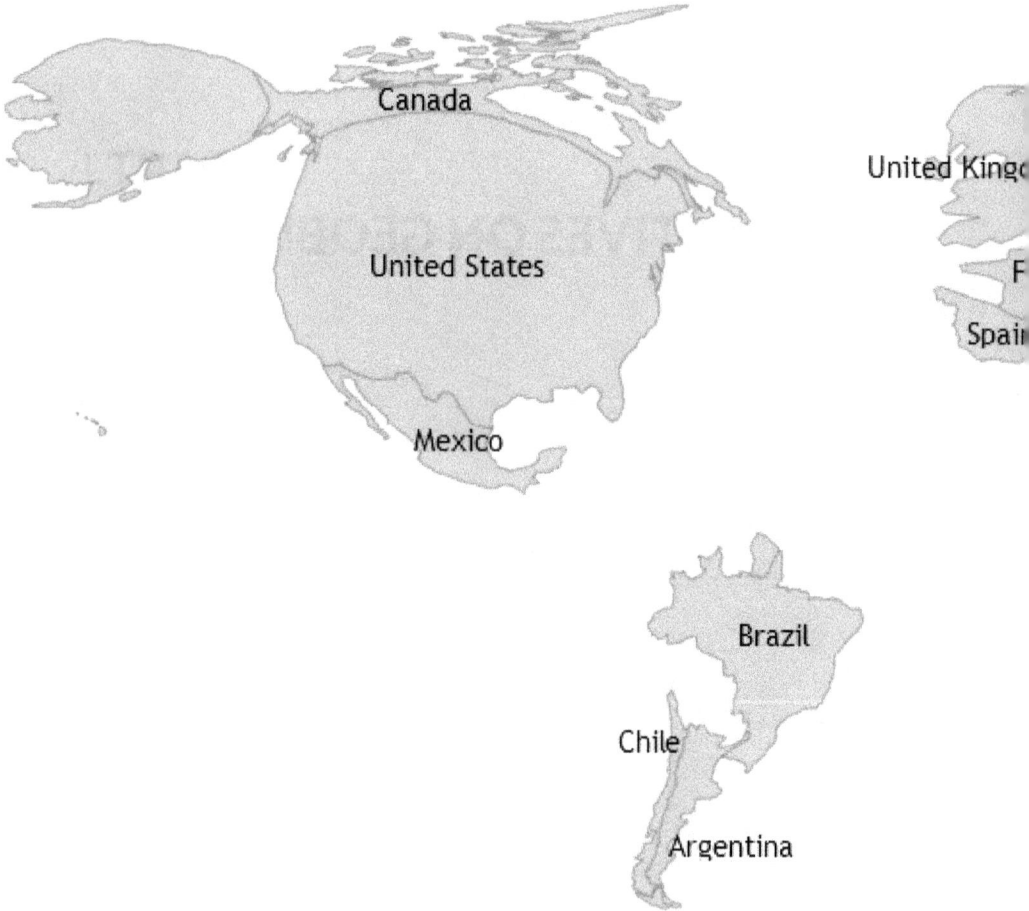

GLOBAL STREAMING: SCALE AND INFRASTRUCTURE

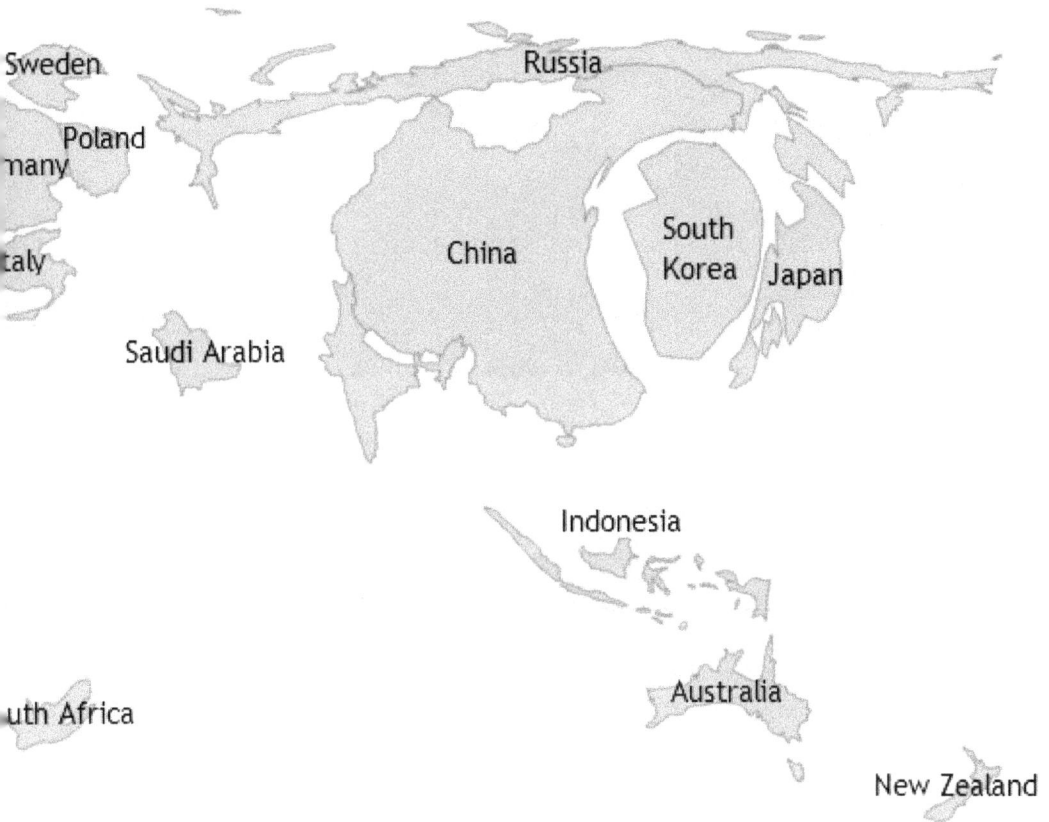

Figure 1. A cartogram of consumer internet video traffic. Data source: Cisco Visual Networking Index: Global IP Traffic Forecast, 2014–2019

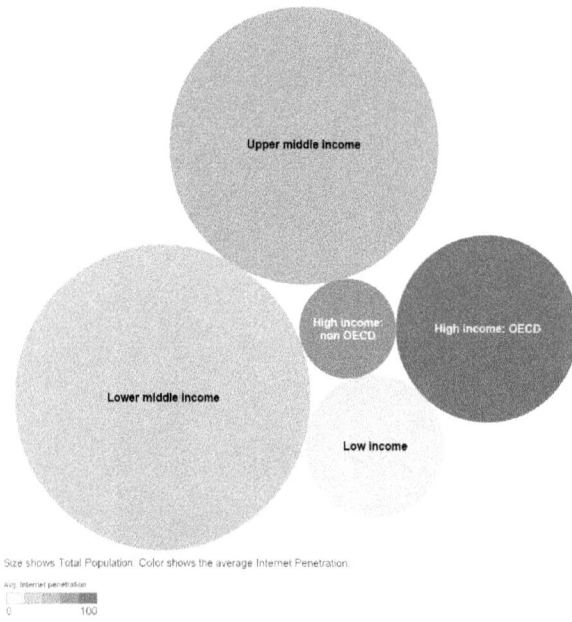

Size shows Total Population. Color shows the average Internet Penetration.

Avg. Internet penetration

0   100

Figure 2. Income status of global internet users. Data source: The World Bank

Internet speed (Mbps)

Figure 3. Average internet connection speeds around the world. Data source: Akamai State of the Internet Report Q4 2014

NETFLIX BY NUMBERS

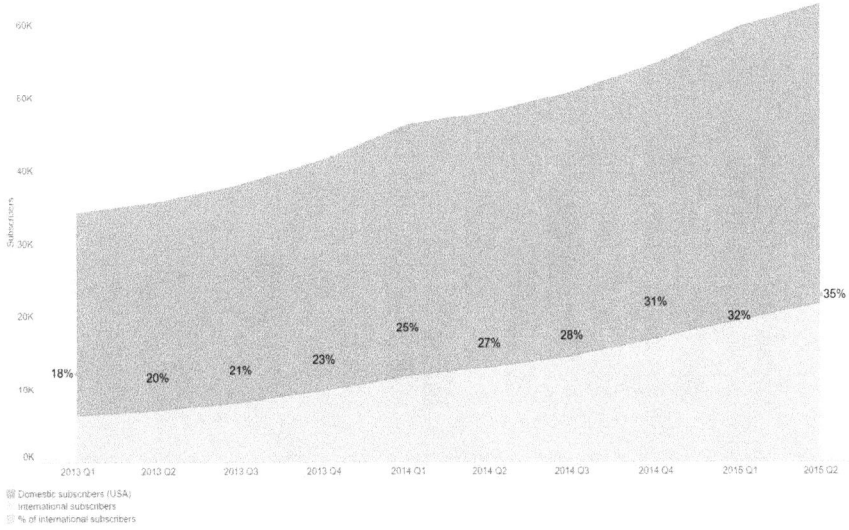

Figure 4. U.S. and international Netflix subscribers, 2013-2015. Data source: Netflix Inc. quarterly reports

Figure 5. Countries where Netflix is officially available. Data source: Netflix, https://help.netflix.com/en/node/14164

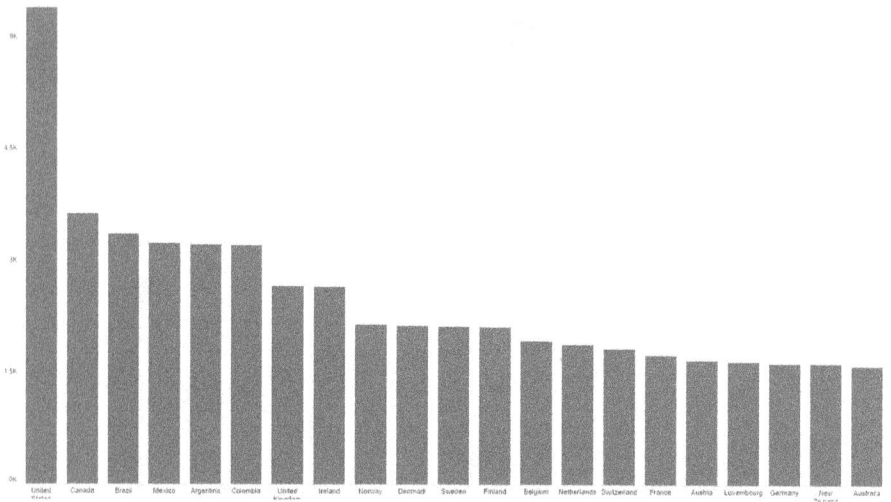

Figure 6. Size of Netflix catalogue in various countries (Number of available titles). Data source: UnblockUS, https://blog.unblock-us.com/how-many-titles-are-available-in-each-netflix-region

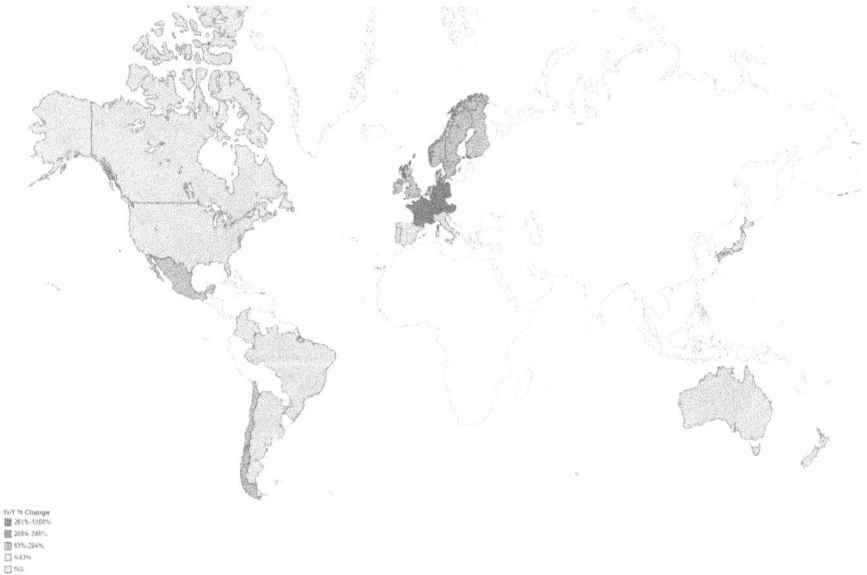

Figure 7. Countries with highest Netflix subscriber growth since 2014. Data source: Digital TV Research forecast

VPN GEOGRAPHY

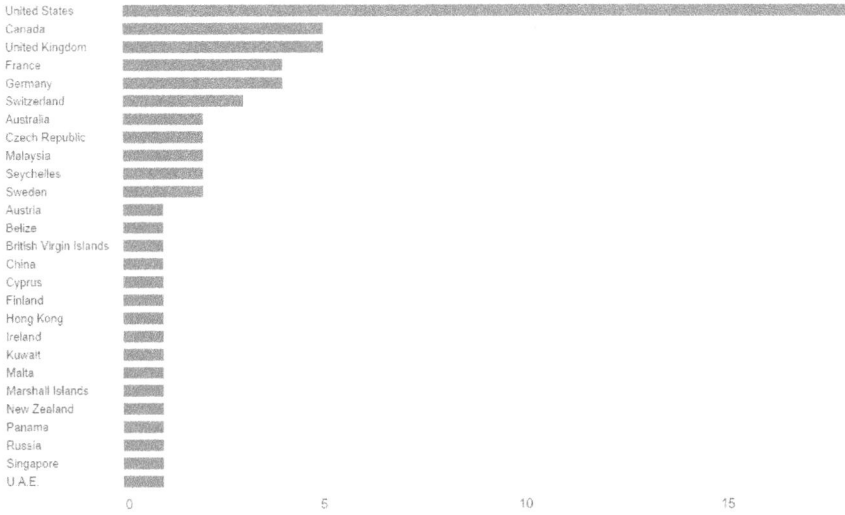

Figure 8. Number of VPNs by host country. Data source: Swinburne University

Figure 9. Most popular VPN server locations. Data source: Swinburne University, Berkman Center for Internet and Society

TUNNELING MEDIA: GEOBLOCKING AND ONLINE BORDER RESISTANCE

JUAN LLAMAS-RODRIGUEZ

The highway functioned as an early metaphor for the increasingly transnational network we now call the internet. The 'information superhighway' promised interconnectivity that was faster and freer than anything the world had seen before. In the decades since this initial euphoria, the infrastructural metaphor for the internet has morphed into variants like pipe-lines, tubes, and rhizomes, language that contests and recalibrates what types of access and communication are possible. Despite some residual techno-utopianism, the promise of a free network of connectivity has turned out to be anything but in the midst of net neu-trality debates across the world. The internet is now a site for struggles over sovereignty, surveillance, and control, concerns that were once the domain of the offline world (or at least *imagined* as such).[1] The web's fall from grace is mirrored in the metaphors used to describe it. It is hardly surprising that the creators of Tor, an online browser that allows for anonymous browsing in various websites, liken their work to a 'series of virtual tunnels'. As the power struggles of the offline sphere become increasingly salient in the online one, an alternative language that counteracts this dominant sense of control has begun to coalesce. The metaphorical shift in the cultural imaginary from a highway to a tunnel illustrates the death of that initial fantasy of free, unfettered connectivity.

Metaphors are powerful means for understanding social life. Spatial metaphors in particular proliferate across social theory and cultural criticism, often without appropriate examination of their implications.[2] Yet the tunnel metaphor invoked by the creators of Tor, as well as consumer-friendly VPNs such as TunnelBear, is instructive to think through the practices that circumvent 'geofences' since it likens these practices to the underground tunnels that allow for bypassing borders in the physical realm. Surely there are many other ways to describe alternative modes of online connectivity, but tunneling is significant for a number of reasons. First, it alludes to a symbolic vertical differentiation between channels of connectivity – these 'dark tunnels' are not in some online elsewhere but they remain just below the channels used for everyday navigating. As well, this vertical differentiation reveals a struggle for legiti-macy, where only accepted channels are deemed (metaphorically) 'above ground'. Vertical metaphors for operations of power are all too common, especially for those subordinated. The symbolic and material creation of vertical spaces in turn produces sites for exposing and contesting these relations. Thinking of these divergent forms of network connectivity as tunneling practices signals one such space of contestation.

---

1   As Paul Edwards argues, struggles over sovereignty and control were always a constitutive part of the
     internet despite claims otherwise. See Paul N. Edwards, *The Closed World*, Cambridge: MIT Press,
     1997.
2   Neil Smith and Cindi Katz, 'Grounding Metaphor – Towards a Spatialized Politics', in Michael Keith
     and Steve Pile (eds) *Place and the Politics of Identity*, New York: Routledge, 1993, p. 68.

The intellectual task is therefore to pursue the metaphorical implications of tunneling prac-tices in order to theorize emergent and resistant configurations of online connectivity. In par-ticular, it is to follow the example of physical border tunnels as a blueprint for understanding the discourses around, and the technological restraints of, contemporary borders as well as the methods for circumventing them. At stake is not a comparison between two pur-portedly distinct spaces of human activity, but rather a consideration of the consequences of bordering processes in each of these spaces. If the aim is to analyze how geoblocking technologies shape the cultural and political geographies of the internet – in other words, how they de- and re-territorialize the online world, then analyzing the methods for de- and re-territorializing physical boundaries prove a generative starting point. Metaphor, as a con-ceptual vehicle, allows for profound affinities and adjacencies to be uncovered without differences being lost. Since the verticality of the virtual sphere remains more symbolic and less material than that of the physical sphere, the allusion to tunneling translates the lessons and complications of the physical practice of tunneling into the virtual realm while foregrounding the key differences between them.

In essence, tunneling reorganizes geographies of control for a stretch of time. If geoblocks, like borders, function not to protect sovereignty but to sort populations, to categorize users and provide content based on these categories, then tunneling provides an opportunity for change. Yet not all tunneling is the same. Degrees of technological sophistication for physical and virtual tunneling create a hierarchy between those that can 'hack' their way around a geofence and those that need the help of others. These various levels of differ-entiation constitute users in relation to their distinct experiences of the internet. Tunneling thus responds to, and counteracts, the control enacted through borders, the hierarchization performed through technical expertise, and the power imbalances engendered through different user experiences.

Borders on/off the Internet

Newfound spaces have always replicated the structures of already existing ones. Tracing the connections between a pre-World War II conception of air space, a Cold War era conception of outer space, and a contemporary one of cyberspace, James Hay argues that each subsequent invention of a space was tied to a reinvention of the liberal ideals of governmentality.[3] If the notion of air space was integral to supporting national sovereignty, the advent of outer space was key to formulating questions about the reach and rule of new communication technologies with a global reach. Cyberspace extends these questions once again, projecting a virtual arena in which to rethink national dominance and power. In accounting for both the physical and digital realms, scholars write about 'living in two planes'[4] or the production of a 'doubling of place',[5] but these analyses posit the internet as a 'vehicle

---

3   James Hay, 'The Invention of Air Space, Outer Space and Cyberspace', in Lisa Parks and James
     Schwoch (eds), *Down to Earth: Satellite Technologies, Industries and Cultures*, New Brunswick:
     Rutgers University Press, 2012, p. 19.
4   Serra Tinic, *On Location: Canada's Television Industry in a Global Market*, Toronto: University of
     Toronto Press, 2005, p. 17.
5   Shaun Moores, 'The Doubling of Place: Electronic Media, Time-Space Arrangements, and Social

of mobility' allowing you to end up somewhere else from where you physically start. Instead, VPNs – as well as other sorts of tunneling technologies – change the place you start at, a critical difference since the regulation of online activities begins at the national level.[6] Yet 'changing the place you start at' is more than a feature enacted by user-friendly VPNs that provide the option of choosing a location and mask an IP address to make it happen. It is a characteristic that speaks to the changing nature of borders writ large.

The proliferation of information and communication technologies (ICTs) have increased the function of borders as regulatory mechanisms. Immigration agencies and border check-points operate as trackers of movement, differentially regulating access to specific spaces for specific subjects.[7] Oscar Gandy refers to these practices as the 'panoptic sort', where complex surveillance systems collect swathes of information in order to 'coordinate and control [individuals'] access to the goods and services that define life in modern capitalist economy'.[8] Given the sorting of both physical and virtual borders, Didier Bigo suggests a dynamic conception of borders where it is the borders themselves that are on the move. Borders, as we experience them, are 'concretions of power struggles in a specific space [that are] materialized within a territory'.[9] A dynamic conception of borders also demands a reconsideration of the movement that occurs across these, the channels that restrict this movement, and the tunneling practices that enable new forms of mobility.

While ICTs make border sorting faster and more efficient, they also '*add* friction, barriers or logistical costs to the mobility and everyday lives of those deemed by dominant states or service providers to be risky, unprofitable, or undeserving of mobility'.[10] The fact that both nation states and service providers are implicated in these practices speaks not only to the outsourcing of sovereign control – the border tracking technologies used by countries are often privately developed – but also to the blurring of the distinction between risky citizens and risky consumers. Populations that are deemed unprofitable become tantamount to undeserving citizens. Worse, they might be deemed dangerous to the idealized freedoms of circulation promised for other, more deserving consumers. The discursive slippage of the 'dark web', for instance, groups into this concept both those users trying to avoid spying from commercial trackers and those specialized in providing illegal services online.

Thus, despite the sensationalism over building towering fences at national borders, these

---

Relationships', in Nick Couldry and Anna McCarthy (eds) *MediaSpace: Place, Scale, and Culture in a Media Age*, New York: Routledge, 2003, p. 21.

6   Benjamin Burroughs and Adam Rugg, 'Extending the Broadcast: Streaming Culture and the Problems of Digital Geographies', *Journal of Broadcasting & Electronic Media* 58.3 (2014): 377.

7   Andrea Brighenti, 'Visibility: A Category for the Social Sciences', *Current Sociology* 55.3 (May, 2007): 337.

8   Oscar Gandy, *The Panoptic Sort: A Political Economy of Personal rInformation*, Boulder, CO: Westview, 1993, p. 15.

9   Didier Bigo, 'Globalized (In)Security: The field and the Ban-Opticon', in Didier Bigo and Anastassia Tsoukala (eds) *Terror, Insecurity and Liberty: Illiberal practices of liberal regimes after 9/11*, London: Routledge, 2008, p. 28.

10   Stephen D.N. Graham, 'The Software Sorted City: Rethinking the Digital Divide', in Stephen Graham (ed.) *The Cybercities Reader*, Oxford: Blackwell, 2004, p. 329.

boundaries are predicated less on 'fencing off' the national territory than on regulating what can be allowed through at any given time. Global video culture is indicative of this shift in bordering practices. The DVD market that once divided the globe into sections required specific production characteristics (DVDs with the appropriate language options, special features, and artwork depending on the region) and targeted infrastructures (DVD players that were region-specific or multi-region). The current video streaming markets depend on local differences only in the last instance. Because they capitalize on existing internet infrastructure and on centralized data servers for storing content, the differently coded regions of the world are thus only distinguished when verifying an IP address. The virtual data point replaces the physical line. Much like ICT-enabled, 'remote control' borders that can 'jump scale' into transnational space and 'touch down' in various nodes across the globe,[11] in contemporary online video culture, content travels across the world only to be sorted at endpoints. IP addresses become virtual passports to be presented at the border checkpoints represented by various kinds of online geoblocks. It is within this context of disaggregated, data-driven borders that tunneling practices thrive, capitalizing on existing infrastructures to create an alternative world of connectivity.

A World of Tunnels

Tunnels come in multiple forms. The U.S. Department of Homeland Security identifies at least three different types of underground border tunnels. Rudimentary tunnels are small, shallow, often crudely constructed and used to travel only a short distance. These are usually detected when they cause a sinkhole, or ground surface collapse. In December 2013, officers from the U.S. Immigration and Customs Enforcement and Homeland Security Investigations found one of these tunnels in the backyard shed of a residence in Nogales, Arizona. It was a crude, hand-dug tunnel, approximately 52 feet long and roughly two feet wide by three feet tall, with some wood shoring.[12] In contrast to rudimentary ones, sophisticated tunnels, also called 'super tunnels', are elaborately constructed systems. They usually stretch more than 2,000 feet and may include shoring, ventilation, electricity, and rail systems. In April 2014, one such tunnel was discovered inside Otay Mesa, a neighborhood in southern San Diego.[13] The San Diego Tunnel Task Force inspected a warehouse and discovered a small hole in the floor that led to a 15-foot walkway which connected to a 68-foot vertical shaft that dropped into the tunnel, one of the longest straight-down drops the agency had ever seen. The tunnel itself was 600 yards long and included a multi-tiered electric rail system and an array of ventilation equipment. The exit point was sealed with material that made it seem like it was painted concrete, and there was a half-ton winch pulley system to hoist up goods up the vertical shaft.

11   Neil Brenner, *New State Spaces: Urban Governance and the Rescaling of Statehood*, London: Oxford University Press, 2004, p. 57.

12   U.S. Immigration and Customs Enforcement, 'Nogales Tunnel Task Force shuts down drug tunnel in backyard shed', 18 December 2013, http://www.ice.gov/news/releases/nogales-tunnel-task-force-shuts-down-drug-tunnel-backyard-shed.

13   Debbi Baker and Sandra Dibble, 'Two Drug Smuggling Tunnels Found', *San Diego Union-Tribune*, 4 April 2014, http://www.utsandiego.com/news/2014/apr/04/cross-border-drug-tunnels-investigation/.

Figure 1. Tunnel found in Otay Mesa, California, in 2011: dug through soil and sand. Source: U.S. Customs and Border Protection

The third type of tunnel is the interconnecting one, which is intended to make use of existing subterranean infrastructure such as storm drains or sewers. During a routine inspection of the city's main storm drain system, authorities in Nogales found a concrete access panel embedded in the storm drain floor and discovered a tunnel when they removed the panel. U.S. Border Patrol, in partnership with Mexican federal police, inspected the unfinished tunnel and guessed it was intended to end underneath a public parking lot a few miles north. The passageway was almost 160 feet long and was roughly two feet wide by three feet tall. In its wake, a water line, storm drain pipe and two fiber optic lines were exposed.[14] These types of tunnels are suspected to proliferate across the Mexico-US border, prompting the creation of a specialized 'tunnel task forces', but because they include existing storm drains and sewers as parts of their structure, they have become the hardest type of tunnel to detect and shut down.

The interconnecting tunnel best corresponds to the type of digital practices that fall under 'tunneling' since the latter also use existing infrastructure – in this case, that of the internet – to create loopholes or roundabouts that allow for distinct avenues of communication. Exploiting the existing infrastructure has advantages for avoiding detection. Because they utilize storm drains and sewers, users of interconnecting tunnels depend less on creating their own channels. This reduced effort benefits tunnels users both because they take less time to construct the tunnel and because they are less likely to be found. There is no complete mapping of the existing sewage drains around the Mexico-U.S. border, a region that extends almost 2000 miles, so authorities need to evaluate whether an underground construction is legitimate on an individual basis. In addition, interconnecting tunnels take advantage of the geological affordances of the border region. The physical characteristics of the local soil, for instance, vary tremendously across the southern U.S. border. Any tunnel detection technology would need to adapt to different levels of porosity and texture, and tunnel task forces would have to map the variations in types of soil across the entire area they wanted to surveil. These features mean that standardizing border tunneling detection

14   U.S. Immigration and Customs Enforcement, 'US, Mexican authorities shut down smuggling tunnel under construction in Nogales', press release, 26 June 2013, https://www.ice.gov/news/releases/us-mexican-authorities-shut-down-smuggling-tunnel-under-construction-nogales.

highly costly and cumbersome, which explains why finding and shutting down these tunnels has been a slow process focused on one tunnel at a time.[15]

Figure 2. Tunnel found in Naco, Arizona, in 2015: dug through soil and clay. Source: U.S. Customs and Border Protection

Tunneling online follows similar deflection techniques. Small-scale exploits, such as ad-blocking plugins or DNS proxies, capitalize on the technologically taxing methods of real-time, extensive tracking, allowing for restrictions can be temporarily circumvented. As well, VPNs function by harnessing the complex system of IP address allocation and user privacy laws in order to protect their users, making user targeting a case-by-case ordeal. Large-scale tunneling structures such as Silk Road can further obfuscate entire networks of activity from the surveilled channels of the internet. This level of complexity once meant that only people with sophisticated technological expertise could bypass existing geoblocks. Yet the rise of consumer-friendly VPNs has made this type of circumvention more accessible. It has also made it more trackable. The rise of 'anti-piracy industries' such as P2P traffic measurement and packet inspection businesses has depended on the centralization of contravention methods.[16] In the past, prosecuting any one user bypassing geoblocking measures was almost never economically or practically feasible, except in cases of users with strong influence on multiple networks or deemed high security threats. Now, the proliferation of technologies for geoblocking circumvention results both in an increase of users and of methods to track and surveil these users. Although tunneling by using existing infrastructure has its advantages, the very fact that tunneling depends on structures that are already in place means that these tunnels, physical or virtual, are not intrinsically emancipatory solutions but rather temporary alternatives to dominant forms of control.

---

15   Department of Homeland Security Science and Technology Directorate, 'Tunnel Detection: Going Underground to Enhance Security', 31 October 2014, http://www.dhs.gov/sites/default/files/publications/Tunnel%20Detection-Going%20Underground%20to%20Enhance%20Security.pdf.

16   Ramon Lobato and Julian Thomas, 'The Business of Anti-Piracy: New Zones of Enterprise in the Copyright Wars', *International Journal of Communication* 6 (2012): 613.

Temporalities of Tunneling

It is this temporal aspect that provides the last zone of overlap between physical border tunnels and virtual tunneling practices. Recall that tunneling reorganizes geographies of control for a stretch of time. If borders have become dynamic, as Didier Bigo argues, then tunneling takes advantage of this fluctuation to allow for previously restricted traffic flow – but only temporarily. The dynamism of borders does not imply an imbalance: tunneling creates new routes that are eventually foreclosed again. The stretch of time that tunnels occupy thus becomes a crucial aspect to their successful implementation. In the case of physical tunnels, this 'stretch of time' acquires a double significance: first, it refers to the span of time that the tunnel is active before it is found and shut down; second, it alludes to the spatial stretch, that is, to the time it takes to cross the tunnel. Tunnels are therefore transitory both because they create conditions that enable fugitive flows and because they exist for a reduced amount of time. In the case of virtual tunnels, these two meanings of the 'stretch of time' of tunneling are conflated. Here the time it takes to 'cross the tunnel' – to transfer whatever communication was previously prevented by geoblocking – is one and the same as the time that this tunneling protocol is active.

Nowhere is this temporal correspondence better exemplified than in the case of the con-sumer-friendly VPN TunnelBear. Promoted for its ease of use, TunnelBear consists of a simple interface with two user inputs, a dropdown menu to select the geographical loca-tion of the IP address desired and a switch button to turn the application on or off. All the user has to do is turn the knob 'On' and the VPN is activated. The tunnel is active as the data transmission occurs and becomes inactive once the user switches the knob 'Off'. The simplification of this protocol into an on/off knob metonymizes the temporal aspect of tunneling: there is a beginning and an end, and this stretch of time is finite and measurable. The second user input, the selection of IP address location, represents the reorganization of geography intrinsic to tunneling. It also evidences the fact that tunnels reorganize, rather than alter, these political and cultural geographies. VPNs undermine but do not undo practices of geoblocking. Similarly, physical tunnels bypass borders but do not permanently erase these geopolitically enforced boundaries. Acknowledging the 'stretch of time' that tunneling entails means realizing that the structural imperatives that make tunneling necessary remain in place, disturbed but not disrupted.

The temporality of tunneling shows the structures of power of the internet beyond their spatial characteristics. It also reveals the internet's power-chronographies, Sarah Sharma's conception for how time is 'worked on and differentially experienced at the intersections of inequity'.[17] Time as lived experience is always political, argues Sharma, because it is produced at the intersection of a range of social differences and institutions. Tunneling exhibits not only how users experience these power differentials based on their geographical location but also how they constitute themselves in time. To some extent, this is analogous to the temporalities that media industries call 'windowing', schedules that release media at

---

17   Sarah Sharma, *In the Meantime: Temporality and Cultural Politics*. Durham: Duke University Press, 2014, p. 13.

different times in different formats and locations. But tunneling allows for the multiplication of these temporalities. Affluent users can afford VPNs that shorten the windows when they can watch content, and technologically savvy users can access this content even faster than mainstream users. When, and for how long, any user can view previously geoblocked content is a consequence of their economic or cultural capital. Tunneling therefore has implications for the cultural geography *and* the cultural chronography of the internet.

Finally, the temporal aspect of virtual tunneling methods carries implications for theorizing media objects themselves. Film, television, and video are considered time-based media because of how they produce structures of temporarily in our culture. Early accounts theorized how these media captured and represented duration. Later, the time of reception came into focus, particularly the disjointed and disorganized forms of temporality enabled by the advent of digital technologies for recording and storage. The rise of geoblocking and methods of circumventing it add another layer of temporality to the consumption of these time-based media. If in online spheres the time needed to circumvent geoblocking mechanisms is often the time required for data transmission, then running time becomes tunneling time. The chronographies of power that differentially produce subjects become projected on the moving image, shaping its reception and composing hierarchies of audiences. Theorizing contemporary media will increasingly necessitate accounting for this third temporality, the time that geographies of control are reorganized for media reception to occur.

References

Baker, Debbi, and Sandra Dibble, 'Two Drug Smuggling Tunnels Found',*San Diego Union-Tribune*, 4 April 2014, http://www.utsandiego.com/news/2014/apr/04/cross-border-drug-tunnels-investigation/.

Bigo, Didier. 'Globalized (In)Security: The field and the Ban-Opticon', in Didier Bigo and Anastassia Tsoukala (eds) *Terror,Insecurity and Liberty: Illiberal practices of liberal regimes after 9/11*, London: Routledge, 2008, pp. 10-48.

Brenner, Neil. *New State Spaces: Urban Governance and the Rescaling of Statehood*, London: Oxford University Press, 2004.

Brighenti, Andrea. 'Visibility: A Category for the Social Sciences',*Current Sociology* 55.3 (2007): 323-342.

Burroughs, Benjamin, and Adam Rugg. 'Extending the Broadcast: Streaming Culture and the Problems of Digital Geographies', *Journalof Broadcasting & Electronic Media* 58.3 (2014): 365-380.

Department of Homeland Security Science and Technology Directorate, 'Tunnel Detection: Going Underground to Enhance Security', 31 October 2014, http://www.dhs.gov/sites/default/files/publications/Tunnel%20Detection-Going%20Underground%20to%20Enhance%20Security.pdf.

Edwards, Paul N. *The Closed World*, Cambridge: MIT Press, 1997.

Gandy, Oscar. *The Panoptic Sort: A Political Economy of Personal Information*, Boulder, CO: Westview, 1993.

Graham, Stephen D.N. 'The Software Sorted City: Rethinking the Digital Divide', in Stephen Graham (ed) *The Cybercities Reader*, Oxford: Blackwell, 2004, pp. 324-330.

Hay, James. 'The Invention of Air Space, Outer Space and Cyberspace',in Lisa Parks and James Schwoch (eds) *Down to Earth: Satellite Technologies, Industries and Cultures*, New Brunswick: Rutgers University Press, 2012, pp. 19-42.

Lobato, Ramon, and Julian Thomas. "The Business of Anti-Piracy: New Zones of Enterprise in the Copyright Wars," *International Journal of Communication* 6 (2012): 606-625.

Moores, Shaun. 'The Doubling of Place: Electronic Media, Time-Space Arrangements, and Social Relationships', in Nick Couldry and Anna McCarthy (eds) *MediaSpace: Place, Scale, and Culture in a Media Age*, New York: Routledge, 2003, pp. 21-36.

Mosco, Vincent. *The Digital Sublime: Myth, Power, and Cyberspace*, Cambridge: MIT Press, 2005.

Parks, Lisa. 'Mapping Orbit: Towards a Vertical Public Space,' in Chris Berry, Janet Hardon, Rachel Moore (eds) *Media Space, Public Space,* New York: Palgrave Macmillan, 2013, pp. 61-87.

Sharma, Sarah. *In the Meantime: Temporality and Cultural Politics*, Durham: Duke University Press, 2014.

Smith, Neil, and Cindi Katz, 'Grounding Metaphor – Towards a Spatialized Politics', in Michael Keith and Steve Pile (eds) *Place and the Politics of Identity*, New York: Routledge, 1993, pp. 66-81.

Tinic, Serra. *On Location: Canada's Television Industry in a Global Market*, Toronto: University of Toronto Press, 2005.

U.S. Immigration and Customs Enforcement, 'US, Mexican authorities shut down smuggling tunnel under construction in Nogales', 26 June 2013, https://www.ice.gov/news/releases/us-mexican-authorities-shut-down-smuggling-tunnel-under-construction-nogales.

U.S. Immigration and Customs Enforcement, 'Nogales Tunnel Task Force shuts down drug tunnel in backyard shed', 18 December 2013,http://www.ice.gov/news/releases/nogales-tunnel-task-force-shuts-down-drug-tunnel-backyard-shed.

THE LOGICS AND TERRITORIALITIES OF GEOBLOCKING

CAMERAN ASHRAF AND LUIS FELIPE ALVAREZ LEÓN

Introduction

The internet is often represented as an open network threatened by the aberrations of internet censorship and control. However, its historical development and architecture belie this binary model. The early split of the ARPANET by the U.S. Department of Defense into MILNET and ARPANET in order to protect sensitive military communications demonstrates that the ability to close and control the internet was by design part of its very foundation. Indeed, few states would embrace the internet were there not sufficient technical mechanisms to ensure an acceptable degree of management, surveillance, and control. In order to produce a better understanding of the political dimensions of the internet, the binary model of an open or closed system should be seen as part of a broader range of geopolitical and geoeconomic logics espoused by states and other actors, such as firms, who envision and construct the internet through different territorial perspectives.

The purpose of this chapter is to examine the territorialities associated with the internet through the lens of geoblocking. Geoblocking, from this perspective, is a phenomenon that brings together various actors, each with particular logics of action, and maps their corresponding territorialities onto the internet. The geopolitical and geoeconomic logics behind geoblocking and their resulting territorialities will be illustrated by a comparative examination of states and markets through two specific examples: state-sponsored internet censorship and online video distribution markets. These two perspectives reveal how geoblocking and its corresponding logics of deployment produce a range of territorialities that transcend the open/closed binary through which the internet is often understood.

States

The international state system is predicated upon geographical concepts which establish territorial states as distinct and discrete entities. The state is free to act within its territory, which is demarcated by borders, and its freedom to act within those borders is its sovereignty. Territory, borders, and sovereignty are the geographical assumptions underpinning the international state system. While these geographical concepts manifest themselves in many familiar ways, such as passport controls at airports or border fences, they need not be bound to the explicitly physical domain of land. Indeed, they have been adapted through airspace, territorial waters, and subterranean rights. The development of the internet, however, represents a new space for states to act and to reassert traditional notions of territory. For example, early cyber-utopians such as John Perry Barlow, co-founder of the Electronic Frontier Foundation, envisioned cyberspace as a radical space where borders and states no longer mattered: 'Governments of the Industrial World, you weary giants of flesh and steel, I come from Cyberspace, the new home of Mind. On behalf of the future, I ask you of the past to leave us alone. You are not welcome among us. You have no sovereignty where we gather.'[1] In cyberspace one could be something radically different and no longer be constrained by any of the perceived drawbacks of the physical world, such as physical appearance or geography.

Contrary to this vision, states have engaged with cyberspace by adapting the ideas of territory, borders, and sovereignty to this environment through the development of internet censorship and control. This is a view of the internet as an extension of existing territory in the new informational space through the development of laws and technical systems to territorialize cyberspace. In effect, many aspects of the international state system became duplicated online, such that the internet experienced from within one state could radically differ from the internet experienced from another. Through utilizing internet controls states are able to restrict the flow of information inside and outside of their borders, regardless of political circumstances. In cyberspace internet filtering is the primary way states assert their geopolitical visions, which are founded on the principles of sovereignty and borders. This is the 'information curtain' first articulated by Secretary of State Hillary Clinton in 2010.[2]

The rise of state internet controls and internet filtering has led many scholars and critics to assert that the modern state has found renewed vigor and life online.[3] The libertarian and utopian visions surrounding the birth of cyberspace have given way to a colder realism whereby cyberspace as a prototypical global public sphere[4] or global cyber commons[5] is becoming increasingly balkanized and segmented geopolitically. Censorship implementation and circumvention are a major and growing industry, worth at least $1.2 billion dollars in 2012 and including well-known corporations such as Cisco Systems and McAfee.[6]

Activity Regulations

According to Jonathan Zittrain and John Palfrey, activity regulations embody the many levels in which state territorialities are mapped onto cyberspace. Rather than internet-specific laws, activity regulations often stem from extensions of pre-existing restrictions on freedom

---

1   John Perry Barlow, 'A Declaration of the Independence of Cyberspace', 8 February 1996, https://projects.eff.org/~barlow/Declaration-Final.html

2   Rebecca MacKinnon, 'China's "Networked Authoritarianism"', *Journal of Democracy* 22.2 (2011): 32-46.

3   Ronald Deibert, 'The Geopolitics of Internet Control: Censorship, Sovereignty, and Cyberspace', in Andrew Chadwick and Philip N. Howard (eds) *The Routledge Handbook of Internet Politics*, Abingdon: Routledge, 2009, pp. 323-336; Nart Villeneuve, 'The Filtering Matrix: Integrated Mechanisms of Information Control and the Demarcation of Borders in Cyberspace', *First Monday* 11.1 (2006); Jack Goldsmith and Tim Wu, *Who Controls the Internet?*, New York: Oxford University Press, 2008.

4   Zizi Papacharissi, 'The Virtual Sphere: The Internet as a Public Sphere', *New Media & Society* 4.1 (2002): 9-27.

5   Nazli Choucri, *Cyberpolitics in International Relations*, Cambridge, Mass: The MIT Press, 2012. Choucri, *Cyberpolitics in International Relations*.

6   Orans and Firstbrook. 2011. 'Magic Quadrant for Secure Web Gateways.', Gartner Inc., available at https://www.gartner.com/doc/3064318/magic-quadrant-secure-web-gateways.

of speech or other media controls with the specific forms they take vary depending on social and political factors. For example, some states, such as Saudi Arabia or Iran, choose to enact content regulations to restrict or forbid citizens from developing, consuming, or distributing certain types of content. On the other hand, states may choose to 'relocate' content regulations by requiring internet service providers (ISPs) to filter content on behalf of the state in order to get a business license. Companies that do not filter on behalf of the state may be subject to various liabilities and penalties until they are in compliance. Finally, in states with pervasive surveillance regimes, users may engage in self-monitoring as a form of self-censorship echoing Foucault's panopticon whereby the user, company, ISP, or other user or provider censors themselves or the content and internet access they provide without prompting or intervention by the state. [7] This is often accompanied by a general level of surveillance and monitoring by the state that facilitates self-monitoring and surveillance as a social norm.

As with content classification, these filtering categories are not necessarily demarcated clearly, nor are their existence mutually exclusive. A state may implement some or all of these categories in their own interpretation of how best to protect and create informational sovereignty. In Iran, ISPs must obtain licenses, web hosting and mobile data plans require home addresses and personal registration, and cyber cafes must also register users while being under the threat of liability or licensing requirements.[8] In China the state includes its content restrictions in domestic copyright laws, creating a sheen of legitimacy and the appearance of working with international copyright norms while regulating content domestically. [9] Further, content restrictions may not be aimed solely at an individual user; a university or other organization may be held liable by a state for facilitating objectionable activities online as evidenced by the numerous copyright lawsuits filed by the Recording Industry Association of America (RIAA) against U.S. university students. While these activity regulations are often enforced to preserve state sovereignty, they can exist at the confluence of multiple logics. For example, the use of copyright by industry groups and enforced by the state can simultaneously advance a specific kind of market logic while also enacting state territoriality.

Technical Regulations

While activity regulations focus on *what* is controlled through the process of internet blocking, technical regulations focus on the instruments used to achieve this aim. Technical regulations and the technical specifics of internet filtering are expansive and vast. They can be grouped into four broad categories: in-line, DNS/domain tampering, denial of service, and national cyberzones.[10] Each category approaches filtering from a different perspective and each has

---

7   Michel Foucault, *Discipline and Punish: The Birth of the Prison*, 2nd edition, New York: Vintage, 1995.
8   Jonathan Zittrain and John Gorham Palfrey, 'Internet Filtering: The Politics and Mechanisms of Control', in Ronald Deibert et al. (eds), *Access Denied: The Practice and Policy of Global Internet Filtering*, Cambridge, MA: MIT Press, 2007, pp. 29-56.
9   Ibid.
10   Steven J. Murdoch and Ross Anderson, 'Tools and Technology of Internet Filtering', in Ronald Deibert et al. (eds), *Access Denied: The Practice and Policy of Global Internet Filtering*, Cambridge, MA: MIT Press, 2008, pp. 57-72.

unique structural advantages and disadvantages. For example, in moments of political crisis the easiest method to intimidate and control information flows can be to attempt a denial of service attack either conventionally or through identifying weaknesses in an offending server/website and bringing it down.

In-line filtering is comprised of two methods: proxy filtering and TCP/IP filtering. Proxy filtering seeks to insert another server between the user and the internet. Users access this server, which retrieves content on behalf of the user. Doing so allows the proxy server to cache content, increasing performance and speed for the end user while allowing administrators to have detailed abilities to block specific assets rather than entire domains.[11] This approach limits the user's ability to connect directly to the internet, ensuring that virtually all content is localized within the territorial state, a technique used by Syria after the Arab Spring uprising.[12]

TCP/IP filtering is the most commonly known method of internet filtering. Data packets are inspected for specific attributes (IP address, domain name, service port number, etc.) and this is checked against a defined block list, usually provided by the state. This level of analysis can occur at a router level or require a deeper level of inspection. Filtering at the router level will examine just the header of the information packet – equivalent to the address on an envelope – and block or allow that packet to continue to its destination. Examining the content of the data packet – equivalent to opening the envelope and reading its contents – requires more sophisticated technologies, called Deep Packet Inspection (DPI), which is currently believed to be in use in Iran.[13]

In the DPI method of TCP/IP filtering, the data packets are checked not only at the header level, but the actual content of the packet is checked for prohibited content, search queries, words, or other information. These are then checked against another list automatically via algorithm, to determine whether the packet should continue to its destination or be dropped or blocked. Depending on the sophistication of the algorithm, the censor can capture or monitor a tremendous amount of information at a highly granular level. This system can be used to not only identify content, but to address specific signatures and patterns in encrypted communications and block those packets, as evidenced by the repeated blocking of the Tor circumvention and anonymity tool in Iran.[14]

Most websites and online content are accessed using domain names, such as Google.com or UCLA.edu. In order to effectively translate the human readable domain names into machine readable IP addresses, users must access their ISP's DNS server when requesting a website. This process is normally invisible to the user, but within a filtering regime the

11 Ibid.
12 T. Eissa and Gi-hwan Cho, 'Internet Anonymity in Syria, Challenges and Solution', in Kuinam J. Kim and Kyung-Yong Chung (eds), *IT Convergence and Security 2012*, Dordrecht: Springer Netherlands, 2012, pp. 177-86.
13 Simurgh Aryan, Homa Aryan, and J. Alex Halderman, 'Internet Censorship in Iran: A First Look', *Proceedings of the 3rd USENIX Workshop on Free and Open Communications on the Internet*, Washington, August 2013, https://jhalderm.com/pub/papers/iran-foci13.pdf.
14 Ibid.

ISP's DNS server is fed with a list of specific domain names that should be blocked. When a user attempts to access a website in a filtering regime with DNS tampering, they will be unable to see the page.

Domain modifications and tampering are the counterparts to DNS tampering. DNS tampering works to block a user within a national filtering regime from accessing specific content. However, users outside of the territorial filtering regime are still able to access that content. If, for example, a website located in the Sudan is reporting on atrocities within the country, then users in the home country would be unable to access the content, but international media, such as CNN or the BBC, would still be able to do so. Domain modifications prevent this by removing the DNS entry for the domain name from the national DNS servers, which outside users access in order to retrieve a domain.

The final category, denial of service, involves a range of actions undertaken by states to filter both domestically and internationally. It includes distributed denial of service (DDoS) attacks, hacking, surveillance, and content takedown. The central logic of the denial of service category is that it uses cyber-attacks and infiltration to remove or alter undesirable content, regardless of where it is located geographically.

Content takedowns are a relatively new method of filtering which reflects the explosion of user-generated content in the web. In this method, states and citizen sympathizers or paid actors 'flag' or report objectionable content to content providers in the hopes of having the offending content removed and the uploader banned.[15] If, for example, a protest video were uploaded to video sharing site YouTube, a content takedown would see state-affiliated actors register accounts and report the video to YouTube so that it would be removed automatically.

The previous examples impose the territoriality of states by actively filtering, blocking or removing content, thus altering information flows. Surveillance, on the other hand, employs social, political, legal, and technical means to observe, collect, and classify information from the general populace and other targets of interest to the state. In-line filtering, especially through DPI, aids in surveillance as all aspects of data packets can be examined and then routed for storage and further investigation. Surveillance supports filtering because it acts as a digital panopticon whereby users are uncertain if they are being observed or monitored, and thus practice self-censorship of content for fear of punishment or other sanction.[16] Thus, surveillance as a filtering method must be supported by social or legal consequences otherwise it lacks ability to facilitate filtering.

Finally, the creation of national cyberzones marks an approach where 'hard' territoriality that

---

15   Erica Newland et al., 'Account Deactivation and Content Removal: Guiding Principles and Practices for Companies and Users', Berkman Center Research Publication, Harvard University, 2011, no. 2011-09.
16   Ronald Deibert, 'Black Code: Censorship, Surveillance, and the Militarisation of Cyberspace', *Millennium-Journal of International Studies* 32.3 (2003): 501-30; Ronald Deibert and Rafal Rohozinski, 'Liberation vs. Control: The Future of Cyberspace', *Journal of Democracy* 21.4 (2010): 43-57.

mirrors the land boundaries of the state is deployed through internet controls[17] to fence in flows of information. This approach seeks to develop an internal or "national internet" whereby users can only access information located within their territorial borders by disconnecting from the broader internet and relying on an exclusively domestic one. International connections still exist, but are restricted to elites or those with other forms of government approval. North Korea's Kwangmyong network is the oldest example of a national cyberzone where users can only access websites and resources located within North Korea and approved by state information ministries.[18] As with many of the blocking techniques previously discussed, national cyberzones can also intersect state with market logic by creating market spaces that are free from external competition, thus producing conditions that favor specific (often state-backed) actors.

Geographical concepts such as borders, territory, and sovereignty thus have both technical and legal analogues that have supported and extended their conceptual development, mutation, and maturation throughout human history. The Treaty of Westphalia's principle of mutual recognition, for instance, was dependent upon surveying technologies that could accurately demarcate and communicate borders. Technology plays a critical role for states in demarcating their limits and extents as well as communicating and defending those extents. To achieve this, states must combine activity regulation within their geographies with demarcation of these geographies through technical regulation. In spite of ethereal metaphors such as 'the cloud', the internet is a tremendously territorial medium grounded in space with easily identifiable packets, standardized national domain registrars, transnational data agreements and configuration, and national or sub-national networks (autonomous systems) whose deployment is the foundation of the internet and the purview of states.[19]

Cyberspace is increasingly territorialized by states through activity and technical regulations. States see cyberspace as an extension of the existing geographical status quo and have extended their legal and technical domains to encompass this, while simultaneously beginning to pursue international conventions in cyberspace. However, states are not alone in mapping their territorialities onto cyberspace. Indeed, states often see markets and firms as integral to efforts to normalize territorialized cyberspace. Through the transactions of myriad actors, markets deploy their own specific territorialities onto information flows. While mostly guided by a profit-seeking logic, these territorialities are constantly in dialogue, interaction, and sometimes tension with those of the state. The following section discusses the guiding logics of markets and their associated territorialities on the internet, and in doing so demonstrates a non-state centric logic through which geoblocking produces a broad range of territorialities which transcend attempts to understand the internet through an open/closed binary perspective.

17   Ronald Deibert et al. (eds), *Access Controlled: The Shaping of Power, Rights, and Rule in Cyberspace*, Cambridge, Mass: MIT Press, 2010.

18   Barney Warf, 'The Hermit Kingdom in Cyberspace: Unveiling the North Korean Internet', *Information, Communication & Society* 18.1 (2015): 109-20.

19   Hal Roberts, David Larochelle, Rob Faris, and John Palfrey. 2011. "Mapping Local Internet Control." In Computer Communications Workshop (Hyannis, CA, 2011), IEEE.

Markets

While states can control or record flows of information to preserve their sovereignty and territorial power online, market actors pursue a different type of territorialization: one that allows them to maximize profit. Often this involves 'locking information' through technical means, such as Digital Rights Management technologies, in order to target specific authorized spaces or devices. This means that the territorialities of information markets can be determined by the extent of market segmentation, distribution and enforcement of intellectual property rights, or the compatibility of technical means with particular digital goods.

In order to understand how market actors territorialize information, this process has to be put into the broader context of governance structures, such as regulatory frameworks. Intellectual property regimes, for example, have become instrumental in creating informational market spaces by limiting the distribution of content to specific jurisdictions. However, while this enables copyright holders, such as film studios, to secure revenue from distribution rights, it also presents new challenges. One of these is the difficulty of ensuring that only 'legitimate' content flows within the territorialized information markets. In digital environments it is very difficult to eradicate market-anomalous behavior such as piracy and file-sharing due to the low costs of reproduction and distribution online.

Another challenge for the construction of territorialized markets across digital information networks is the globalizing scale of information flows. This requires technical and governance frameworks such as payment systems and intellectual property protections to be coordinated across time and space at transnational scales. This level of coordination has made it more difficult to maintain a strategy long used by film distributors: the windowed release of products according to geographic region, and even by medium, such as theater and then home video. This strategy was designed to 'manage time and control speed through space so as to minimize the threat posed by new technologies'.[20] Consistent with the logic of market actors, the ultimate goal in this stepwise control of information is to reach the highest possible price each segmented market is capable of bearing.[21]

The distribution potential of digital networks presents a paradox to copyright holders and their efforts to map their particular territorialities onto these environments. While they present platforms for wider distribution and expanded markets, they also enable the development of actors who operate outside the bounds of those markets. Configured in fluid, decentralized assemblages such as P2P file-sharing networks and user communities, these actors often have the ability to circumvent the territorial and legal controls imposed by states and copyright holders.

---

20   Shujen Wang, 'Recontextualizing Copyright: Piracy, Hollywood, the State, and Globalization', *Cinema Journal* 43.1 (2003): 30.
21   Brett Christophers, 'The Territorial Fix: Price, Power and Profit in the Geographies of Markets', *Progress in Human Geography* 38.6 (2014): 754-770.

Operating beyond the bounds established by territorialized information markets, another type of information represents a potential for disruption to profit-maximization in markets. This is the spread of information outside the markets (through channels such as media outlets and social networks) *about* content circulating within those markets. The dissemination of this information may create network effects outside the markets that increase demand for content circulating inside them. Since digital goods such as films or TV shows are subject to the territorial limits of the market, but reviews, commentary and memes are not, this creates a spatial mismatch between the supply and demand. This means that some demand may not be satisfied by legal means outside of the markets due to either lack of authorized distribution or prices higher than most consumers will pay. As Shujen Wang points out, in the case of films and entertainment media, this has created an instant demand for pirated products.[22]

This tension between market territorialization and increased demand through digital networks *outside of the market* is an example of how new territorialities are extending old ones. While windowing the release of content by territory was an old strategy of copyright holders such as film studios, this is increasingly difficult in an era of global information flows. This has led to a multiplicity of coexisting strategies such as hard territorial markets through geoblocking, hybrid release campaigns across platforms, and simultaneous global releases.

Much like the controls of information enforced by states, the 'geographic rights management' approach behind geoblocking has been successful in producing territorialized spaces of information through exclusion. This process can be self-reinforcing because its deployment in a digital network environment expands the scope of its control with every digital copy. Lawrence Lessig has made the point that, through the use of DRM and the internet

> […] it is possible for [copyright holders] to centralize control over access to their content. Because each use of the Internet produces a copy, use on the Internet becomes subject of the copyright owner's control. The technology expands the scope of effective control because the technology builds a copy into every transaction.[23]

Yet, like states' control of information, which is often contested (and subverted) by groups of actors, the territorialities of information markets advanced by copyright holders are not permanently settled. In spite of the technical success of geoblocking technologies in territorializing content markets, copyright holders cannot permanently uphold their bid for control and centralization unless they offer audiences alternatives that meet their demands. This has forced copyright holders to seek different approaches that go beyond centralized control of information and punishment of violations.

As shown by the millions of takedown notices collected by the Chilling Effects project of the Berkman Center and the Electronic Frontier Foundation, it is common practice for copyright holders such as media companies, film studios, and states to demand the removal of

---

22   Shujen Wang, 'Recontextualizing Copyright', p. 31.
23   Lawrence Lessig, *Free Culture*, New York: The Penguin Press, 2004, p. 147.

copyrighted content from video streaming websites such as YouTube. However, while states seek to map their sovereignty and borders onto information networks, the profit-seeking logic of market actors is reflected in more malleable territorialities of information. For example, while the punishment of piracy was a key strategy to keep digital market spaces under control, copyright holders have opted to complement this approach with strategies aimed at capturing the lost revenue outside of the borders of these markets. Several studios have realized that if consumers are demanding video streaming online then the takedown notices and restrictions on streaming sites should be coupled with legitimate supply alternatives that address such unmet demand. That is how the service Hulu was born in 2008, which offers free streaming audiovisual copyrighted content available anytime with reduced commercial breaks. In a similar fashion, the television network websites are now offering part of their media catalogs in streaming content free of charge.

These alternatives are premised on the capacity of the copyright holders and distributors to enforce access controls on a territorial basis. These video platforms are offered within the bounds of states or regions that can provide a legal framework, a technological infrastructure, and a target audience receptive to the media products they offer and the advertisements that accompany them. Hulu, for example, detects if the IP number – which identifies the physical location of a computer – is within the United States or Japan, the two markets where this service operates. While for some time users abroad were able to circumvent these controls through the use of Virtual Private Networks or other technologies[24], Hulu has now blocked this possibility[25] – further demonstrating the territorialized construction of their market.

These video platforms present building blocks in territorialized information markets that have the dual aim of restricting access to a specific territory for legal purposes and also of providing highly differentiated marketing opportunities for their sponsors at a local level. Since markets cannot be created only through exclusion, but require the negotiation of supply and demand, this means that content is not only restricted through geoblocking, but also tailored by the information provided by geo-targeting and geographic rights management systems. This process of delimiting an audience geographically and constructing territorial information markets is a step towards creating "a well-mannered marketplace", the fabled walled garden of the internet.

Geoblocking and DRM are technical means used by market actors to achieve territorialities that can maximize their profit. These territorialities do not substitute existing political geographies, such as state borders, but complement and often correlate with them. As was argued above, the territorialities of information markets necessitate the regulatory protection that can be offered by confining the dissemination of (supposedly borderless) information to the physical boundaries of particular jurisdictions. This of course allows for the application of jurisdiction-specific copyright laws jointly with the deployment of Digital Rights Management,

24   Hulu, 'Why Can't I Use Hulu Internationally?', n.d., http://www.hulu.com/help/articles/171122.
25   Jeff Stone, 'Hulu Streaming: How To Evade The Ban On VPNs And Continue Watching Online
       TV',*IB Times,* 7 July 2014, http://www.ibtimes.com/hulu-streaming-how-evade-ban-vpns-continue-
       watching-online-tv-1620940.

which would be much more difficult to oversee in users and markets in other locations.

The complexities of enforcement highlight the continued presence of state institutional frameworks on the internet and the intersections between the territorialities of states and market actors in this environment. An example that illustrates this intersection is the recent Megaupload case, where millionaire Kim Dotcom was apprehended in New Zealand in 2012 at the behest of US authorities for illegally hosting copyrighted content in his storage service. In this case the reason why the United States Department of Justice could claim jurisdiction was due to the location of Megaupload's hired servers in Virginia. This conflu-ence of factors resulting in a claim of territorial jurisdiction and extraterritorial prosecution is, however (for now), an exceptional case. Needless to say, much extra-legal copyrighted content distribution takes place outside of the bounds of jurisdictions actively protected by legal regimes and law enforcement agencies.

In an age of intense global competition the territorialities of online markets are increasingly important for copyright industries. Market segmentation strategies with rigid territorialities that rely on windowed releases are becoming increasingly difficult in light of the fluidity and reach of digital networks. These technologies have the potential to bring new competitors and enable current market leaders to deploy a multiplicity of territorial strategies. While the infrastructural advantages of Hollywood studios and Anglo-European media conglomerates are undeniable, the competition from emerging competitors such as Korean and Chinese media industries highlights the imperative to adapt in order to survive. The American film pro-duction system successfully navigated a structural reconfiguration in the middle of the 20th century, when its transformation from a vertically integrated industry to a network dominated by flexible specialization ensured its survival.[26] However, the challenge copyright holders face today is unprecedented in the sense that it entails a fundamental reconfiguration of media markets through the coexistence of multiple and shifting territorialities.

If new and established copyright holders aim to develop markets internationally, they must do so increasingly through digital networks. The successful construction and profitable operation of digital markets requires a balancing act between two countervailing forces. On the one hand, copyright holders enact territorialities through enforcement and control (by combining technical and legal means, such as geoblocking and copyright law). On the other hand, (legal and illegal) competition forces them to negotiate unmet market demand by developing alternative territorialities through new forms of distribution. These territoriali-ties are built on the logic of profit-seeking, but also intersect with technical capabilities and politico-legal frameworks necessary to establish functioning markets. Thus, a key challenge in this project is the construction of stable territorialities of information markets. This requires considerable maneuvering and negotiation between judicial systems, technology firms, con-tent providers, business strategies and consumer demands.

---

26   Allen J. Scott, *On Hollywood: The Place, The Industry*, Princeton: Princeton University Press, 2005.

Conclusion

Different actors have different territorial logics through which the internet is envisioned and created. Certain actors, such as states and firms, articulate clear territorialities based on intellectual property regimes, markets, and internet censorship or control. The existence of an "open" internet can be considered a techno-utopian vision at odds with the historical development of this network.[27] Indeed, the word 'geoblocking' presupposes that there is something to be blocked, necessitating a binary open/closed model of the internet. This idea represents yet another frame of territorial logic mapped onto the internet. However, as this chapter demonstrates, multiple actors envision the internet less as an open network and more structured around territorialized logics in pursuit of their own economic, political, and social goals. Thus, the internet as a medium of experience is heterogeneous rather than binary with multiple actors co-existing with and creating multiple internets. This is the internet of lived experience rather than one which is only conceptual or rhetorical: an internet whose terrain is as varied as the globe it spans.

References

Aryan, Simurgh, Homa Aryan, and J. Alex Halderman. 'Internet Censorship in Iran: A First Look', *Proceedings of the 3rd USENIX Workshop on Free and Open Communications on the Internet,* Washington, August 2013, https://jhalderm.com/pub/papers/iran-foci13.pdf.

Bendrath, Ralf, Johan Eriksson, and Giampiero Giacomello. 'From "Cyberterrorism" to "Cyberwar", Back and Forth', in Johan Eriksson and Giampiero Giacomello (eds), *International Relations and Security in the Digital Age*, Abingdon: Routledge, 2007, pp. 57-82.

Barlow, John Perry. 'A Declaration of the Independence of Cyberspace,' 8 February 1996, https://homes.eff.org/~barlow/Declaration-Final.html.

Choucri, Nazli. *Cyberpolitics in International Relations*, Cambridge, Mass: The MIT Press, 2012.

Christophers, Brett. 'The Territorial Fix: Price, Power and Profit in the Geographies of Markets', *Progress in Human Geography* 38.6 (2014): 1-17.

Deibert, Ronald. 'Black Code: Censorship, Surveillance, and the Militarisation of Cyberspace', *Millennium-Journal of International Studies* 32.3 (2003): 501-30.

Deibert, Ronald. 'The Geopolitics of Internet Control: Censorship, Sovereignty, and Cyberspace', in Andrew Chadwick and Philip N. Howard (eds) *The Routledge Handbook of Internet Politics*, Abingdon: Routledge, 2009, pp. 323-336.

Deibert, Ronald et al. *Access Controlled: The Shaping of Power, Rights,and Rule in Cyberspace.* Cambridge, Mass: MIT Press, 2010.

Deibert, Ronald, and Rafal Rohozinski. 'Liberation vs. Control: The Future of Cyberspace', *Journal of Democracy* 21.4 (2010): 43-57.

Digital Element, 'Geographic Rights Management', http://www.digital-element.net/our_technology/our_technology.html.

Eissa, T., and Gi-hwan Cho. 'Internet Anonymity in Syria, Challenges and Solution', in Kuinam J. Kim and Kyung-Yong Chung (eds), *IT Convergence and Security 2012*, Dordrecht: Springer Netherlands,

---

27   Roberts, Hal, David Larochelle, Rob Faris, and John Palfrey. 2011. 'Mapping Local Internet Control.' In Computer Communications Workshop (Hyannis, CA, 2011), IEEE

2012, pp. 177-86.

Foucault, Michel. *Discipline and Punish: The Birth of the Prison*, 2nd edition, New York: Vintage, 1995.

Goldsmith, Jack, and Tim Wu. *Who Controls the Internet?: Illusions of a Borderless World*, New York: Oxford University Press, 2008.

Hulu, 'Why Can't I Use Hulu Internationally?', n.d., http://www.hulu.com/help/articles/171122.

Lessig, Lawrence. *Free Culture*, New York: Penguin, 2004.

MacKinnon, Rebecca. 'China's "Networked Authoritarianism"' *Journal of Democracy* 22.2 (2011): 32-46.

Murdoch, Steven J., and Ross Anderson. 'Tools and Technology of Internet Filtering', in Ronald Deibert et al. (eds), *Access Denied: The Practice and Policy of Global Internet Filtering*, Cambridge, MA: MIT Press, 2008, pp. 57-72.

Newland, Erica et al. 2011. 'Account Deactivation and Content Removal: Guiding Principles and Practices for Companies and Users', *Berkman Center Research Publication*, Harvard University, no. 2011-09.

Orans, L., and P. Firstbrook. 2011. 'Magic Quadrant for Secure Web Gateways.' *Gartner Inc.*, http://www.gartner.com/technology/research/methodologies/magicQuadrants.jsp.

Papacharissi, Zizi. 'The Virtual Sphere: The Internet as a Public Sphere', *New Media & Society* 4.1 (2002): 9-27.

Roberts, Hal, David Larochelle, Rob Faris, and John Palfrey. 2011. "Mapping Local Internet Control." In Computer Communications Workshop (Hyannis, CA, 2011), IEEE.

Scott, Allen J. *On Hollywood: The Place, The Industry*. Princeton: Princeton University Press, 2005.

Stone, Jeff, 'Hulu Streaming: How To Evade The Ban On VPNs And Continue Watching Online TV', *IB Times*, 7 July 2014, http://www.ibtimes.com/hulu-streaming-how-evade-ban-vpns-continue-watching-online-tv-1620940.

Stryszowski, Piotr and Danny Scorpecci. *Piracy of Digital Content*, Paris: OECD, 2009.

Thomas, Julie. 'Ethics of Hacktivism.' *Information Security Reading Room* 12 (2001).

Villeneuve, Nart. 'The Filtering Matrix: Integrated Mechanisms of Information Control and the Demarcation of Borders in Cyberspace', *First Monday* 11.1 (2006), http://firstmonday.org/ojs/index.php/fm/article/view/1307/1227.

Wang, Shujen. 'Recontextualizing Copyright: Piracy, Hollywood, the State, and Globalization', *Cinema Journal* 43.1 (2003): 25-43.

Warf, Barney. 'The Hermit Kingdom in Cyberspace: Unveiling the North Korean Internet', *Information, Communication & Society* 18.1 (2015):109-20.

Zittrain, Jonathan, and John Gorham Palfrey. 'Internet Filtering: The Politics and Mechanisms of Control', in Ronald Deibert et al. (eds), *Access Denied: The Practice and Policy of Global Internet Filtering*, Cambridge, MA: MIT Press, 2007, pp. 29-56.

GEOBLOCKING, TECHNICAL STANDARDS AND THE LAW

MARKETA TRIMBLE

Introduction

In a world where countries cannot agree on a single set of laws that would apply uniformly around the globe, most national laws need to be territorially confined. Without territorial limits, laws have extraterritorial effects that often, although not always, impinge upon other countries' sovereignty and freedom to set their own laws and policies. For example, what might work as law in the United States might not work in France, and therefore French law might be different from U.S. law. Some legal rights and responsibilities exist only within countries' jurisdictional limits, and therefore persons and entities may enjoy the rights and must fulfill the responsibilities within the defined territory. For example, copyright is territorially limited; someone who owns copyright to a work in the United States under U.S. law might not be the owner of copyright to that same work in France under French law.[1] As long as the world operates on the basis of national laws, there will be a need to replicate national borders on the internet to comply with these corresponding physical limitations.[2] Geoblocking is being used with increasing frequency to achieve this compliance.[3]

The relationship between geoblocking and legal compliance has undergone significant development in recent years. Legislators, courts, and agencies previously did not view geoblocking as a reliable method of achieving legal compliance. They assumed that the internet was inherently borderless and geoblocking was invariably unreliable, and they adopted laws, rendered judgments, and issued decisions with the conviction that these would inevitably have global effects.[4] Recently, however, legislators, courts, and agencies have begun to consider geoblocking as a viable tool for delineating the effects of their laws, judgments, and decisions, and for territorially limiting actions on the internet in general.

The idea that geoblocking could be used as a compliance tool is one part of the development of the relationship between geoblocking and legal compliance. This chapter outlines the three stages through which this development will proceed. In the first stage, geoblocking will be accepted as a tool of regulation and enforcement. While acceptance has already occurred in some countries in some contexts, this acceptance is certainly not yet general

---

1   Marketa Trimble, 'The Multiplicity of Copyright Laws on the Internet', *Fordham Intellectual Property, Media & Entertainment Law Journal* 25.2 (Winter, 2015): 345-346.

2   Jack L. Goldsmith and Tim Wu, *Who Controls the Internet?: Illusions of A Borderless World*, New York: Oxford University Press, 2006, at p. viii and 152.

3   On other methods of imposing borders on the internet *see* Marketa Trimble, 'The Future of Cybertravel: Legal Implications of the Evasion of Geolocation', *Fordham Intellectual Property, Media & Entertainment Law Journal* 22.3 (2012): 583-585.

4   Michael Geist, 'Cyberlaw 2.0', *Boston College Law Review* 44 (2003): 335-347.

or widespread. In the second stage, minimum standards for geoblocking will be promulgated because the use of geoblocking for purposes of legal compliance necessarily calls for minimum technological standards that geoblocking tools must meet in order to create virtual borders sufficiently precise and impermeable to satisfy the law. In the third stage, circumvention of geoblocking and the tools that facilitate circumvention will be targeted by countries' regulation. The three stages will likely begin at different times in different countries, industries, and contexts, but will eventually overlap and thereafter develop concurrently.

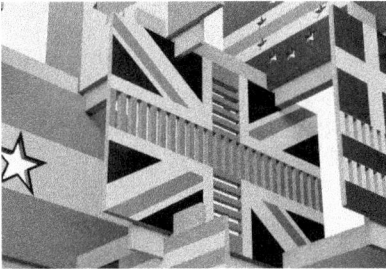

Figure 1. Geoblocking has a complicated relationship with national legal systems but it is starting to be increasingly recognized as a useful tool for legal compliance. Credit: Karen Roe (CC BY 2.0)

Geoblocking as a Tool of Regulation and Enforcement

The first stage of the development of the relationship between geoblocking and legal compliance – the process of accepting geoblocking as a tool of regulation and enforcement – is already under way. Here, three specific developments are notable: First, private party contracts are including geoblocking to secure territorial limitations on contractual obligations; second, regulators have turned to geoblocking as their preferred means of achieving compliance with territorially-limited regulatory requirements; and, third (the most remarkable development so far), the legal profession is exploring the potential for geoblocking as the *only* valid means to comply with laws that create territorially-limited rights and responsibilities. We now look at these developments in detail.

Parties enter contracts that include obligations to geoblock for various reasons, not all of which are based in legal requirements.[5] Geoblocking may be used to customize localized services through supply of content in a particular language, culturally-sensitive content, and localized advertising. Geoblocking may be also used to enforce price differentiation in various markets. Contractually-prescribed geoblocking need not follow national borders; parties may define other, completely different territorial limits if they wish – such as only the West Coast of the United States, or the Flemish-speaking region of Belgium. Additionally, parties include geoblocking in their contracts in order to comply with obligations related to territorial limitations arising by law. For example, when a content provider owns copyright to content in only some countries and licenses that content only for some of the countries

---

5   On the various reasons for which parties turn to geolocation and geoblocking *see* Trimble, *supra* note 3, pp. 586-589.

in which it owns copyright, its license may require that the licensee geoblock users who connect from outside the particular countries for which the license is issued. For instance, when Czech Television obtains a license from BBC to the *Doc Martin* TV show, BBC might limit the license to the territory of the Czech Republic with the result that the Czech Television must use geoblocking to prevent users who connect from outside the Czech Republic from viewing the show on their platform.

The acceptance of geoblocking as a tool of regulation is another important development. For example, online gambling regulators in some jurisdictions require their licensees to use geoblocking tools and to allow users to access content only within the jurisdictions where online gambling is legal. In Germany, when doubts arose as to whether geoblocking was and is a sufficiently reliably tool to meet the territorial limitations set by law for online gambling, courts have confirmed that geoblocking is sufficiently reliable for that purpose.[6] In the United States, a Kentucky court issued an order directing an online gambling website to geoblock users connecting from Kentucky in order for the website to comply with Kentucky law.[7]

As these court decisions suggest, geoblocking may eventually be recognized by courts as *the* indispensable compliance tool. This development is important because it could result in geoblocking being accepted as standard practice on the internet – the standard measure that every actor on the internet would be expected to employ in order to satisfy an obligation to territorially restrict access to content on the internet.

Typically, the law expects persons and entities to employ measures that are reasonable according to the law to comply with the law, including its territorial limitations. An example of an offline distribution of a book is illustrative: When a distributor obtains a license to sell copies of a book in one particular country, the law requires the distributor to take reasonable measures to comply with the territorial limitation of the license. The distributor takes a reasonable measure, for example, when it checks the address of a purchaser before it ships a copy of the book to the purchaser. The law does not require the distributor to attach a weight to every copy to make transportation of the copies more difficult, nor does the law expect the distributor to attach a radio frequency identification tag to every copy and install a surveillance system to monitor the movement of each copy and prevent copies from leaving the country. The latter two measures are technically feasible but are clearly not reasonable; a contract could in theory bind the publisher to employ such measures, provided that the publisher would agree to such unusual contractual terms. However, absent such contractual terms or absent an explicit requirement in the law, no one would read in the law – for example in copyright law in the present example – an obligation to employ such extreme measures.

---

6   Oberlandesgericht Münster, 13 B 775/09, 3 December 2009; Oberverwaltungsgericht Nordrhein-
     Westfalen, 13 B 646/10, 2 July 2010; Oberverwaltungsgericht Nordrhein-Westfalen, 13 B 676/10, 13
     July 2010.
7   Jazette Enterprises Ltd. v. Commonwealth of Kentucky, Court of Appeals of Kentucky, 2014 WL
     689044, 21 February 2014, p. 2.

Is geoblocking today more consistent with checking purchasers' addresses or is it more like attaching weights and radio frequency identification tags to books? If geoblocking is more like checking purchasers' addresses and is a reasonable measure, then any territorial limitations mandated by law should implicate the required use of geoblocking. If geoblocking is more like a weight or radio tag, it is not a reasonable measure and will not usually be required by law. The following dispute involving video content made available on the internet highlights the issue that needs to be clarified.

A dispute arose between *Spanski Enterprises, Inc.*, a Canadian television distributor, and *Telewizja Polska, S.A.*, a Polish government-owned corporation that operates several television channels in Poland. *Spanski Enterprises* obtained an exclusive license from *Telewizja Polska* to broadcast Polish television programming in North and South America; later the parties updated the license to include broadcasting on the internet. However, approximately seven years into the license, *Spanski Enterprises* objected to the fact that internet users in North and South America could access the *Telewizja Polska* website and watch content on the website for which *Spanski Enterprises* held an exclusive license.

The first lawsuit that *Spanski Enterprises* filed (in 2007) resulted in a 2009 settlement agreement in which the parties agreed to 'maintain and continue all internet geo-blocking which is currently in effect, and [...] use their best efforts to conform their respective future geo-blocking efforts to the latest widely disseminated and financially practicable geo-blocking technologies.'[8] Then, in 2012, *Spanski Enterprises* returned to court with allegations that *Telewizja Polska* had 'turned off the geoblocking feature and thereby intentionally made available to viewers in the United States via the internet thousands of episodes of shows to which [*Spanski Enterprises*] had the exclusive distribution rights in the United States.'[9] As of September 2015 the case was still pending before the U.S. District Court for the District of Columbia with the trial date set for December 7, 2015.[10]

If *Telewizja Polska* did indeed disable geoblocking (an allegation it denied), it would likely violate the settlement agreement. The more difficult question is whether *Telewizja Polska*'s alleged actions would violate U.S. copyright law – whether the use of geoblocking is a reasonable measure that the law today should expect to be employed by content providers to avoid infringing the copyrights of others. *Spanski Enterprises* claims that *Telewizja Polska* infringed copyright under U.S. law; *Telewizja Polska* contends that its 'obligation to geo-block is a contractual covenant to protect the rights actually licensed to [*Spanski Enterprises*] – it is not part of the licensed rights themselves.'[11]

---

8   Spanski Enterprises, Inc. v. Telewizja Polska, S.A., D.D.C., 1:12-cv-00957-TSC, document 1, Complaint, 11 June 2012, p. 4.
9   *Id.*, pp. 4-5.
10   Spanski Enterprises, Inc. v. Telewizja Polska, S.A., D.D.C., 1:12-cv-00957-TSC, document 37, Amended Pretrial Order, 20 August 2015, p. 1.
11   Spanski Enterprises, Inc. v. Telewizja Polska, S.A., D.D.C., 1:12-cv-00957-TSC, document 29, Defendant's Consolidated Memorandum of Points and Authorities, 27 February 2015, p. 4. For the purposes of the present discussion we leave aside the question whether the agreement's provision on geoblocking was a covenant or a condition.

Telewizja Polska argues that an obligation to geoblock is a contractual covenant. If *Spanski Enterprises* can prove its allegations, a breach of a contractual covenant would result only in monetary remedies for a violation of the agreement; a finding of copyright infringement would presumably be more costly for *Telewizja Polska*. The outcome of the case could be of general importance for the future of geoblocking because it should clarify whether geoblocking is *the* reasonable measure – *the* standard means that internet actors must employ to meet territorial limitations on rights and responsibilities imposed by law.

Minimum Standards for Geoblocking

Minimum standards for geoblocking – the hallmark of the second stage of the development in the relationship between geoblocking and legal compliance – have been the subject of debate. A range of geoblocking tools exists, and more advanced tools are constantly being developed.[12] The difficulty, of course, is setting minimal legal standards with sufficient precision, while still allowing improvements in current tools and the development of new tools. To facilitate and propel improvements, minimum standards must not include specific technical details that would entrench old technology; to safeguard the potential to develop new technology, minimum standards should follow the principle of technological neutrality.

As mentioned earlier, minimum standards for geoblocking exist in contracts between parties that have agreed to the use of geoblocking. For example, the language of the 2009 settlement agreement between *Spanski Enterprises* and *Telewizja Polska* sets a minimum standard for geoblocking; the parties agreed to 'the latest widely disseminated and financially practicable geo-blocking technologies.'[13] In a licensing agreement concluded between Sony and Netflix, the parties agreed on very general language according to which Netflix would 'utilize an industry standard geolocation service'[14] and language that specified that the geolocation service employed must, for example, 'provide geographic location information based on DNS registrations, WHOIS databases and Internet subnet mapping' and 'provide geolocation bypass detection technology designed to detect IP addresses located in the Territory, but being used by Registered Users outside the Territory.'[15] For the purposes of legal compliance, courts and regulators will play an important role in defining the minimum standards of geoblocking.

The general understanding is that geoblocking cannot be perfect; geoblocking tools are not 100 percent reliable, particularly given that users have access to readily available tools to

---

12   James A. Muir and Paul C. Van Oorschot, 'Internet Geolocation: Evasion and Counterevasion', *ACM Computing Surveys* 4 (December 2009).

13   *Supra* note 8.

14   Michael Geist, 'Nobody's Perfect: Leaked Contract Reveals Sony Requires Netflix to Geo-Block But Acknowledges Technology is Imperfect', Michael Geist's blog, 17 April 2015, http://www.michaelgeist. ca/2015/04/nobodys-perfect-leaked-contract-reveals-sony-requires-netflix-to-geo-block-but-acknowledges-technology-is-imperfect/.

15   *Id.*

circumvent geoblocking.[16] For example, users can use VPNs, such as Chameleon, simpler tools, such as MyExpatNetwork, or more complicated tools, such as Tor, to bypass geoblocking and access content on the internet that is otherwise inaccessible to them because of their location. Not only might it be unrealistic to expect perfect geoblocking, it might also be illogical to require perfect geoblocking for purposes of legal compliance. The offline physical borders on which legal compliance relies are not impermeable, and the law accepts some cross-border spillover. For example, countries recognize an intellectual property law exception for small quantities of materials protected by intellectual property rights that travelers carry in their luggage for personal use.[17] Similarly, some leakage through national borders on the internet should be acceptable. The question is what an acceptable volume of leakage is; the acceptable volume may vary depending on the area of law and regulation. In other words, when does VPN or proxy use become too much?

The fact that geoblocking circumvention tools exist does not mean that geoblocking is incapable of meeting some minimum standards of territorial restrictions sufficient for legal compliance. The approaches that courts have taken to evaluate the effectiveness of technological protection measures designed to protect access to copyrighted works is instructive, given that, in the case of technological protection measures, tools also exist that enable circumvention of these measures. For example, the Regional Court of Munich, in a discussion of the secondary liability of an online journal provider for providing a link to a circumvention tool, noted that the ineffectiveness of a technological measure cannot be concluded from the existence of a circumvention tool; it might be sufficient for the measure to prevent *average* users from accessing protected content.[18] The U.S. District Court for the Northern District of California rejected an argument proposing that a measure not be considered effective if tools to circumvent the measure are 'widely available on the Internet.'[19] The court said that the argument is 'equivalent to a claim that, since it is easy to find skeleton keys on the black market, a deadbolt is not an effective lock to a door.'[20]

Regulating the Circumvention of Geoblocking

In the third stage of the process, the law will start to respond to the easy availability of VPNs, proxies and other circumvention tools. Their widespread use, as shown throughout this book, suggests that ongoing evasions can no longer be considered negligible spillover.[21]

---

16   Dan Jerker B. Svantesson, 'Geo-Location Technologies and Other Means of Placing Borders on the Borderless Internet', *The John Marshall Journal of Information Technology & Privacy Law* 23 (2004): 111 ff.

17   Agreement on Trade-Related Aspects of Intellectual Property Rights, WTO, 1994, Article 60.

18   Oberlandesgericht München I, 21 O 6742/07, 14 November 2007.

19   *321 Studios v. Metro Goldwyn Mayer Studios, Inc.*, 307 F.Supp.2d 1085, 1095 (N.D.Ca. 2004).

20   *Id.*

21   For example, Liana B. Baker and Yinka Adegoke, 'Olympics Fans Find Ways to Circumvent NBC's Online Control', *Reuters*, 31 July 2012, http://www.reuters.com/article/2012/07/31/us-olympics-tech-workaround-idUSBRE86U02R20120731; Aaron Gell, 'Reinventing the Web: A New App Lets You Watch Whatever TV Program You Want, Including the Olympics, Anywhere in the World', *Business Insider*, 25 January 2014, http://www.businessinsider.com/hola-tv-watch-olympics-vpn-blocker-netflix-world-2014-1.

Some content providers now include provisions in their terms of service that prohibit internet users from evading geoblocking. For example, German television station *Sat.1* in its terms of service for the use of its online video portal makes it a violation of the terms of service for users to 'alter, evade or otherwise disregard' the technical measures that the station uses to territorially limit the access to content on the portal.[22] If a user does use a VPN or other tool to circumvent geoblocking, the user violates this provision of the terms of service and is in breach of his contract with *Sat.1*, thus exposing himself to a response by *Sat.1*, who may terminate the contract with the user, or, although unlikely, file suit against the user for violation of the contract.

Absent a contractual provision prohibiting circumvention, the status of geoblocking evasion under the law of various countries is currently unclear.[23] Specific legislation on the evasion of geoblocking does not exist; whether the evasion of geoblocking is covered by copyright law provisions on technological protection measures or retransmission has been disputed,[24] and anti-computer-hacking laws may be applicable in some countries, to a limited degree.[25] In some countries the providers of geoblocking circumvention tools could be held liable for facilitating access to restricted content.[26] A dispute that arose in New Zealand between the media companies SKY, TVNZ, Lightbox, and MediaWorks on one side and ByPass Network Services on the other side seemed to have provided impetus for a clarification – or at least a fruitful discussion – of the status of circumvention of geoblocking in New Zealand.[27] The dispute over the Bypass *GlobalMode* product – a 'geo-unblocking solution' for ISPs – was settled in June 2015 and therefore provided no guidance on the status of the evasion of geoblocking in New Zealand; nevertheless, it is notable that the practical result was the promise to withdraw the geoblocking circumvention tool from the New Zealand market as of 1 September 2015.[28]

The development of approaches to geoblocking circumvention tools by legislators, courts, and agencies has been complicated by the fact that many existing circumvention tools were developed for and still serve another purpose – anonymization. Safeguarding privacy, protecting personal data, and securing the freedom of speech and the right to access information are among the concerns that suggest that a simple proscription against geoblocking circumvention tools might be undesirable.

---

22   Nutzungsbedingunen für die Nutzung des Videoportals von Sat.1, § 4.1(g), http://www.sat1.de/
      service/nutzungsbedingungen/nutzungsbedingungen-fuer-die-nutzung-des-videoportals-von-sat-1.
23   Trimble, *supra* note 3.
24   *Id.*, pp. 612-620 and 630-634; Christopher Hilliard, 'Evaluating the Legitimacy of Geo-Location
      Circumvention in the Context of Technical Protection Measures', *Queen Mary Journal of Intellectual
      Property* 5(2) (2015): 157-182.
25   Trimble, *supra* note 3, pp. 625-627 and 630.
26   *Id.*, pp. 628-630.
27   Jeremy Kirk, 'Geoblocking Question Unresolved After New Zealand Lawsuit Ends', PCWorld, 23 June
      2015, http://www.pcworld.com/article/2939972/geoblocking-question-unresolved-after-new-zealand-
      lawsuit-ends.html.
28   *Supra* note 27.

Conclusion

In discussing the three stages in the development of the relationship between geoblocking and legal compliance this chapter presumes that geoblocking will be more pervasive and eventually become the only means to achieve compliance with territorial limitations of the law. The presumption is rooted in the conviction that legal compliance on the internet cannot be achieved without replicating national borders online. A single global law that would eliminate the need for national borders is unlikely to develop anytime soon, and the alternative – the harmonization of national laws – is unlikely to result in the uniformity necessary to make national borders obsolete for legal purposes. Because differences among national laws persist, a need for borders on the internet, and therefore for geoblocking, seems unavoidable.

There is, of course, much opposition to geoblocking. Users complain about the inaccessibility of geoblocked content, and their increasing use of geoblocking circumvention tools evidences their displeasure with territorial limitations. In May 2015 the European Commission criticized the use of geoblocking in the European Union in 'A Digital Single Market Strategy for Europe – Analysis and Evidence'[29] and launched a related inquiry into the e-commerce sector.[30] In the document the Commission referred to geoblocking as one of the 'barriers that hold back cross-border e-commerce.'[31] A preference for unencumbered cross-border access to content on the internet is also apparent from the draft 'Trade in Services Agreement'[32] that is being negotiated by a group of countries – members of the World Trade Organization. However, all official initiatives throughout the world concerning cross-border access on the internet recognize that there are areas of law – such as intellectual property law and gambling law – in which countries will continue to have legitimate grounds for imposing restrictions on the cross-border flows of goods and services.[33] Although some stakeholders desire a liberalization of cross-border access to internet content, the fact cannot be ignored that countries have major differences in some areas of law, and therefore good reasons to maintain control of content flows.

Business models that respond to consumer demand for cross-border access will continue to emerge, and countries can facilitate the development of new business models by providing favorable legislative and regulatory environments. The 2014 European Union's Collective Rights Management Directive[34] is one effort to improve the environment for businesses

---

29 A Digital Single Market Strategy for Europe – Analysis and Evidence, European Commission, SWD(2015) 100 final, 6 May 2015, pp. 21-25.

30 Commission Decision of 6 May 2015 initiating an inquiry into the e-commerce sector pursuant to Article 17 of Council Regulation (EC) No 1/2003.

31 *Supra* note 30, p. 3.

32 Draft Trade in Services Agreement (TiSA), Annex on Electronic Commerce, 16 September 2013. *See also* Marketa Trimble, Local Hosting and the Draft "Trade in Services Agreement", Technology & Marketing Law Blog, 22 September 2015, http://blog.ericgoldman.org/archives/2015/09/local-hosting-and-the-draft-trade-in-services-agreement-guest-blog-post.html.

33 For example General Agreement on Trade in Services, Article XIV(a); North American Free Trade Agreement, Chapter 21; Treaty on the Functioning of the European Union, Article 36.

34 Directive 2014/26/EU of the European Parliament and of the Council of 26 February 2014 on collective management of copyright and related rights and multi-territorial licensing of rights in musical

that seek to provide cross-border online access to music, at least within the borders of the European Union. Because some geoblocking is required by law, contracts will not be able to eliminate geoblocking entirely; however, contracting parties can eliminate some geoblocking, and limited geoblocking evasion could mitigate some of the effects of geoblocking where the use of geoblocking exceeds what is required by law. For example, a system of 'digital passports' could facilitate access to users who travel abroad.[35]

References

'A Digital Single Market Strategy for Europe – Analysis and Evidence', European Commission, SWD (2015) 100 final, 6 May 2015.

Agreement on Trade-Related Aspects of Intellectual Property Rights, WTO, 1994.

Baker, Liana B., and Yinka Adegoke. 'Olympics Fans Find Ways to Circumvent NBC's Online Control', *Reuters*, 31 July 2012, http://www.reuters.com/article/2012/07/31/us-olympics-tech-work-around-idUSBRE86U02R20120731.

Commission Decision of 6 May 2015 initiating an inquiry into the e-commerce sector pursuant to Article 17 of Council Regulation (EC) No 1/2003.

Directive 2014/26/EU of the European Parliament and of the Council of 26 February 2014 on collective management of copyright and related rights and multi-territorial licensing of rights in musical works for online use in the internal market.

Draft Trade in Services Agreement (TiSA), Annex on Electronic Commerce, 16 September 2013.

Geist, Michael. 'Cyberlaw 2.0', *Boston College Law Review* 44 (2003): 335-347.

Geist, Michael. 'Nobody's Perfect: Leaked Contract Reveals Sony Requires Netflix to Geo-Block But Acknowledges Technology is Imperfect', Michael Geist's blog, 17 April 2015, http://www.michaelgeist.ca/2015/04/nobodys-perfect-leaked-contract-reveals-sony-requires-netflix-to-geo-block-but-acknowledges-technology-is-imperfect/.

Gell, Aaron. 'Reinventing the Web: A New App Lets You Watch Whatever TV Program You Want, Including the Olympics, Anywhere in the World', *Business Insider*, 25 January 2014, http://www.businessinsider.com/hola-tv-watch-olympics-vpn-blocker-netflix-world-2014-1.

General Agreement on Trade in Services.

Goldsmith, Jack L., and Tim Wu. *Who Controls the Internet?: Illusions of A Borderless World*, New York: Oxford University Press, 2006.

Hilliard, Christopher. 'Evaluating the Legitimacy of Geo-Location Circumvention in the Context of Technical Protection Measures', *Queen Mary Journal of Intellectual Property* 5(2) (2015): 157-182.

Jazette Enterprises Ltd. v. Commonwealth of Kentucky, Court of Appeals of Kentucky, 2014 WL 689044, 21 February 2014.

Kirk, Jeremy. 'Geoblocking Question Unresolved After New Zealand Lawsuit Ends', PCWorld, 23 June 2015, http://www.pcworld.com/article/2939972/geoblocking-question-unresolved-after-new-zealand-lawsuit-ends.html.

Muir, James A., and Paul C. Van Oorschot. 'Internet Geolocation: Evasion and Counterevasion', *ACM Computing Surveys* 4 (December 2009).

---

works for online use in the internal market.

35   Trimble, *supra* note 3, p. 639.

North American Free Trade Agreement.

Oberlandesgericht München I, 21 O 6742/07, 14 November 2007.

Oberlandesgericht Münster, 13 B 775/09, 3 December 2009.

Oberverwaltungsgericht Nordrhein-Westfalen, 13 B 646/10, 2 July 2010.

Oberverwaltungsgericht Nordrhein-Westfalen, 13 B 676/10, 13 July 2010.

Scarlet Extended SA v. SABAM, CJEU, C-70/10, 24 November 2011.

Spanski Enterprises, Inc. v. Telewizja Polska, S.A., D.D.C., 1:12-cv-00957-TSC, document 1, Complaint, 11 June 2012.

Spanski Enterprises, Inc. v. Telewizja Polska, S.A., D.D.C., 1:12-cv-00957-TSC, document 29, Defendant's Consolidated Memorandum of Points and Authorities, 27 February 2015.

Spanski Enterprises, Inc. v. Telewizja Polska, S.A., D.D.C., 1:12-cv-00957-TSC, document 37, Amended Pretrial Order, 20 August 2015.

Svantesson, Dan Jerker B. 'Geo-Location Technologies and Other Means of Placing Borders on the Borderless Internet', *The John Marshall Journal of Information Technology & Privacy Law* 23 (2004): 101.

Treaty on the Functioning of the European Union.

Trimble, Marketa. 'The Future of Cybertravel: Legal Implications of the Evasion of Geolocation', *Fordham Intellectual Property, Media & Entertainment Law Journal* 22.3 (Spring, 2012): 567-657.

Trimble, Marketa. 'Local Hosting and the Draft "Trade in Services Agreement"', Technology & Marketing Law Blog, 22 September 2015, http://blog.ericgoldman.org/archives/2015/09/local-hosting-and-the-draft-trade-in-services-agreement-guest-blog-post.htm.

Trimble, Marketa. 'The Multiplicity of Copyright Laws on the Internet', *Fordham Intellectual Property, Media & Entertainment Law Journal* 25.2 (2015): 339-405.

PERISCOPE, LIVE-STREAMING AND MOBILE VIDEO CULTURE

ADAM RUGG AND BENJAMIN BURROUGHS[1]

On 26 March 2015, Twitter released Periscope, its recently acquired live-streaming mobile app, on the Apple app store. Despite widespread praise and media attention for the app's potential to usher in the era of mobile live-streaming, Periscope initially experienced slow uptake amongst mobile users. However, within a few months of launch, the perils and promise of Periscope were on full display as users found novel and sometimes illegal ways of using the app. Perhaps the most infamous use of Periscope occurred on 2 May 2015, during a much-hyped boxing match between Floyd Mayweather and Manny Pacquiao. After thousands of users used Periscope to watch unsanctioned streams - rather than pay an unprecedented $100 for the official PPV feed of the fight - *The New York Times* observed that the app had 'barged its way onto sports' biggest stage', while the CEO of Twitter controversially declared the app the real winner of the night.[2] While most discussion of Periscope since then has focused on the app's potential for piracy, we suggest it also represents a broader, escalating tension between traditional media industries, informal digital media practices, and mobile technologies.

Just three months later and across the world in Turkey, an unemployed math teacher named Ekol Hoca was utilizing the app as an educational tool to reach thousands of Turkish students. After the Turkish government shut down prep schools affiliated with the Gülen religious movement as part of a political crackdown, Hoca turned to Periscope to continue the lessons the government sought to end.[3] In so doing he circumvented state authority and disrupted the strategic place of the government through this emergent mobile technology. With around 1,500 students sometimes turning into his broadcasts, Hoca has shown how live-streaming technologies can themselves be political tools, bypassing state controls to communicate and interact with other citizens.[4]

Elsewhere we have looked at the rise of 'streaming culture' and competing claims of sanctioned and unsanctioned streaming media.[5] Operating across the formal and informal media

---

1   Both authors are first authors.
2   Richard Sandomir, 'Periscope, a Streaming Twitter App, Steals the Show on Boxing's Big Night', *New York Times,* 4 May 2015.
3   Bethan McKernan, 'This Turkish Maths Teacher is Defying a Government Ban By Using Periscope to Teach 1000s of Students', *The Independent,* 22 August 2015, http://i100.independent.co.uk/article/this-turkish-maths-teacher-is-defying-a-government-ban-by-using-periscope-to-teach-1000s-of-students--Z1CzJZFJBg.
4   Ayşenur Ereker, 'Ekol Hoca Center of Attention on Periscope with his Online Prep School', *Todays Zaman,* 13 August 2015, http://www.todayszaman.com/national_ekol-hoca-center-of-attention-on-periscope-with-his-online-prep-school_396440.html
5   Benjamin Burroughs and Adam Rugg, 'Extending the Broadcast: Streaming Culture and the Problems of Digital Geographies', *Journal of Broadcasting and Electronic Media* 58:3 (2014): 365-380.

economy,[6] Periscope is a manifestation of these claims within a mobile context and a demonstration of how streaming culture is increasingly entering into wider public awareness and use. Periscope harnesses advances in compression, hardware, and mobile bandwidth to surpass earlier desktop-oriented live-streaming platforms like *Justin.tv*, which was originally designed for streaming original content from a user's everyday life before becoming a space for pirated sports broadcasts.[7] Further, Twitter's acquisition of Periscope (and the subsequent integration of Periscope into the Twitter platform), has given the app a significant edge in the US over mobile competitor Meerkat, which launched shortly before Periscope. As of August 2015, Periscope had over 10 million users that were watching over 40 years of video per day.[8]

As a mobile video sharing infrastructure based on the individual, yet utilizing global smartphone platforms, Periscope challenges broadcast logics of content production and circulation. The intimacy of the app, combined with its immediacy, also fosters new types of live video content, potentially reinvigorating mobile journalism and crisis reporting. Ultimately, Periscope is the product of this complicated duality. It is a platform for citizens to bypass state and corporate control while simultaneously enmeshing users within the very production processes of the digital media industries. In doing so, these nascent streaming technologies reflect the interlocking discontinuities of the evolving media landscape where traditional and digital media industries continue to struggle over the future of video production and circulation.

Periscope, Locational Piracy, and the Circumvention of Media Institutions

Since its launch, Periscope has been linked to piracy. The app first made news when people used it to live-stream the U.S. premiere of the 5th season of the HBO series *Game of Thrones,* allowing non-subscribers and those living outside the U.S., where the program had a later premiere date, to view the first episode for free. The incident resulted in HBO labeling the app as a site for 'mass copyright infringement' and lobbying for more 'proactive' tools to remove copyrighted material from the platform and 'not be solely reliant on upon notifications'.[9] Shortly afterward, the app hit the headlines again during the aforementioned Mayweather-Pacquiao boxing match. HBO's calls have been echoed by many in the sports media industry as well, namely the former chairman of NBC Sports, Dick Ebersol, who derided the use of Periscope for live and televised sporting events as 'theft'. 'Are you going

6   Ramon Lobato and Julian Thomas, *The Informal Media Economy*, Cambridge: Polity Press, 2015.
7   James Meese and Aneta Podkalicka, 'Practices of Media Sport: Everyday Experience and Audience Innovation', *Media International Australia* 155 (2015): 89-98.
8   Periscope, 'Periscope by the Numbers', *Medium*, 12 August 2015, https://medium.com/@periscope/periscope-by-the-numbers-6b23dc6a1704.
9   Natalie Jarvey, 'HBO Criticizes Over "Game of Thrones" Live Streams, Issues Takedown Notices', *The Hollywood Reporter,* 14 April 2015, http://www.hollywoodreporter.com/news/hbo-criticizes-periscope-game-thrones-788734.

to let them steal the signal?', he asked.[10]

While Periscope has quickly become a new platform for the old practice of distributing copyrighted video, it has also given greater prominence to a new form of copyright circumvention – the 'on-site' livestream. Most acutely seen in the sports world, Periscope has quickly become a controversial app for spectators and journalists alike. Golf reporter Stephanie Wei had her PGA tour credentials revoked after using Periscope to showcase golfers teeing off in practice. As Wei defended herself by pointing out that the practice shots were not going to be televised, the Tour's chief marketing officer argued that the tour owns the rights to all media produced in and around the event, adding that Wei was 'stealing'.[11] Following the PGA tour's lead, the NHL, NFL, EPL, and Wimbledon have all banned the use of Periscope from stadiums. Outside of sports, Comic-Con, the largest popular culture convention in the world, also instituted a Periscope ban for its 2015 gathering. Key players on the film festival circuit are similarly wary. While Cannes Film Festival already bans any form of video recording inside the festival, Mark Gill, the president of Millennium Films, has declared the app, 'a whole new brand of terrifying' as organizers have promised extra vigilance to prevent any live-streaming of any films shown at the festival.[12] These emphatic statements and actions illustrate the expanding ability of networked individuals to not only redistribute copyrighted content from their television screens, but straight from the source as well.[13]

Figure 1. The live-streaming app Periscope allows individuals to distribute and consume content in new ways that circumvent existing corporate and state media infrastructures Source: Anthony Quintano (CC BY 2.0).

10   Eric Chemi and Jessica Golden, 'Fan Streaming Apps have Sports World Debating TV Rights', *CNBC*, 21 May 2015, http://www.cnbc.com/2015/05/21/fan-streaming-apps-have-sports-world-debating-tv-rights.html.
11   Alan Shipnuck, 'The Real Loser In Wei Vs. PGA Tour Is The Golf Fans', *Golf.com*, 3 May 2015, http://www.golf.com/tour-and-news/pga-tour-revokes-stephanie-weis-credentials.
12   Scott Roxborough and Rhonda Richford, 'Cannes: Are Periscope and Meerkat Threats to the Fest?', *The Hollywood Reporter*, 13 May 2015, http://www.hollywoodreporter.com/news/cannes-2015-are-periscope-meerkat-795342.
13   Brett Hutchins, James Meese and Aneta Podkalicka, 'Media Sport: Practice, Culture and Innovation', *Media International Australia* 155 (2015): 66-69.

In 2007, Viacom waged a long legal battle against YouTube, seeking damages for profiting off of the viewing of infringing content. The Second Circuit court ruled that YouTube was indeed protected by the safe harbor provision because the 'DMCA requires knowledge or awareness of specific infringing activity in order to find a party liable for hosting [...] the district court found that YouTube was protected by the safe harbor provision'.[14] However, to bolster their legal positioning and dissuade other lawsuits YouTube started filtering videos and posting takedown notices. In the case of Periscope the safe harbor provision largely protects Twitter as a corporate parent and hosting platform from any legal liability (part of the reason Twitter's CEO could be so brazen in declaring Periscope the winner of the Mayweather/Pacquiao fight despite rampant piracy and rights infringement). Thus, Periscope is free to publicly decry streaming piracy on its platform while continuing to reap the piratical benefits of its users streaming concerts, television programs, sporting events, and conferences. However, when everyone with a smartphone can potentially become a spontaneous distributor of copyrighted material, the existing convention of 'taking down' infringing streams or posts after they are detected will increasingly be less effective, resulting in greater calls from content owners for modifying app policies and practices in order to address the exponentially increasing difficulty of preventing copyright infringement.

Periscope is also emerging as a circumvention tool for citizen journalism and civic streaming. Civic streaming is a form of digital witnessing that bypasses traditional media restraints, which lock down the place and location of reporting. Periscope has quickly become a tool for journalists to bypass traditional media industry infrastructure and connect directly with audiences. Journalists routinely host Periscope sessions where they answer audience questions and display their expertise on current issues. In an era of social media, live-streaming becomes a part of journalists building their own personal brands to navigate post-Fordist labour markets. Journalists are extending the workplace as new technologies facilitate greater audience connection, but this, in turn, leads to increased audience expectations of seemingly omnipresent reporting. Journalists are required to tweet and be 'live' as Periscope augments the demands of immediacy. There is no excuse not to be constantly broadcasting. The audience as a group of networked individuals spurs the need for an active, temporal, always-already connected coverage.[15]

On March 26th, the same day as Periscope's initial unveiling to the public, a large downtown fire in Manhattan, New York caused a discussion about the implications of live-streaming on citizen journalism and crisis reporting. Predictability, the ability to almost instantaneously broadcast and view the unfolding of a crisis was heralded as a 'new form of ubiquitous live broadcasting', with one observer suggesting that '[w]ith the smartphones in our pockets, we're all citizen journalists now'.[16] Certainly this ubiquity and immediacy enable new forms

---

14   John Palfrey, Jonathan Zittrain, Kendra Albert, and Lisa Brem, 'From Sony to SOPA: The Technology-Content Divide', *Harvard Law School Case Studies* 23 (2013), p. 9.

15   An Nguyen, 'Journalism in the Wake of Participatory Publishing', *Australian Journalism Review* 28.1 (2006): 47-59.

16   Ben Popper, 'There was an Explosion in New York City, and Seconds Later I was Watching it Live on Periscope', *The Verge*, 26 March 2015, http://www.theverge.com/2015/3/26/8296537/explosion-east-village-periscope-live.

of participation as citizens broadcast the spectacular as an emergent form of crisis report-ing. However, this spectacle of distant suffering as civic streaming presents a complicated duality, on the one hand enabling participation and immediacy while on the other generating proximity at a distance, intensifying a kind of voyeurism.

Civic streaming is also a circumvention of the information control of the state and media institutions. An increased sense of proximity means that the viewing public feels like they can be present amidst a crisis, natural disaster, or riot. Periscope is circumventing state and traditional media structures of power that filtered audiences' proximity to scenes of tragedy. Citizens live-streaming are no longer wholly reliant on news organizations to disseminate stories and broadcast dissenting viewpoints and values. This is especially important within communities that have a longstanding distrust of government surveillance and control from law enforcement officers. Increased usage of smartphone technology to film police officers in a string of incidents that depict questionable police behavior have served to ignite a national debate in the United States about the role of body cameras, cellular technology, and live-streaming. Paradoxically, live-streaming increases the capacity of state and local gov-ernments to ramp up surveillance of citizens, while still allowing for citizen journalism through the same tools. Streaming and increased surveillance can lead to surveilling the surveillers.

The Future of Live-Streaming Apps: Assimilation, Regulation, and Geoblocking

Our discussion of Periscope-enabled circumvention and civic streaming exemplify the unique possibilities of mobile live streaming and reveal the competing discontinuities of emergent mobile video culture. Further, they illustrate the increasing divergence of the mobile video space from existing broadcast and desktop platforms. Within the realm of desktop access to internet video, distribution has historically been modeled according to existing television broadcast logics that divide control of content by nation and enforce those divisions through the use of geofences. Even platforms with large amounts of amateur content have instituted geographic restrictions on content, as in the case of YouTube and its Content ID system. However, recent popular mobile video sharing platforms have been much more global in nature. Instagram, Vine and Periscope (along with other popular live-streaming apps such as Meerkat and Twitcast) are conceptualized as geographically agnostic in terms of content rights, with no current tools for geographical restrictions in place. Perhaps owing to the premise and promise of mobile computing, the use of geofencing within mobile apps is often utilized as an inclusive, positive measure rather than one of restriction, such as in the use of location based games, proximity-based alerts and notifications, and in the functioning of location-dependent service apps like Uber.

While there are plenty of websites and desktop-oriented video platforms that are global in nature, the ubiquity of mobile devices along with the prominence of these smartphone apps is the crucial difference. With 70 percent of the world's population predicted to own a smartphone by 2020, and the accelerating expansion of mobile bandwidth across the world, Periscope's infamous rise to fame during the Mayweather-Pacquiao fight and *Game of Thrones* premiere, then, is less a surprise than it is a culmination of the increasing migration of producers and consumers to mobile video platforms.[17] Vine, another Twitter-owned platform for the sharing of six-second video clips, has also received major criticism from content owners, especially the English Premier League which has sought to stop the proliferation of goal highlights that spread across the platform seconds after they appear on television.

Periscope, and similar live-streaming smartphone apps, exist at the forefront of mobile video culture and expand the ways that technology and physical space interact. Whether through original content, authorized and unauthorized behind-the-scenes moments, news reporting, or the distribution of copyrighted material, live-streaming apps have come to bypass many governmental, corporate, geographic, and technical restrictions on producing and distributing live video. While Periscope and other live-streaming platforms display how global networks of individuals with media producing and distributing devices in their pockets can disrupt the geographical and technological logics of broadcasting, journalism, and piracy, it ultimately remains to be seen how the media industries, national governments, and the cultures around the world will adapt and respond to these disruptions. On the one hand, Periscope is frequently heralded as opening new doors for global communication and content sharing, but it is unlikely these doors of rupture will stay open forever. Despite the positioning of the app as a global video sharing platform, legal and corporate pressure may potentially force the app to succumb to geographically based restrictions that have long been in place for other live broadcasters.

As new media industries continue to mature, they will increasingly integrate with old media industries, establish partnerships with content providers, and participate in the structures of global capital and financing. As such, the policies and purpose of popular live-streaming apps will increasingly be beholden to pressures from content providers, investors, and parent companies. While Periscope has not yet gestured toward implementing any geofencing or copyright detection methods, it may find itself in this position sooner rather than later. Already, its parent company Twitter began partnering with major video content providers under its Twitter Amplify program that launched in May 2013.[18] Included in these partnerships is the NFL and PGA, which already have a contentious relationship with Periscope, banning the app from their respective live events.

As seen by HBO's quick demand for more proactive tools to combat piracy on the platform, large corporations are already placing pressure on Periscope to not only eliminate copyright circumvention after it happens, but provide prevention tools as well. Vine's trouble in purging soccer goal videos illustrates the difficulty in preventing the proliferation of television content on social media platforms. However, Periscope could still utilize geofences in order to prevent unauthorized broadcasts of events at physical locations, such as sport stadiums, film festivals, and concerts.

---

17   Ericsson, 'Ericsson Mobility Report: On the Pulse of the Network Society', June 2015, http://www.ericsson.com/res/docs/2015/ericsson-mobility-report-june-2015.pdf.

18   Kathleen Chaykowski, 'Twitter Automates "Amplify" as it Pushes the Live-Video Ad Product into News, Entertainment', Forbes, 28 May 2015, http://www.forbes.com/sites/kathleenchaykowski/2015/05/28/twitter-automates-amplify-as-it-pushes-the-live-video-ad-product-into-news-entertainment/.

A model for this voluntarily geographic restricting already exists in mobile social media application Yik Yak. The app, which allows users within the same geographic area to post public
messages, faced a public backlash after elementary and high school students used the app
to anonymously cyber-bully other students. Eventually, Yik Yak partnered with Maponics, a
mapping company, to institute geofences around all schools below college level to restrict
younger students from using the app at school.

Legal pressures may also force live-streaming apps such as Periscope to install government-mandated geofences around 'sensitive' or 'secure' areas. As Cristina Alaimo and Jannis Kallinikos argue, social media is 'actively involved in the production of new types of data
that have commonly remained outsid the regulative purview of institutions'.[19] Live-streaming
is no exception. The quick proliferation of smartphones across the world combined with rapid technological advances in phone hardware and mobile bandwidth capacity have brought
about a recent expansion of live-streaming video within social networks, both existing (in
the case of the recently introduced Facebook Live feature) and new (such as Periscope and
Meerkat). The short period of time in which this happened has made many live-streaming
apps solely responsible to broadly applied copyright laws and their own internal policies.

As Marketa Trimble states, many governments across the world have just started grap-
pling with the physical and digital mobility of internet users and are still early in the process
of figuring out how to legislate and regulate the concept of geographical territories and
borders within the constructed geography of the front facing internet.[20] While many apps
and techniques currently take advantage of this legal grey area to bypass geofences and
other restrictions, governments and regulatory bodies could pass laws or restrictions that
give greater weight to territorial boundaries on the internet and establish mechanisms for
authorizing temporary and permanent geofences that restrict the use of media-sharing
platforms in certain locations. Recent patents developed by Apple already point toward the
technological means these restrictions could be enforced.[21]

We have already seen nation-states show a willingness to restrict internet platforms that spur
communication outside of official channels. China and North Korea already block or heavily
restrict a wide swath of social media apps at the national level. Moments of crisis have also
prompted other nation-states to temporarily restrict social media apps as well, most notably
during the Arab Spring uprisings that began in 2010.[22] During the uprisings, Twitter and
Facebook became central conduits for the organizing of protest actions, the proliferation
of revolutionary ideas, and communication with international sympathizers, leading Tunisia,

---

19   Cristina Alaimo and Jannis Kallinikos, 'Encoding the Everyday: Social Data and its Media Apparatus',
     in Cassidy R. Sugimoto, Hamid Ekbia, and Michael Mattioli (eds) *Big Data is not a Monolith: Policies,
     Practices, and Problems*, Cambridge: The MIT Press, (forthcoming).
20   Marketa Trimble, 'The Future of Cybertravel: Legal Implications of the Evasion of Geolocation',
     Fordham Intellectual Property, Media, and Entertainment Law Journal 22 (2012): 654.
21   Lance Whitney, 'Apple Patent May Foreshadow iPhones That React to Location', *CNET*, 28 August
     2012, http://www.cnet.com/news/apple-patent-may-foreshadow-iphones-that-react-to-location.
22   Manuel Castells, *Networks of Outrage and Hope: Social Movements in the Internet Age*, Hoboken:
     John Wiley & Sons, 2013.

Egypt, and other Middle Eastern countries to restrict citizen access to the social networks or even the internet as a whole.[23] While the efforts of these countries to install geofences around Twitter and Facebook were partially subverted by the use of VPNs and the digital attacks of the hacker group Anonymous, they starkly revealed the importance of social media apps in conflicts between states and their citizens.[24] As live-streaming continues to enmesh itself within the structures of social media platforms and as civic streaming increasingly becomes an important tool to communicate and share information in times of crisis, it was will be subject to increased efforts by states to restrict and control its use.

Periscope is just one of a suite of emerging technologies used to circumvent copyright, access, and distribution restrictions. All of these technologies contain user-friendly interfaces, branding, and marketing efforts that reject the technical difficulty of previous circumvention technologies to position themselves instead as user-friendly computing tools. Some of these technologies, like VPNs, DNS proxies, and IP maskers, utilize the geographical ambiguity of the internet to bypass geofences and access content authorized to users in different locales. Others, such as Periscope, Ustream, and Vine, provide mobile users with live video publishing tools, allowing them to become hosts of original and copyrighted content that can be streamed across geographically agnostic platforms. All of these tools, however, reflect the tension emerging as digital platforms make the production, consumption, and distribution of video content exponentially easier for corporations and consumers alike.

References

Alaimo, Cristina and Jannis Kallinikos. 'Encoding the Everyday: Social Data and its Media Apparatus', in Cassidy R. Sugimoto, Hamid Ekbia, and Michael Mattioli (eds) *Big Data is not a Monolith: Policies, Practices, and Problems*, Cambridge: The MIT Press (forthcoming).

Burroughs, Benjamin and Adam Rugg. 'Extending the Broadcast: Streaming Culture and the Problems of Digital Geographies', *Journal of Broadcasting and Electronic Media* 58.3 (2014): 365-380.

Castells, Manuel. *Networks of Outrage and Hope: Social Movements in the Internet Age*, Hoboken: John Wiley & Sons, 2013.

Chaykowski, Kathleen. 'Twitter Automates "Amplify" as it Pushes the Live-Video Ad Product into News, Entertainment', *Forbes,* 28 May 2015, http://www.forbes.com/sites/kathleenchaykowski/2015/05/28/twitter-automates-amplify-as-it-pushes-the-live-video-ad-product-into-news-entertainment/.

Chemi, Eric and Jessica Golden. 'Fan Streaming Apps have Sports World Debating TV Rights', *CNBC,* 21 May 2015, http://www.cnbc.com/2015/05/21/fan-streaming-apps-have-sports-world-debating-tv-rights.html.

Ericsson. 'Ericsson Mobility Report: On the Pulse of the Network Society', June 2015, http://www.ericsson.com/res/docs/2015/ericsson-mobility-report-june-2015.pdf.

Ereker, Ayşenur. 'Ekol Hoca Center of Attention on Periscope with his Online Prep School', *Todays Zaman,* 13 August 2015, http://www.todayszaman.com/national_ekol-hoca-center-of-attention-on-

---

23 Philip N. Howard et al., 'Opening Closed Regimes: What was the Role of Social Media During the Arab Spring?', 2011, http://ssrn.com/abstract=2595096.
24 Philip N. Howard and Muzammil M. Hussain, 'The Role of Digital Media', *Journal of Democracy* 22 (2011): 35-48.

periscope-with-his-online-prep-school_396440.html.

Howard, Philip N. et al. 'Opening Closed Regimes: What Was the Role of Social Media During the Arab Spring?', 2011, http://ssrn.com/abstract=259509.

Howard, Philip N. and Muzammil M. Hussain. 'The Role of Digital Media', *Journal of Democracy* 22 (2011): 35-48.

Hutchins, Brett, James Meese, and Aneta Podkalicka. 'Media Sport: Practice, Culture and Innovation', *Media International Australia* 155 (2015): 66-69.

Jarvey, Natalie. 'HBO Criticizes Over "Game of Thrones" Live Streams, Issues Takedown Notices', *The Hollywood Reporter*, 14 April 2015, http://www.hollywoodreporter.com/news/hbo-criticizes-periscope-game-thrones-788734.

Lobato, Ramon and Julian Thomas. *The Informal Media Economy*, Cambridge: Polity Press, 2015.

Meese, James and Aneta Podkalicka. 'Practices of Media Sport: Everyday Experience and Audience Innovation', *Media International Australia* 155 (2015): 89-98.

McKernan, Bethan. 'This Turkish Maths Teacher is Defying a Government Ban by Using Periscope to Teach 1000s of Students', *The Independent,* 22 August 2015, http://i100.independent.co.uk/article/this-turkish-maths-teacher-is-defying-a-government-ban-by-using-periscope-to-teach-1000s-of-students--Z1CzJZFJBg.

Nguyen, An. 'Journalism in the Wake of Participatory Publishing', *Australian Journalism Review* 28.1 (2006): 47-59.

Palfrey, John. et al. 'From Sony to SOPA: The Technology-Content Divide.' *Harvard Law School Case Studies*, 23 February 2013.

Periscope. 'Periscope by the Numbers', *Medium*, 12 August 2015, https://medium.com/@periscope/periscope-by-the-numbers-6b23dc6a1704.

Popper, Ben. 'There was an Explosion in New York City, and Seconds Later I was Watching it Live on Periscope', *The Verge,* 26 March 2015, http://www.theverge.com/2015/3/26/8296537/explosion-east-village-periscope-live.

Roxborough, Scott and Rhonda Richford. 'Cannes: Are Periscope and Meerkat Threats to the Fest?', *The Hollywood Reporter,* 13 May 2015, http://www.hollywoodreporter.com/news/cannes-2015-are-periscope-meerkat-795342.

Sandomir, Richard. 'Periscope, a Streaming Twitter App, Steals the Show on Boxing's Big Night', *New York Times,* 4 May 2015.

Shipnuck, Alan. 'The Real Loser in Wei Vs. PGA Tour is the Golf Fans', *Golf.com,* 3 May 2015, http://www.golf.com/tour-and-news/pga-tour-revokes-stephanie-weis-credentials.

Trimble, Marketa. 'The Future of Cybertravel: Legal Implications of the Evasion of Geolocation', *Fordham Intellectual Property, Media, and Entertainment Law Journal* 22 (2012): 654.

Whitney, Lance. 'Apple Patent may Foreshadow iPhones that React to Location', *CNET*, 28 August 2012, http://www.cnet.com/news/apple-patent-may-foreshadow-iphones-that-react-to-location.

CIRCUMVENTION, MEDIA SPORT AND THE FRAGMENTATION OF VIDEO CULTURE

JAMES MEESE AND ANETA PODKALICKA

Introduction

Lurid tales of football officials pocketing millions hit the headlines following the recent FIFA scandals. The reporting rightly shone a light on corruption in football, but also drove home a basic fact: sport is awash with money. This is largely because television networks spend a significant amount on purchasing rights to major sporting events. To provide a few brief examples, Fox Sports has paid over $400 million (USD) in 2011 for the rights to the 2018 and 2022 FIFA World Cups[1] and NBC has paid $7.65 billion (USD) for the right to broadcast the Olympics from 2022 to 2032 in the U.S.[2] These sums are so large that nowadays professional sporting clubs at the highest level earn the bulk of their income from the influx of money earned from the sale of broadcasting rights, rather than from gate receipts or merchandising.

Sport is able to demand this level of investment because there is a strong viewer preference for mediated live sport, which in turn is a unique form of modern screen content. Live sport is one of the last program genres that require people to watch it at a particular time. This is unlike most other programs, which can be provided on-demand (as we have seen elsewhere in this collection). This in turn means that live sport stands as a reasonable financial investment for media companies. By purchasing exclusive rights to popular sporting contests, networks will have access to an interested audience, which can be on sold to advertisers.

Rights deals between sporting organisations and television networks are managed through a complicated geography of contractual agreements. Sporting organisations maximize their income by selling limited exclusive rights to networks, allowing them to sell the same content to multiple national markets. For example, the aforementioned $400 million World Cup deal made in the United States of America, sits alongside other deals FIFA makes with broadcasters in Australia, India and so on. This relationship provides benefits for both parties. Sport offers television networks compelling content that can help build a loyal audience and rights deals stand as a direct source of revenue for sporting organisations as well as a marketing and public relations outlet.

---

1   Jere Longman, 'Fox and Telemundo Win U.S. Rights to World Cups', *New York Times*, 21 October, 2011, http://www.nytimes.com/2011/10/22/sports/soccer/fox-and-telemundo-win-us-rights-to-2018-and-2022-world-cups.html.
2   'IOC Awards Olympic Games Broadcast Rights to NBC Universal through to 2032', *Official Website of the Olympic Movement,* 7 May, 2014, http://www.olympic.org/news/ioc-awards-olympic-games-broadcast-rights-to-nbcuniversal-through-to-2032/230995.

In order for this system to work, both television networks and sporting organisations depend on geographical exclusivity. However, these claims to geographic exclusivity are currently being challenged by a range of alternative models and viewing practices that circumvent these broadcast arrangements: live-streaming; using circumvention technologies such as VPNs to access geoblocked content; uploading highlights on social media platforms; and purchasing cheap overseas cable decoder boxes. We examine these circumvention practices, which vary in their scope and levels of informality, and explore how they are fragmenting the sporting video landscape and offering new sites of consumption for fans.

Beyond the Traditional Sporting Broadcast: Challenging Exclusivity

Media sport stands as an interesting case study to explore changing media geographies because of the sector's resilience and longevity. It has arguably managed to weather the digital transition with more aplomb than other screen cultures and genres (for example, film or television serials). Television networks are investing heavily in broadcasting rights for sporting contests, without having to worry about Netflix-like competitors. But as a consequence of this apparent lack of competition, television networks generally assume that audiences' engagement is granted through the provision of high-quality, innovatively produced sporting content, which feeds this sense of exclusivity. But as a consequence of this apparent lack of competition, television networks tend to hold a series of assumptions about how people will watch sport. In short, it is presumed that audiences will engage with high-quality, innovative broadcasts. So these days most sporting broadcasts feature high definition cameras, novel camera angles, and a range of visual and audio content, from heat maps to theme songs.

Sports organisations also often stream games online either under a paid subscription model or for free depending on the rights arrangement. For example, the Australian Open tennis championship is customarily broadcast free to air on the national commercial station *Channel 7*. However, in 2015 the station's Seven Sport website also featured live streaming, which during the tennis tournament, and for Australia-based audiences, showed parallel matches played across multiple courts. The stream also provided real-time coverage from hot spots from around the Melbourne Park such as players' backstage entrance or training sessions. The 2014 FIFA World Cup offers another example. The event offered live streaming as part of its global coverage and was retrospectively promoted as 'the biggest multimedia sporting event in history, with more people watching matches and highlights online than ever before'.[3] However, this live streaming is still something that happens under the auspices of the sporting organisation and their broadcast partners. It provides flexibility and diversity to viewers and can expand the audience of an event or competition, but the control and branding of this content is still of paramount concern to the media, event organisers and promoters.

Furthermore, while these rights deals are structured around exclusivity, it is important to note that in the current media landscape 'exclusivity' is a malleable concept. Live sport is

3   '2014 FIFA World Cup Breaks Online Streaming Records', *FIFA.com*, 7 July 2014, http://m.fifa.com/aboutfifa/news/newsid=2401405.html.

seen as a particularly precious resource and the *in situ* broadcast is strongly protected by rights-holding networks. This ability to broadcast the game live is a major drawing card for networks. But once the result is known, the game itself becomes less valuable, both in an economic sense, and in terms of the sporting competition. Highlights start circulating on the news programmes of competing networks, the event's tension dissipates and the original network's exclusivity immediately diminishes. Furthermore, the live blogging and tweeting of sporting broadcasts (or indeed, of live games), as well as the commentary that takes place on radio stations, contributes to this dilution of the game's exclusivity by offering another location for fans to engage with the game. This commentary could supplement an official broadcast, but in some circumstances it could just as likely replace it (for example, if it was difficult to access an official broadcast).

Geography also plays a role in the diminishing this exclusivity. The British Broadcasting Corporation (BBC) – a public broadcaster – broadcasts Match of the Day (MotD), a popular Association Football highlights show, and also streams it on their VoD service. However, their streaming service is restricted to the United Kingdom ostensibly so individuals who have not paid a television license fee are unable to get access to it. Similarly, the United States cable network ESPN geoblocks their Watch ESPN streaming service for non-US audiences. MLB.TV goes so far as to enforce 'online blackouts in the geographical area covered by a baseball club's local television market when they play'.[4] This of course drives circumvention, as subscribers aren't able to watch the team they care about most online: their local one. Other geo-sequestering is more nuanced. The 2006-2007 Ashes series was broadcast online for 'free to Australian users, while overseas users were charged a fee'.[5] This is not so much a 'block' as a 'hurdle', one that still allows for access but only through a tiered system defined through geography.

While many fans are happy to pay for live sports, these examples show why some fans might willingly circumvent geoblocking. Our study of these various practices not only give us some insight into how and why circumvention takes place in a particular media industry, but also show the implications of circumvention. The mediation and corporatisation of sport has generally been premised on the delivery of a unified video broadcast in real time, with some localization (such as local commentary). However, circumvention drastically fragments these points of reception with audiences now able to watch sport in a number of different ways. As we will see below, these options are often quite different from the existing broadcast and so we suggest that circumvention is not just about access, but about sustaining alternative consumption preferences, which are often not catered for in the dominant forms of sporting broadcast.

4   Brett Hutchins, 'Robbing the World's Largest Jewellery Store'? Digital Sports Piracy, Industry
     Hyperbole, and Barriers to an Alternative Online Business Model', ANZCA 2011, Waikato, New
     Zealand, 5-8 July, 2011, http://www.anzca.net/documents/anzca-11-1/refereed-proceedings-3/495-
     hutchins-anzca-2011-1/file.html, p. 6.
5   Brett Hutchins and David Rowe, *Sport Beyond Television: The Internet, Digital Media and the Rise of
     Networked Media Sport*, New York, Routledge: 2012, p. 362.

Circumvention Practices in Media Sport

Circumvention in media sport occurred from the 1970s onwards, thanks to flexible consumer technologies like VCRs, which gave audiences with greater control over the content they were accessing. Brett Hutchins notes that '[u]nauthorised video dubbing and illegal access to cable and satellite sports television channels was' a practice undertaken in many countries, 'but these activities … had a relatively minor effect upon profitability in the media market'.[6] Unsurprisingly, the internet has intensified opportunities for circumvention practices, and here we outline some of the most common methods. However, we leave a discussion around one of the most novel methods, the use of the live streaming app Periscope, to Adam Rugg and Ben Burroughs in the previous chapter.

Unauthorized live-streaming websites

One prominent practice is the live streaming of sporting content on websites such as *Wiziwig* or *ATDHE*, which offer free unauthorized streams of sporting events as they occur. They provide access to a diverse range of content from UEFA Champions League matches and college basketball games to specialist cable television channels (such as ESPN). The sites are relatively easy to find but they are also unreliable, with feeds occasionally being shut down, suffering playback problems or allowing advertising content that blocks the sporting content. They present content broadcast in a variety of languages, and come across as fairly minimalist in terms of user interface – simply offering links to feeds and no other content. Often, in the middle of viewing, the feed can be cut off entirely, as Florian Hoof details in the chapter that follows. Alternatively sites mimic the aesthetic of a professional sports site, with better website design, in order to attain some legitimacy with their audience. However, the general minimalism of the sites offers a protection against rights holders. The limited information available means that unofficial live streams are notoriously difficult to stop while a sporting event is occurring.

These websites stand as the most serious threat to rights holders. They impinge on the most prized possession of sports TV broadcasters: the live audio/visual broadcast of a sporting event. They also disrupt the carefully organized geography of broadcasting rights, offering an unrestricted broadcast to individuals from across the globe. It is no surprise that 'media sport industry professionals' dislike these sites, which are 'very easy to create and very difficult to shut down'.[7] It is also worth noting that it is not prohibitively difficult to upload a stream of a sporting match for online broadcast, to the extent that walkthroughs are available online.

Circulation of Game Replays

An alternative circumvention tactic is based around a number of websites, which host delayed highlights of games after the match has finished. At first glance these sites look professional and appear to be an authorised place to consume content. Their status as

---

6   Hutchins, 'Robbing the World's Largest Jewellery Store', p.1.
7   Hutchins, 'Robbing the World's Largest Jewellery Store', p. 4.

"grey" locations for sporting content are well disguised through competent web-design, a clear site structure and the prominent display of game highlights. However, these websites often feature copyright infringing content. The only way they stay clear of lawsuits is by sourcing content uploaded by individuals hosted on third party video hosting websites (such as DailyMotion or MetaCafe). We will turn to one of the more prominent sites, Footytube, to show how this negotiation takes place.

Footytube deploys three specifically customized search aggregation bots, which scan the open web for content (bots are small programs that run on the internet). The bot service runs 'through millions of webpages each day, aggregating and semantically analysing … niche specific and timely football related datasets'. They graze a number of intermediary video sharing websites, sourcing edits from users all over the world. However, the bots are unable to tell whether the content is under copyright or not. This method produces an archive of football highlights for sports fans after each game as well as indemnifies Footytube from any claims of copyright infringement.

The global reach of this operation means that Footytube's audience engages with sports content at an awkward angle: poor quality footage and foreign commentary often forms part of their media experience. Roughly edited 'official' broadcasts, such as Sky Sports broadcasts of the F.A. Premier League are likely to be swiftly removed, as the broadcasts contain obviously copyrightable material in the form of graphics, post-match analysis and theme songs. This means that secondary broadcasts from other countries (for example, a Russian broadcast of a Premier League game) tend to be left up the longest on these sites. However, industry professionals tend to see these services as 'an irritation', an issue we will discuss later in this chapter, because unlike live sport, there is a limited audience for delayed content.[8]

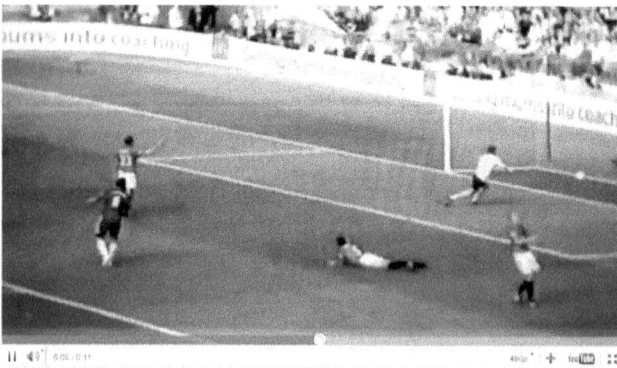

Figure 1. Highlights aggregated by Footytube from Youtube. The YouTube account associated with this footage has since been terminated

---

8   Hutchins, 'Robbing the World's Largest Jewellery Store', p. 4.

Conventional Circumvention Tools

Sporting audiences also use commercial Virtual Private Networks and Domain Name System proxy services in order to evade geoblocking, assigning themselves another location in order to access geoblocked content. These services promote their ability to make sporting content easy to access. UnoTelly for example makes it clear that individuals can access the BBC, Canal+ or ESPN from anywhere in the world. Access to sporting content is also positioned as a predominant use of these products, with advice site *The VPN Guru* providing guides on how to access geoblocked content for the ICC Cricket World Cup 2015 and NCAA March Madness.

This practice engages with legitimate distribution geographies in a strange way. A VPN or DNS allows individuals to access licensed content, which is hosted on an authorized platform such as the BBC or ESPN. Individuals subsequently access content in a radically different fashion from unauthorized third party sites. For all intents and purposes they are recognized as someone with legitimate access to the site, despite the fact that they are residing in an unauthorized geographical location. With the geographic delineation of rights such a central part of the sports broadcasting landscape, the use of circumvention technologies challenges this distribution strategy, which has been in place for some time.

Fan Recordings on Social Media

Another phenomenon that has emerged in recent years is people posting sporting content on social media platforms, either during or after a match. This practice came to mainstream attention during the 2014 FIFA World Cup, when six-second videos of goals from World Cup matches started to appear online. Hosted on the (Twitter-owned) social media platform *Vine*, short six-second videos (or 'Vines') started to be shared across Twitter and Facebook and were also utilized in online sports reporting. The videos were often of goals scored during the match, but also captured humorous moments such as boring commentary or the Columbian team playing a practical joke on their teammate. Often people created Vines by recording footage playing on a television screen, offering a strange double layering to the short video. Vines are particularly conducive to sporting content, allowing fans to quickly view highlights from the previous night, and offering a way for journalists to embed relevant footage into their online reports.

However, during the final week of the World Cup, FIFA and its rights-holding partners ESPN and Spanish-language Univision started to issue takedown notices, arguing that these Vines were infringing their copyright. This frenzy of activity even led to the Vine accounts of major media companies being taken down. These debates around the publication of fan recordings further underlines the tensions between established geographies of rights and the de-territorialization the internet affords. As an aside, it is also interesting to note that while all corporate organisations – including sporting organisations – enjoy it when a deliberately selected piece of content goes viral, losing control over this process is often treated as a direct threat to their business model.

Parallel Imports of Cable Decoders

Our final example is a practice that constitutes, perhaps, one of the most ingenious methods of circumvention: paying for a cheaper cable service from a foreign cable provider. Portsmouth publican Karen Murphy stands out as the most prominent example of this strategy. She challenged the FA Premier League's agreement with Sky to provide the station with exclusive rights by signing up with the Greek television provider NOCA who provided her with 'a decoder box and a NOVA viewing card'.[9] This allowed her to screen the Greek broadcast of Premier League matches in her pub. Her reason for doing so was because while SKY commercial subscriptions cost £700 per month, Murphy only paid £700 a year for the Greek Nova subscription.

The Premier League hired Media Protection Services (MPS) to conduct an investigation, and MPS went on to sue Murphy. She was found guilty of copyright infringement. However, Murphy appealed the decision, until it eventually found its way to the High Court of England. The High Court then asked the European Court of Justice (ECJ) to provide advice how these issues related to the EU Treaty. The ECJ found that Murphy as an individual was legally able to purchase a subscription. However, the EJC noted that publicans could not use this loophole in order to support commercial activities. Following this advice, the High Court quashed Murphy's conviction but noted that the case was incredibly complex and the finer legal points of the issue were still yet to be determined.

It is worth noting that many pubs use unauthorized live-streaming websites *in addition* to parallel imported cable or legally obtained subscriptions in order to meet the demands of their patrons. Matthew David and Peter Millward discovered that if football games couldn't be found through their parallel imported cable, publicans would often hook a computer up to the television and watch it from an online stream. Alternatively, a publican noted that if fans from different teams were attending his pub, he would show one broadcast through the parallel imported broadcast and another 'through on that screen or that screen [points to two large televisions] from the computer [an internet live-stream]'.[10]

This shows how circumvention practices often work in tandem with each other and one suspects, perhaps even with legal methods of distribution. These practices are often about supplementing existing distribution infrastructures rather than replacing them. In the case of the two sets of fans, we can also see how circumvention assists in what could be viewed as both a social and economic transaction. The publican is expanding their own customer base, addressing audience demand and managing social relationships. When we consider the history of football fan violence or even the good-natured tensions between two local teams, the provision of multiple games at a local pub is no small matter.

---

9   The details of this case can be found at *Murphy v. Media Protection Services* [2012] EWHC, 466, http://www.bailii.org/ew/cases/EWHC/Admin/2012/466.html.
10   Matthew David and Peter Millward, 'Football's Coming Home?: Digital Reterritorialization, Contradictions in the Transnational Coverage of Sport and the Sociology of Alternative Football Broadcasts', *The British Journal of Sociology* 63.2 (2012): 360.

(Un)authorised Circumvention Practice

These circumvention practices don't emerge out of thin air. Sporting organisations and media networks are actively cultivating some of them, even though they run counter to their dominant narratives of fidelity, quality and exclusivity. For example, while takedown notices used to be sent to third-party sites in order to prevent the circulation of game replays, sporting organisations are starting to manage these practices in more nuanced ways. A sporting executive noted that rather than taking down content posted on YouTube, through the platform's Content ID system, it's easier for 'content creators to register [...] content as theirs' and then any money made from the content, 'goes back to the content creator rather than the person who has uploaded it'.[11]

However, when it comes to live streaming websites, which directly challenges authorized geography of live sporting event broadcasts, rights holders take a more punitive stance. Third party companies are regularly employed to not just shut down illegal streams, but to also recoup any advertising money that had been earned from the adverts placed 'against those illegal streams'.[12] U.S. Homeland Security went so far as to seize ATDHE's original domain in 2011, although the site has continued to operate under a new domain name. These examples reinforce the point made throughout this article, that the threats to live broadcasts, are the ones that rights holders respond most strongly to.

The Fragmentation of Digital Sporting Video Cultures

The circumvention practices outlined above directly challenge assumptions about content, which are embedded in the geographically exclusive agreements made between sporting organisations and media companies. The traditional sports broadcasting model presumes that fans want to watch live sports in high definition, with fidelity and quality are presented as standardized and idealized forms of content consumption. However, as the table below shows, when it comes to circumvention technologies, only accessing live-streamed FTA broadcasts through VPN provides a level of quality equivalent to a legitimate broadcast. In contrast, other methods, such as watching Vines or accessing highlights on Footytube dramatically impact on the quality of the sporting content. Viewers regularly come across pixelated footage, foreign language commentary and delayed coverage. Even cable that has been parallel imported suffers from a decline in audio and visual quality. While the broadcast is of a high standard the fact that the commentary is in a foreign language might impact on the enjoyment of the game.

---

11   Raymond Boyle, 'Battle for control? Copyright, Football and European Media Rights', *Media, Culture & Society* 37.3 (2015): 370.
12   Boyle, 'Battle for control?', p. 371.

Platform	Do you need to pay?	Timing	Geographic restriction	'Quality'
TV (Satellite)	Yes	Live	Yes	Excellent
TV (FTA)	Sometimes	Live	Yes	Excellent
Parallel Import TV	Yes	Live	No	Average
TV (FTA) through VPN	Yes	Live	No	Excellent
Live Streaming	No	Live	No	Average to Poor
Vine	No	Slight Delay	No	Poor
YouTube/Other Third Party Site	No	Delay of a few hours	No	Average to Poor
Skype	No	Live	No	Poor
Website	No	Delay of a few hours	No	Average to Poor

Figure 2: A breakdown of the relationship between geographic restriction, cost and quality

Collectively, this shows that when it comes to watching sport, audiences tend to weigh up quality against other factors. Obviously, when it comes to geoblocking and circumvention, access is a key motivator. This means that people might accept 'poor' or 'average to poor' coverage (see the above table) in order to circumvent geoblocking and watch a sporting match. However, as David and Millward's interviews with publicans show,[13] economic and social factors also play into decisions about quality and circumvention practices. One publican only set up an online live-stream when two sets of fans came to the pub wanting to watch two separate games. While being able to cheaply provide for two groups of fans is clearly a boon for the publican financially, the willingness of fans to watch an unreliable live-stream shows how particular forms of sociality and long-standing sporting cultures can also drive access (i.e. wanting to watch your team at your local pub), as opposed to purely economic considerations (i.e. not wanting to pay for access to sporting content).

The considered rejection of quality for economic or social reasons by audiences has implications for how we think about the consumption of sporting content. Firstly, it challenges the dominant narrative of innovation that typifies broadcast media outlets, which revel in showing audiences the latest data analytics tools or replay cameras. While these features are of interest to sporting audiences, due to poor quality of the feed or recording, they are often not easily discernible when engaging in many of circumvention practices detailed above, However, the fact that these circumvention practices keep occurring, show that these top-down ideas about innovation and the general turn towards high-definition sport,

---

13   Matthew David and Peter Millward, 'Football's Coming Home?', p. 360.

is not an essential part of the mediated sporting experience.

Secondly, this rejection of quality sets up alternate sites of consumption which points to the interesting fact that people are experiencing mediated sport in a range of different ways. When it comes to video content, a person may just follow a football league through Vine highlights, with each goal commentated by a fervent fan in front of their television (rather than by a jaded ex-pro). The footage will be pixelated and the edits jumpy, but the heart of the game – the goal – will be legible. A fan might jump on Footytube and regularly watch highlights of their favourite team with additional Russian commentary. Alternatively, a tennis fan might watch an obscure ATP tour match on a live-streaming service and join in a live chat box that pops up alongside the stream. In each of these cases we see new constellations of media sport cultures forming and a series of diverse fan engagements occurring online.

Further to this, the fact that sport does not rely on language as much as a narrative driven drama means that this consumption occurs in a much more flexible cosmopolitan fashion than other consumption achieved through geoblocking circumvention. Much of the media accessed through circumvention is either diasporic in its nature, with expats often sourcing media content from their home country, or read through a particular form of Western hegemony (e.g. everyone trying to access U.S. Netflix). However, while there is still a Western bias present, sports fans are likely to engage in more transnational forms of consumption. This is because sports can still be understood without the restrictions of spoken language, as a sort of lingua franca. Circumvention practices may help a hardcore football fan watch the African Nations Cup or an Australia tennis fan watch an ATP tour match in Swedish. This suggests that sport is more amenable to these sort of transnational exchanges than other forms of media.

As a final point, we note that the access of authorized sites through circumvention tools, presents conceptual (rather than economic) challenges for broadcasters and sporting organisations, particularly with regards to public-service broadcasters (PSB) like the BBC. Jock Given argues that the 'Online Age' has turned national broadcasters into international broadcasters, and it is an impossible task to try and reinstate the sort of national localism that was predominant the broadcast television era.[14] However, the practice of geoblocking public-service broadcasters does just that. Travelling citizens and expats are unable to access streamed content on national broadcasters without the use of a VPN.

The cultural importance of media for expat and diasporic populations, including sporting content cannot be understated. Tom Evens and Katrien Lefever note that public service broadcasters play a central role in the European sports media landscape, and that these broadcasters 'pioneered sports coverage on grounds of nation-building and cultural citizenship', and suggest that moving sport to 'subscription-based platforms' raises issues around cultural citizenship.[15] This account underlines the historical tensions that circulate around the

14   Jock Given, 'Bringing the ABC Back Home', *Inside Story*, 16 May 2014, http://insidestory.org.au/
       bringing-the-abc-back-home/.
15   Tom Evens and Katrien Lefever, 'Watching the Football Game: Broadcasting Rights for the European

geoblocking of public service media. On occasion, small-scale infringement has assisted in supporting the media consumption habits of diasporic populations or in archiving old media texts. One could potentially view the use of VPNs and DNS proxies to access PSB by these citizens in a similar fashion. Of course, the circumvention of geoblocking by non-citizens is a different matter and raises a more complex set of questions for PSBs.

Conclusion

Thanks to the preponderance of various circumvention practices, sporting video culture has fragmented. Because of this we see other interesting trends emerge. Audiences are displaying a negotiable approach to quality when looking to access geoblocked content. New forms of consumption also emerge from these practices, with six-second Vines of goals and amateur edits of highlights uploaded on video hosting platforms, letting people engage with sport in a different way. The use of VPNs also contributes to both a diasporic and at times opportunistic cosmopolitan sporting video culture, with both expats and international audiences watching and in turn 'de-territorialising' sporting content. All of this suggests that when it comes to locating media sport in the future, we will be addressing a growing selection of distinct but interrelated sites rather that a sole 'official' broadcast. Paradoxically, in the search for access to official broadcasts, sports fans have conjured up an emergent petri dish of sporting video cultures – ripe for further study.

References

'2014 FIFA World Cup Breaks Online Streaming Records', FIFA.com, 7 July 2014, http://m.fifa.com/aboutfifa/news/newsid=2401405.html.

Boyle, Raymond. 'Battle for control? Copyright, Football and European Media Rights', *Media, Culture & Society* 37.3 (2015): 359-375.

David, Matthew and Peter Millward. 'Football's Coming Home?: Digital Reterritorialization, Contradictions in the Transnational Coverage of Sport and the Sociology of Alternative Football Broadcasts', *The British Journal of Sociology* 63.2 (2012): 349-369.

Evens, Tom and Katrien Lefever. 'Watching the Football Game: Broadcasting Rights for the European Digital Television Market', *Journal of Sport & Social Issues* 35.1 (2011): 33-49.

Gantz, Walter and Nicky Lewis. 'Sports on Traditional and Newer Digital Media: Is There Really a Fight for Fans?', *Television & New Media* 15.8 (2014), p. 760-768.

Given, Jock. 'Bringing the ABC Back Home', *Inside Story*, 16 May 2014, http://insidestory.org.au/bringing-the-abc-back-home/.

Hutchins, Brett. 'Robbing the World's Largest Jewellery Store'? Digital Sports Piracy, Industry Hyperbole, and Barriers to an Alternative Online Business Model', ANZCA 2011, Waikato, New Zealand, 5-8 July, 2011, http://www.anzca.net/documents/anzca-11-1/refereed-proceedings-3/495-hutchins-anzca-2011-1/file.html, p. 6.

Hutchins, Brett and David Rowe. *Sport Beyond Television: The Internet, Digital Media and the Rise of Networked Media Sport,* New York, Routledge: 2012, p. 362.

'IOC awards Olympic Games Broadcast Rights to NBC Universal through to 2032', Official Website

Digital Television Market', *Journal of Sport & Social Issues* 35.1 (2011): 37.

of the Olympic Movement, 7 May 2014, http://www.olympic.org/news/ioc-awards-olympic-games-broadcast-rights-to-nbcuniversal-through-to-2032/230995.

Longman, Jere. 'Fox and Telemundo Win U.S. Rights to World Cups', New York Times, 21 October 2011, http://www.nytimes.com/2011/10/22/sports/soccer/fox-and-telemundo-win-us-rights-to-2018-and-2022-world-cups.html.

LIVE SPORTS, PIRACY AND UNCERTAINTY: UNDERSTANDING ILLEGAL STREAMING AGGREGATION PLATFORMS

FLORIAN HOOF

Geoblocked in Australia

Experiencing live football without having access to live TV coverage can be exceptionally thrilling – even though it might not be the preferred way to watch a match. On the sixth of May 2002, just after midnight, I was sitting nervously in a run-down internet cafe in Potts Point, Sydney, Australia. I was not here to watch a Champions League game, but was hoping to follow a football drama that unfolded live back in Germany's second division. My club VfL Bochum, Germany's most boring football team, had a chance to make it into the first division and one goal could make all the difference. As a fan of this rather insignificant team, I followed the score via live text ticker on a German sports web page.

Several circumstances brought me to this internet cafe. In 2002 options for accessing live football coverage were scarce. There was no way to live-stream the match. Of course in an era of analogue television, there were no digital live images available. Even if there were, the bandwidth provided by a 56k dial-up modem could not cope with that amount of data anyway. At that time TV coverage of German Bundesliga football in Australia was available only via the multicultural public broadcaster, SBS (the Special Broadcasting Service). They broadcast the German news every Sunday morning as a service for the German immigrant community in Australia, but only the highlights would have been shown, and with a one-week delay. There might have been the option to access live coverage via the satellite service Sky Sports Australia – but in that case I would have needed to find a sports bar that would turn their screens to a German second-division football match. This seemed unlikely in a country obsessed with Australian Rules Football, rugby and cricket, and I might have ended up having no access to the match at all. So as I was completely geoblocked from live TV coverage, I was forced to sit in front of a grey monitor, operating a dirty mouse that was sitting on an even dirtier mouse pad, pushing the reload button of the live ticker hoping that VfL Bochum would prevail.

In 2002 geoblocking was not an optional digital rights management feature that could be imposed on a given 'information good',[1] in this case a German football match. It was inherent in the materiality of the situation I found myself in, as a result of geographic, cultural and infrastructural circumstances that could not be circumvented – at least not with the resources available to me. Of course, circumstances have changed dramatically since then.[2] Digital

---

1   Michael Hutter, 'Information Goods', in Ruth Towse (ed.), *A Handbook of Cultural Economics*, Cheltenham: Edward Elgar, 2006, pp. 263-268.
2   See, for example, Michael Curtin, Jennifer Holt, and Kevin Sanson (eds), *Distribution Revolution:*

video broadcasting has become the new standard and the broadcast television industry is struggling to adapt to this changed environment. Bandwidth is no longer only a restricting factor but, due to advances in video compression, has turned into a negotiable and scalable question of image resolution and quality. Furthermore, a whole array of different options for viewing live sports events has evolved. Now the German branch of Sky Sports has an app and a pay-tv subscription plan (Sky Go), allowing you to follow every match of Germany's second division on your computer, tablet or mobile phone.

Despite these advances, if I wanted to watch a VfL Bochum match in Australia today, I would still struggle. Six matches per week of Germany's first division are broadcast by beIN SPORTS Australia, a subsidiary of the Al Jazeera Media Network, but there is still no live coverage of the second division. Furthermore, all the aforementioned Sky Sports live-streaming services are geoblocked in Australia. There is still no legal way for Australians to access live sports coverage from Germany's second division. However, if we move beyond live sports coverage provided by legal distribution channels a wide range of informal options are available which did not exist in 2002.

If in Australia today, I would most likely end up in front of a laptop or tablet in my apartment watching illegal live streams that can easily be accessed via streaming aggregation platforms such as Rojadirecta.me and Stream2watch.me. I might even be tempted to ask friends back in Germany to stream this live broadcast to me via a live-streaming service such as Periscope. For the consumer or sports fan, the increased availability of illegal distribution channels significantly changes the viewing situation. Information about these illegal options including the legal and security risks involved is widespread, with pay-TV circumvention practices discussed openly in mainstream newspapers, such as the Munich-based *tz*.[3] Illegal live sport streams are not exact copies of the authorized live experience. Offered for free, they deliver a highly unstable live experience, one that may disappear unexpectedly mid-match, and with noticeably poor image quality. Moreover, structures and mechanisms – such as legal measures or technological circumstances – that affect the availability of these streams remain an inaccessible black box to the user. As a result, the user is confronted by an uncertain situation that they cannot control or manage. Thus, even though such streams are literally 'for free' they also involve costs for the user precisely because of their unreliability.

Illegal Live Sport Streams as 'Digital Lemons'

I am specifically interested in understanding these costs and how they relate to consumers and market structures. Therefore, I analyze how quality, instability and uncertainty affect markets for digital information goods by focusing on live sports consumption via illegal streaming aggregation platforms. To theorize the productivity of uncertainty for digital network mar-

---

Conversations about the Digital Future of Film and Television, Berkley: University of California Press, 2014.

3   See: Sophie Rohringer, 'Hier sehen Sie Borussia Dortmund gegen FK Krasnodar jetzt im TV und Live-Stream', *tz*, 30 September 2015, https://www.tz.de/sport/fussball/europa-league-borussia-dortmund-gegen-fk-krasnodar-tv-live-stream-sky-sport1-5515199.html.

kets, I combine media and social theory with information economics. I use the concept of 'lemons', originally established by information economics to understand uncertainty in the market for used cars.[4] It describes the situation of a buyer with insufficient information about the quality of a vehicle he is offered by the car dealer. This used car might be a bargain but could also turn out to be a lemon – a product that is actually overpriced due to hidden quality deficiencies. The latter results in costs to the buyer as he pays more than normal market prices would indicate. The mechanisms at play can be transferred to the case of live sport streaming. In both cases uncertainty relates to – if not restricted to a purely monetary definition – additional costs for the user or consumer.

My framework specifically focuses on the costs that accrue to users in the process of locating, accessing and watching illegal information goods and services without knowing if the resource is a 'digital lemon'. I use this term to refer to poor quality streaming sites, often containing malware, and offering an unreliable and unstable streaming resource – one which could carry legal implications for the user. In the same way that the term lemon is used to describe uncertainty and quality in the market for used cars, a 'digital lemon' is a sport stream of poor or uncertain quality.

Sports broadcasting is well suited to an analysis of the 'digital lemons' phenomenon because of its inherent liveness.[5] Unlike music or movies, which have a much longer commodity lifespan, live sports cannot be replicated through classical forms of piracy – such as recording and circulating copies after the match – because its value will have diminished greatly after the final score is known. Consequently, illegal sport streams are more likely to be affected by the phenomenon of 'digital lemons'. While reproducible information goods can simply be downloaded and stored for later consumption, a dysfunctional live stream poses a much higher risk. If a stream is disrupted due to a technological failure or a copyright takedown request, there are limited options to switch to a legal source. Because of the non-reproducible liveness of sports events, the individual will face costs that are fundamentally different when compared to downloading music or movies. This makes live sports events an extremely valuable resource for content providers. From a theoretical point of view, the high-risk characteristics of 'live' information goods make them a suitable case to study the relations between quality and uncertainty in digital markets.

Legal Risks versus Illegal Uncertainty

Following a legal live ticker in an internet cafe and watching illegal live streams at home are both connected to uncertainty and risks that might interrupt the user experience of 'liveness'. In 2002 my live text ticker experience was disrupted because the owner of the

---

4   G. A. Akerlof, 'The Market for "Lemons": Quality Uncertainty and the Market Mechanism', *Quarterly Journal of Economics* 84.3 (1970): 488-500.

5   Nick Couldry, 'Liveness, "Reality", and the Mediated Habitus from Television to the Mobile Phone', *Communication Review* 7.4 (2004): 353-361.; Elena Levine, 'Distinguishing Television. The Changing Meanings of Television Liveness', *Media, Culture & Society* 30.3 (2008): 393-409; Jane Feuer, 'The Concept of Live Television: Ontology as Ideology', in E.A. Kaplan (ed.), *Regarding Television: Critical Approaches – An Anthology*, Los Angeles: American Film Institute, 1983, pp. 12-21.

internet cafe started to intentionally walk around my desk and began to shut down all the computers around me. As I was the only customer left, he was desperate to close his shop and get some sleep. This posed a serious but measurable risk to my live sports experience. I had plenty of information at hand to grasp the character of the situation and to develop strategies for dealing with it. One option to manage the evolving risk would be to talk to the owner of the internet café, asking him not to shut down my computer. Legitimate channels of distribution such as pay TV offer information goods characterized by a predictable stability in the user experience. To pay for such a subscription plan or to try to start a conversation with the owner of the internet cafe are both risk strategies to lower the probability of a disrupted live experience.

When it comes to live-streaming, this risk emerges in a different way. As it is not visible to the consumer it cannot be turned into a manageable risk strategy. Instead it remains uncertain and unpredictable. In order to comfortably access live football streams consumers rely on live stream aggregation platforms that compile a vast amount of live streaming channels. By systemizing them and making them visible, they provide easy access to these kinds of illegal resources. Platforms such as Stream2watch.me (Fig. 1) provide different categories of live sport events on their starting page. These broad categories can be filtered by country or league. After selecting a certain live sports event a submenu appears (Fig. 2), listing the diverse live streams available. The streams are sorted by resolution, quality, data transfer rate, and language of the commentary.

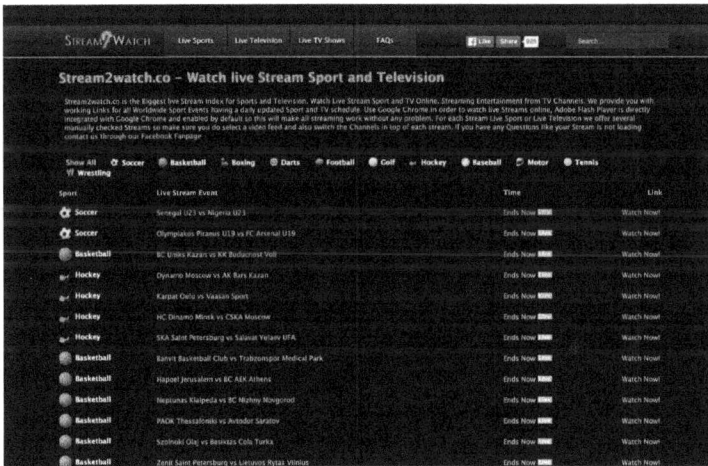

Figure 1. Categories displayed on the starting page of the streaming aggregation platform Stream2watch.me

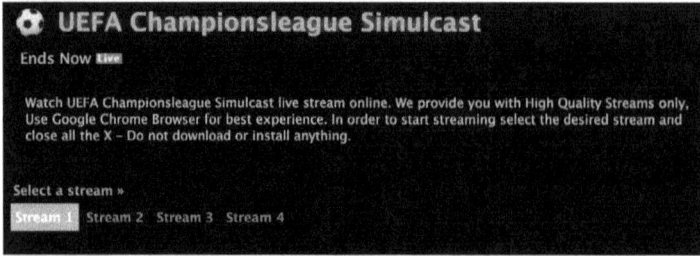

Figure 2. Live stream selection submenu of a streaming aggregation platform

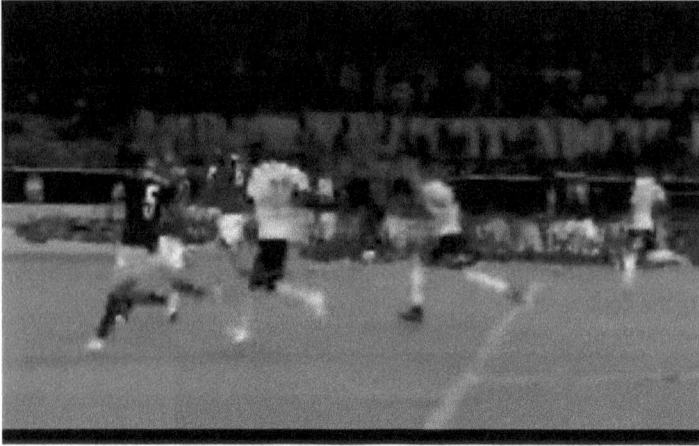

Figure 3. Variable quality, freezing and signal disruption are persistent risks when live-streaming sport

Streams available for the German Bundesliga are either pirated coverage from the German branch of Sky Sports or from foreign broadcasters based in India, Russia, Italy, Spain, United States or China. Some streams are simply filmed from someone's computer or television screen, while others directly access the original digital stream. Depending on the design of the platform and the available streams, between three and fifteen streams are typically listed per match. Popular matches that involve clubs with a worldwide fan base such as FC Bayern Munich tend to attract a larger number of streams. However the quality of these streams is quite diverse, ranging from high-definition resolution to low-quality, heavily compressed video in which it is often difficult to recognize the players. Blurring and compression marks are often visible, making it hard to follow the match (Fig. 3). In addition, streaming channels that infringe the intellectual property of Sky Sports Germany are often disconnected in the last third of a 90-minute football match, reflecting the time it takes to send and process takedown notices. Streams based on foreign broadcast channels are normally not affected by takedown notices. URLs for streaming aggregation platforms change frequently, and platforms often disappear then reappear with a slightly different address.

There is also the risk that there are no streams available at all, or that the quality is too low. Previously stable, high-quality streams can turn into dysfunctional broadcasts if too many users are trying to access them. Other dangers relate to the diverse business models adopted by the streaming providers. Some operators generate profits as part of the 'grey' advertising market and utilize live streaming as an advertising platform, displaying multiple ads via popup windows or Flash content. Others utilize streaming channels as landing pages to spread malware, enabling them to extend bot-networks, conduct identity theft or commit credit card fraud. They use false plug-ins, updates or video player software installers; prepare hidden, transparent buttons; operate with Javascript-based drive-by-download attacks; or take advantage of security holes in software such as Flash. Consumers that rely on illegal live streams significantly increase their risk of being affected by such attacks.

While many people argue that digital network markets are new forms of collaborative capitalism, which can provide free goods, the case of live sports streaming demonstrates that there are significant costs involved. The whole process of locating and consuming illegal 'live' information goods has to be understood as a risky investment of resources that is continuously affected by the problem of 'lemons'. The prevailing uncertainty is a result of different aspects that constitute information goods as 'digital lemons':

1. *searchability* (via well-known streaming platforms; by links that suddenly appear in social networks).

2. *accessibility* (via browser, video player software or via specific software packages; skills required to access streams).

3. *image and sound quality* (compression artifacts; image resolution; time lag issues; foreign language commentaries; loudness; sound modulation).

4. *stability* and *reliability* (interruption of streams due to copyright issues, bandwidth issues or technical problems).

5. *security hazards* (caused by malware and viruses while using illegal streaming platforms).

Conclusion: Uncertain Information Goods and Digital Network Markets

A better understanding of the relations between uncertainty, risk and the consumer provides for a more precise analysis of contemporary digital markets characterized by the phenomenon of piracy as well as by 'freemium' or free-service business models. Live streaming, because of the increased risk of 'digital lemons', offers an exemplary case to investigate uncertainty on the consumer side. Here, the heterogeneous relations between piracy and legitimate consumption structure the gray area between scarcity and abundance of live information goods. The market oscillates between paid and free content and is characterized by information asymmetries that relate to quality and uncertainty. These dynamic structures are not bound to a technologically determined idea of network media that automatically turn goods into public goods. Piracy and measures taken against it – such as geoblocking – are part of continuously fought 'battles and dramas between formal and informal, the ill structured and the well structured, the standardized and the wild'.[6] Here, consumers move continuously 'back-and-forth between ill structured and well structured'[7] situations. If not restricted to the idea of 'free', 'convergence' or 'access', to dualisms such as 'formal' versus 'informal' or 'legal' versus 'illegal', these continuous negotiations between infrastructure, information goods and the market can be understood as a *modus operandi* that structures, stabilizes and changes digital markets. Focusing on the productivity of uncertainty and risk enables us to open up the black box of copy and access culture and to situate it as an intrinsic part of those markets. But it also connects piracy and circumvention practices to a broader perspective that uses risks and uncertainty to explain how stability and change operate in society.[8]

References

Akerlof, G.A. 'The Market for "Lemons": Quality Uncertainty and the Market Mechanism', *Quarterly Journal of Economics* 84.3 (1970): 488-500.

Beck, Ulrich. *Risk Society. Towards a New Modernity*. London: Sage, 1992.

Couldry, Nick. 'Liveness, "Reality", and the Mediated Habitus from Television to the Mobile Phone', *Communication Review* 7.4 (2004): 353-361.

Curtin, Michael, Jennifer Holt, and Kevin Sanson (eds) *Distribution Revolution: Conversations about the Digital Future of Film and Television*, Berkley: University of California Press, 2014.

Feuer, J. 'The Concept of Live Television: Ontology as Ideology', in E.A. Kaplan (ed.) *Regarding Television: Critical Approaches - An Anthology*, Los Angeles: American Film Institute, 1983, pp. 12-21.

Giddens, Anthony. 'Risk and Responsibility', *Modern Law Review* 62.1 (1999): 1-10.

Hutter, Michael. 'Information Goods', in R. Towse and Edward Elgar (eds) *A Handbook of Cultural Economics,* Cheltenham, 2006, pp. 263-268.

Levine, E. 'Distinguishing Television. The Changing Meanings of Television Liveness', *Media, Culture & Society* 30.3 (2008): 393-409.

Luhmann, Niklas. *Risk. A Sociological Theory*, Berlin/New York: De Gruyter, 1993.

Star, Susan L. 'This Is Not a Boundary Object: Reflections on the Origin of a Concept', *Science, Technology and Human Values* 35.5 (2010): 601-617.

Sophie Rohringer. 'Hier sehen Sie Borussia Dortmund gegen FK Krasnodar jetzt im TV und Live-Stream', tz, 17 September 2015, https://www.tz.de/sport/fussball/europa-league-borussia-dortmund-gegen-fk-krasnodar-tv-live-stream-sky-sport1-5515199.html.

---

6   Susan L. Star, 'This Is Not a Boundary Object: Reflections on the Origin of a Concept', *Science, Technology and Human Values* 35.5 (2010): 614.

7   Star, 'This Is Not a Boundary Object', p. 614.

8   See: Ulrich Beck, *Risk Society. Towards a New Modernity*, London: Sage, 1992; Anthony Giddens, 'Risk and Responsibility', *Modern Law Review* 62.1 (1999): 1-10; Niklas Luhmann, *Risk. A Sociological Theory*, Berlin/New York: De Gruyter, 1993. xf

THE FUTURE IN A VAULT OF PLASTIC: PHYSICAL GEOLOCKING IN THE ERA OF THE 16-BIT VIDEO GAME CARTRIDGE, 1988-1993

ROLAND BURKE

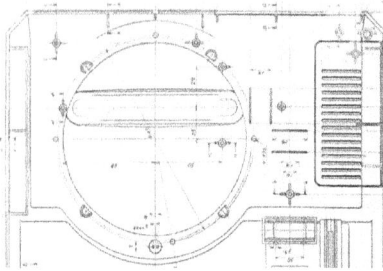

Figure 1. Drawing the Borders: Detail of the original Sega Megadrive design schematic, with the assorted cartridge slot shapes indicated.

Geoblocking has been implemented to partition what would otherwise be potentially borderless worlds of information and entertainment delivered via the internet.[1] Digital media markets, differentiated in price and access to different 'regions' of the globe, now provoke widespread circumvention. Perhaps unsurprisingly, the established hierarchy of digital citizenship has been contested most actively by the citizenry on its margins; particularly in Australia, a wealthy but remote country, with very rapid uptake of technology. Australia's digital citizens, who are amongst the most privileged and prosperous in the physical world, have railed against their digital marginalization with an exceptional intensity.

This is, however, not a wholly new phenomenon. There is a long history of Australian consumers subverting the efforts of their electronic suzerains, not only in the United States, but also Japan, through unauthorised circumvention and parallel importation. Among the most dedicated consumers are Australian gamers, who have been manually modifying game cartridges meant for other markets for at least two decades. This chapter recovers some of that past, and points to a much longer tradition of citizen-led circumvention. It also seeks to

---

1   See, for instance, Michael Strangelove, *Post-TV: Piracy, Cord-Cutting, and the Future of Television,* Toronto: University of Toronto Press, 2015; Brett Christophers, 'Spaces of Media Capital', in Paul Adams et al. (eds), *The Ashgate Research Companion to Media Geography,* Surrey: Ashgate, 2014, 363-376; and Christophers, *Envisioning Media Power: On Capital and the Geographies of Television,* Plymouth: Lexington, 2009. See also the sibling work on parallel, semi-subaltern, circumvention networks, physical and electronic, notably from Ramon Lobato, *Shadow Economies of Cinema: Mapping Informal Film Distribution,* London: Palgrave, 2012; and the large scale survey works from Adrian Johns, *Piracy: The Intellectual Property Wars from Gutenberg to Gates,* Chicago: University of Chicago Press, 2011; Patrick Bukart, *Pirate Politics: The New Information Policy Contests,* Cambridge, MA: MIT Press, 2014; and Hector Postigo, *The Digital Rights Movement: The Role of Technology in Subverting Digital Copyright,* Cambridge, MA: MIT Press, 2012.

restore, in a modest way, an aspect of digital entertainment that has been largely neglected; namely, the creation and circulation of digital information as a discrete physical entity.[2]

The Future Elsewhere: Japan's revival of home video gaming

Video gaming, as a consumer pastime, emeged in the United States. After a number of comparatively unsuccessful precursors, Atari inaugurated a popular culture boom in video games between 1978 and 1983. It was not to last, and after quality control concerns, and catastrophic market oversupply, this first video game efflorescence dramatically darkened, before a slow recovery in the mid to late 1980s.[3] The epicentre of the revival of home video gaming was Japan, a market partially decoupled from the precipitous collapse of the US home gaming industry across 1982-84.[4] As the iconic brands of the preceding Atari age fell, not merely into hardship, but in many cases, bankruptcy, Japan was a kind of sanctuary site. This was where the new custodians of electronic entertainment, Nintendo and Sega, prospered - first at home, and, from late 1985, abroad.[5] Japanese gaming consoles repopulated a desolate American market, and conquered the PAL television system countries of Western Europe and Australia in turn. The Nintendo Entertainment System, and

---

2   The historical milieu of video games, and the labor process by which they were created, produced, and disseminated, has not yet received substantial scholarly investigation. The specialist periodical *Retrogamer* (Imagine) has produced some excellent episodic coverage and interview material, as has the recent work from Keith Stuart and Darren Wall, devoted solely to the Megadrive, with historical drawings, and interviews ranging from its lead software engineers, to the industrial designer who sculpted its casing. See Stuart and Wall, *Sega Mega Drive/Genesis: Collected Works,* n.p: Read Only Memory, 2014. Much of the investigation to date has been focused on the neo-Romantic period of British home computer video games, with recent studies from Christopher Witkins, *The Story of the Sinclair ZX Spectrum in Pixels*, n.p., Fusion Retro Books, 2014; and *The History of Ocean Software,* n.p., Fusion Retro Books, 2014, and a forthcoming book on software publisher US Gold (2015). Given its centrality to the birth of gaming, Atari has been the subject of some extensive historical coverage on labor environment and workplace culture, with a voluminous and insightful empirical account furnished by Curt Vendel and Marty Goldberg, *Atari Inc.: Business is Fun*, Carmel, NY: Syzygy Press, 2012. There appears to be a growing interest in Japan's historical video game production environment, though current work is confined to S.M.G Szczepaniak, *The Untold History of Japanese Game Developers*, n.s., 2014.

3   This story is detailed in numerous narrative histories, see Tristan Donovan, *Replay: The History of Video Games Paperback*, East Sussex: Yellow Ant, 2010; Steven Kent, *The Ultimate History of Video Games: From Pong to Pokemon: The Story Behind the Craze That Touched Our Lives and Changed the World,* New York: Three Rivers, 2001; Mark Wolf, *The Video Game Explosion: A History from Pong to PlayStation and Beyond*, Westport: Greenwood, 2007. See also the dedicated studies of this foundational period, Mark Wolf, Jessica Aldred, Ralph Baer et al., *Before the Crash: Early Video Game History*, Detroit: Wayne State University Press, 2012; Roberto Dillon, *The Golden Age of Video Games: The Birth of a Multibillion Dollar Industry*, Boca Raton, FL: Taylor & Francis, 2011; see especially, the volume from Ralph Baer, inventor of the television game, *Videogames: In the Beginning*, Springfield, NJ: Rolenta, 2005.

4   This Japanese revival is a central waypoint in the periodization of video game history, by near universal consensus across all of the major survey works, see for instance, Chris Kohler, *Power-Up: How Japanese Video Games Gave the World an Extra Life,* Indianapolis, IN: Brady Games, 2004; Leonard Herman, *Phoenix: The Fall & Rise of Video Games*, Springfield, NJ: Rolenta, 1997.

5   Jeff Ryan, *Super Mario: How Nintendo Conquered America*, London: Penguin, 2012; David Sheff and Andy Eddy, *Game Over Press Start To Continue*, Wilton, CT: Cyberactive Press, 1999.

its counterpart, the Sega Master System, restored gaming to its more or less continuous trajectory of growth – a steady gradient which would advance video games to their current, ascendant, position as largest global media industry.

Regional lock-out mechanisms were largely absent from the consoles of the late 1970s and early 1980s. The Atari VCS, Mattel Intellivision, Milton-Bradley Vectrex, and Coleco Toys Colecovision contained no explicit regional locking provisions, though this was no absolute assurance of pan-regional compatibility. In the case of the Atari VCS, the first mass-market system with interchangeable game cartridges, the reality of highly constrained hardware mandated an effective, if inconsistent, region lock. The video display chip and CPU at the heart of the VCS were closely coupled to the raster output of the television: they literally 'raced the beam', or electron gun that painted the TV screen.[6] It followed that the precise timing mattered, and thus, games needed to be finely calibrated for either NTSC (60Hz), or PAL (50Hz).[7] It was a regional lock of sorts, reflecting the difficulty of making a functional, affordable video game system with mid-1970s integrated circuit technology.

In the mid-1980s, with the new Japanese consoles, the relationship between television system and console hardware was less intimate. Newer graphics chips were not so closely coupled to the raster of the television screen. More particularly, there was the emergence of regional coding created independent of television system. Japanese Nintendo games were regionally-locked to the Japanese Nintendo console (Famicom), preventing its cartridges being played on the American Nintendo.[8] This was despite both systems being, in essence, fully compatible, and sharing a common NTSC television output. Nintendo redesigned the form factor of its cartridges to prevent their physical access to American systems, and, for good measure, rerouted the gold pins of the cartridge interface to a new, North American specific, pattern. With the advent of the first Nintendo, the region lock was now much more than a happy, market-segmenting accident derived from television standards – it was a conscious technological strategy crafted by the system vendor.[9]

Between 1988 and 1993, the second wave of Japanese origin consoles, first from Sega in 1988 (Japan, 1990 US, 1991 EU/Australia), and later Nintendo (1990 Japan, 1991 US, 1992

---

6   For an outstanding study of the VCS, and the relationship between material, technological constraint and gameplay, see Nick Montfort, *Racing the Beam: The Atari Video Computer System*, Cambridge, MA: MIT Press, 2009.

7   The differences between PAL and NTSC have been exhaustively parsed, see, for instance, Jim Slater, *Modern Television Systems*, London: CRC Press / Longman, 1991, 1-55; see also Megumi Ogawa, *Protection of Broadcasters' Rights*, Leiden: Brill, 2006, 55.

8   For the most detailed empirical study of the origins, and broader impact, of the original Nintendo, see Nathan Altice, *I Am Error: The Nintendo Family Computer / Entertainment System Platform*, Cambridge, MA: MIT Press, 2015.

9   This was a strategy continued by Nintendo's rival, NEC, which re-badged its popular Japanese console, the PC-Engine, to the Turbografx-16 for US sale. The Turbografx, which had a different plastic shell, and a larger form factor, had its card-shaped cartridges region locked between Japan and the US via differences in the interface pins which connected game to console. The PC-Engine/Turbografx did not receive a PAL territory release, though one was planned, and some inventory prepared for Western Europe.

EU/Australia) – arrived in the historically neglected PAL markets. This chapter will focus on Australia, a geographically isolated region, with no land borders, and no proximate NTSC neighbour – and one which often lagged behind Japan and the United States, in terms of the release of both video game hardware and its requisite software. The second wave of the console contest was the crucible for the modern gaming market, when gaming began to escape to the living room, and to the adult world. With improvements in transistor density, increased global RAM supply after the catastrophic shortages of the late 1980s, and larger markets across which to amortize research and development, video games were markedly more accessible, sophisticated, and aesthetically impressive experiences.[10] A fierce format war between Sega and Nintendo intensified competition, and accelerated the rate of innovation.[11] In this new gaming environment of the 1990s, the issue of region locking became progressively more acute.

The Sega Megadrive was a revealing case. While provisioned with some capacity for an electronic lockout, the console's key region-locking mechanism was a simple variation in the geometry of the cartridge slot.[12] In other words, for much of the Megadrive's commercial life geographic market segmentation was achieved solely by this decidedly flimsy physical countermeasure.

Most cartridges released for the system, and almost all of the most popular titles, would play without incident on both NTSC units, those from Japan and the United States. They would also play on PAL systems, provided they could be inserted into them. As a result, the barrier to importing games was vastly diminished. There was no requirement to purchase a Japanese or American console, a voltage transformer, or a still highly esoteric multi-color system television. In many cases, region-specific languages were also included on the same cartridge, precluding the need for any local language translation for instance, from Japanese to English – a need which was already modest given the comparative narrative simplicity that defined the games of this period.[13] The Megadrive was a rare case where physical blockade

---

10   For the state of the relevant segments of semiconductor industry in the latter 1980s, see Dataquest, 'Report on Asian Semiconductor and Electronic Technology Service (1991)', available at http://archive. computerhistory.org/resources/access/text/2013/04/102723217-05-01-acc.pdf.

11   The early 1990s 'Console War' was regarded as something of a revolutionary period in gaming development, see generally, Blake Harris, *Console Wars: Sega, Nintendo, and the Battle that Defined a Generation*, New York: HarperCollins, 2014; and Sam Pettus et al., *Service Games: The Rise and Fall of SEGA: Enhanced Edition*, Seattle: CreateSpace, 2013.

12   The origins of the Megadrive's lockout policy were within management at Sega Japan, which held an almost imperial control over its regional subsidiaries, including the vast American market. Former director of Sega's US branch, Michael Katz, who presided over a considerable sales success in North America, noted that 'lockout decisions were made in Japan. The Sega Japan International VP handled international sales and marketing'. Sega Japan's reasoning was explicitly designed to foreclose the operation of a flat internationalized market, with its former chief of public relations stating frankly that 'we implemented the security regionally to prevent game software being imported due to gaps of sales time between regions'. Quote reproduced in 'The Megadrive', in *The Videogames Hardware Handbook, Volume 2*, Willenhall: William Gibbons and Imagine Publishing, 2015, 21.

13   Speculatively, this may well have been to mitigate against the inventory risk that inhered to the cartridge format. As a write once, never erase medium for software, the Mask ROM chips which contained the software presented an immense risk to software publishers. An order of too few

was the prime means for seeking a market segmentation; a segmentation that always tended to disfavor the PAL regions of Europe and Australia. Predictably, the unsophistication of the geometrical 'lock out' was rapidly exploited by Australians.

Breeching the Polypropylene Wall: Console Hacking with a Hacksaw and a Heated Carving Knife

Demand for Japanese cartridges in Australia was driven by the long delay between releases in Japan, and those in the PAL countries. In the late 1980s and early 1990s this delay typically amounted to a full fiscal quarter, and often extended to an entire calendar year. Holding back the flood of eager video gamers was, remarkably, a small piece of plastic, which altered the geometry of the cartridge slot – with Japanese cartridges shaped slightly more widely than the slots present on the PAL Megadrive console units. The difference which prevented their use in the Megadrive machines of Britain and Australia, around 12mm, was breathtakingly – perhaps heartbreakingly – close.[14] In essence, slightly more than a centimetre of matte black polypropylene was assigned the weight of defending Australia's cultural borders, or perhaps more accurately, allowing market segmentation by the Japanese parent and its subsidiary. Unremarkably, it was a barrier soon breached by enterprising children, and nervous adults who looked on in fear as their young performed makeshift surgery on the casing of the expensive Megadrive hardware, or provisioned substantial sums of cash to purchase grey market adaptors for the rival console, the Super Nintendo, from dog-eared mail order forms.

For the Megadrive, the process was elegant in concept, and alarming in practice. The outer shell of the cartridge slot, the final sentinel against imported software, had two small tabs of plastic excised. Due care was required that the chosen implement, typically a heated carving knife (for clean margins on the incision), or an electric variant, did not make contact with the motherboard that resided beneath. With these thermoset plastic border posts removed, by a doubtlessly tremulous pair of hands, all cartridges could be inserted without impediment. Marginally more sophisticated was the procedure for the Megadrive's rival, the Super Nintendo. A very crude region checking system had been implemented; but one easily deceived by replicating the cartridge slot. An aftermarket adaptor would accommodate one 'native' region cartridge for chaperone duties (almost always *Super Mario World*), which would present its endogenous credentials; and then immediately defer to the 'foreign' cartridge that was mounted in tandem in the replicated slot alongside it. For the Sega system, circumvention involved punching a hole in the geo-fence; for the Super Nintendo, it required

---

cartridges could produce unrecoverable shortages for key sales periods, such as the Northern Hemisphere winter; a situation which would take months to remedy given the austere limits on Mask ROM production. Conversely, too many units, and the risk of unsold, and expensive, stock, could obliterate any prospect of profit. By consolidating in a central inventory, only the external casing of the cartridge and packaging, manuals, and ephemera – all inexpensive, low lead-time items, needed to be altered to match product to diverse markets.

14   A number of later revisions to the Sega Megadrive did have some software based lock-out mechanisms, which operated alongside anti-counterfeit protection, though it was very inconsistently applied. See *Electronic Gaming Monthly,* September 1992, 76.

a 'native' regional escort providing a fleeting moment of diplomatic cover. In both cases, the breech was easily and cheaply made.

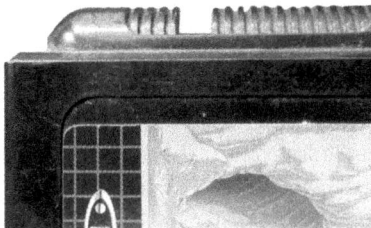

Figure 2. The Japanese Megadrive cartridge with its infuriating rounded edge. The owner is mere millimetres away from fun. Source: Roland Burke

Figure 3. The localized Australian Megadrive cartridge, with its distinctive curved spline. Source: Roland Burke

Circumvention was not a procedure undertaken without considerable deliberation and fore-thought. Inexperienced hands, no matter how nimble, could fatally damage the Megadrive, which was, at the time, an extortionately priced piece of consumer electronics, with a price tag of A$399 in 1991. Acquiring the console required studious petitioning and parental patronage, and even then, the cost involved made it the preserve of the middle class.[15] With Australia entering a very steep and prolonged economic recession shortly after the release of the Megadrive, it took years of depreciation and improving economic conditions before it arrived at a mass market price Breaching the cartridge slot, and thus reaching the 'future' (actually the geographically distant present), was an enterprise that involved great risk. Physical puncture of the motherboard, or electrostatic discharge, could permanently destroy a comparatively massive capital outlay. Australians could leap to the future of Japanese games, but the penalty for a failed attempt would be severe.

---

15 Putting aside the steady stream of game cartridges that would invariably be sought after the Sega Megadrive itself had been secured, at AUD339, the console outlay alone represented a massive fraction of Australian adult average weekly earnings before tax, which stood at AUD568 in August 1991. See Australian Bureau of Statistics, Report on Average Weekly Earnings, August 1991, released 19 December 1991, available at http://www.ausstats.abs.gov.au/ausstats/free.nsf/0/ FAE37DAF57F82D9DCA2574FA00184F33/$File/63020_AUG1991.pdf.

Visible Public Networks: The Classroom VPNs of the early 1990s and the Prestige of Gaming Scarcity

As video game journalism matured during the 1990s, popular knowledge of circumvention increased. Until this point, this gap between promised excitement and local disappointment was present, but manageable. The latency between knowledge of new overseas games, as revealed in effusive print reviews and colorful screenshots, was modest. Almost all dedicated English-language video game journalism was published in the UK or the US.[16] Delivered via the most economical tier of surface mail, the journey of the magazines -- the paper vectors for anticipation, excitement, and, usually, frustration -- consumed much of the latency period between knowledge and release. The games arrived much later than they did in Japan or the United States, but so too did the knowledge of their existence, or in the case of reviews, the assurance of their hedonic virtue.

In the 1990s, this slothful symmetry between printed gaming magazine and printed circuit board was radically disrupted; not by the internet, which remained a mostly inaccessible, text-based curiosity, but by the advent of widespread air mail distribution. Initially confined to hyper-specialist outlets, most famously McGill's Bookshop in Elizabeth Street, Melbourne, the air mailed gaming magazine delivered the future (geographically quarantined present), to the Australian suburbs. There was a substantial price premium, with air-mailed issues almost double the price (A$8.95to A$4.95), but air mail proliferated, particularly through Pacific Computers, a specialist gaming vendor that rapidly spread across suburban malls in southern Australia. Perhaps appropriately, the air-mailed titles had their own informational lock out. They were almost always sealed in plastic -- presumably a measure of prophylaxis against physical damage, but also, a physical membrane which foreclosed access to the knowledge within prior to purchase. This was special, and expensive information. Purchasing a quantum of it was a major outlay – one typically recouped in social capital when latest magazine was circulated by its proud owner amongst school friends.

Beyond the circulation of expensive magazine knowledge, the ownership of highly antici-pated games, well in advance of their domestic launch dates, lent social and cultural capital within school environments, typically amongst late primary and early secondary boys. During the early 1990s, in middle- and upper-middle class suburbs, where almost every want or vaguely expressed material desire could be, and often was, fulfilled, the special supra-mon-etary value of having an 'import' was a socially advantageous asset. Study of the glossy printed materials, which were richly illustrated, and the even the packaging, were privileges to be disbursed judiciously over a playground lunchtime. Indecipherable Kanji characters added an exoticism – though presumably few pondered the sources of the mystique that a Japanese game held. Parsimony in access not merely to the game, but to the material arte-facts of the game cartridge, preserved its scarcity. Custodianship of a high-profile imported

---

16   EMAP Images, publishers of *Computer and Video Games*, and from late 1989, the console focussed sibling, *Mean Machines*, were the most widely distributed in Australian newsagents. Prevalent, but slightly less common, were the American *Electronic Gaming Monthly* (available in Australia in very early 1990), and *Gamepro*.

game, be it *Strider, Bare Knuckle*, or most especially, *Street Fighter 2* was a solemn respon-sibility – albeit one typically wielded with the glib caprice and irresponsibility that inhered in schoolyard politics and classroom diplomacy.

It followed that pricing was not, in the main, driving demand for Japanese or American releases. Very often, imported games, especially highly anticipated titles, were more expen-sive at import than their domestic siblings would be at their official launch. In July 1992, *Street Fighter 2* for the Super Nintendo sold for A$140 as an import, with an additional A$50 for the requisite cartridge adaptor.[17] But it was available – and available at exactly the moment that voluminous reviews, each with praise more superlative than the last, arrived in air-mail imported magazines. The transaction, in the most fundamental form of exchange, repartitioned money into time – time with the game, and in a stroke of serendipity, time which coincided with the two week winter recess in Australian primary schools.[18]

Conclusion: Unlocking the Plastic Gates of the Future

The physical geo-lock of the 16-bit gaming era was an admixture of the then high-tech Motorola 68000 CPU, and ultra-high performance pseudo-SRAM chips, and the decidedly low technology of injection moulding. Its very lack of sophistication marked it out as a profoundly different, and strangely democratized, cultural milieu. Hierarchies were based on depth of enthusiasm; whereby ownership of a prized Japanese title was demonstrative not of greater funds (though plenty were still needed – and always remained insufficient), or of ultra-specialist technical skill, but of daring, and of being privy to seemingly special personal networks. The later era of circumvention, which arrived with optical disk based consoles, notably the Sony Playstation (1995) and the Sega Saturn (1995), altered this arrangement. With the implementation of a digital lockout, the barriers to circumvention were raised dramatically. Bypassing this new generation of software-based geo-locking required custom-made integrated circuits. The energetic resourcefulness of young adults was no longer adequate; and the cross-over with flat out illegality, insofar as the same anti-geolock chips allowed piracy, loomed.

Equally, the 16-bit age represented a more restrained era in the vendor-consumer arms race, a race which has often produced mutually assured irritation. The Megadrive's unso-phisticated physical lock allowed owners a degree of autonomy over their machines – and the constraints on import were mostly those of logistical inconvenience. Enthusiasm and desire could overcome these obstacles, but would only ever do so for a limited market segment, and thus placed an upper ceiling on disruption to local distribution channels and market control. Legislative responses, insofar as they existed, were confined to the sporadic

---

17   Part of this expense derived from the generous amount of ROM employed to deliver a reasonably
      faithful reproduction of original arcade game, which had been wildly successful. The home version
      used 16Mbit of ROM (2Mbyte), twice that of other premium Super Nintendo titles. American reporting
      prior to launch emphasized this vast reservoir of ROM, with a large photograph of the cartridge with
      its top shell removed, and banks of ROM chips visible on the circuit board. See *Electronic Gaming
      Monthly* (April 1992), 42.
18   1992, *Trinity Grammar School Diary*.

and well-publicized confiscation of imported games by Australian Customs (promptly and ostentatiously donated to local children's hospitals), an enforcement measure which was abandoned in the wave of competition reforms which relaxed parallel import rules. Even the expansive, omnibus anti-circumvention provisions of the Digital Agenda Act (2000) would seem ill-armed to counter the threat of a kitchen knife and a determined young video game enthusiast with a poorly developed sense of risk.

The five prime years of the 16-bit video game console also represented a liminal moment in electronic entertainment. Dissemination of information was, emphatically, still physical. News of video games arrived in magazines – initially with considerable delay. The games themselves, although digital, were housed in gaudy plastic carapaces. These cartridge shells protected their contents from static electricity and water (cola) – and, in their territory-specific geometry, sought to prevent their migration from East to West. It was also the last generation where gaming was dominated by the de facto duopoly of Nintendo and Sega, companies with a strong heritage in physical entertainment products. Unlike Sony, which had a large portion of its enterprise tied in the ethereal intellectual property of music rights and film, or Microsoft, which joined the console 'wars' in 2001 having previously been a software company, Nintendo and Sega were experts in producing entertainment objects.

The temptation for Nintendo to approach the new world of software with a vestigial attachment to the physical and material was surely powerful.[19] The Nintendo 64 (June 1996 Japan, September 1996 US, March 1997 Australia/Europe) utilized cartridges, years after its competitors had migrated to optical disks, and despite the complaints of software developers. Nintendo clearly had yet to be persuaded that the delivery medium did not matter. The incredibly high quality of the N64 software library, its resistance to commercial piracy, and the elevated value of these cartridges on the secondary market suggests there was some merit in Nintendo's caution in embracing fully commoditized data formats like optical disc.[20]

The schoolyard circumvention movement of the early 1990s was a fleeting one, and while it presaged aspects of the future – notably, the dramatic rise of the global video game market -- it probably resided more in the last act of a past where entertainment media was unambiguously embodied in a tactile object. The world of the Sega Megadrive and the Super Nintendo consoles marked the zenith in the cartridge as a material entity; with designs which had become, by the early 1990s, truly Baroque. During the last years of cartridge distribution, there were perceptible differences in weight – with the most recent

---

19   For Nintendo's longer genealogy, see the two volumes from Gorges et al. *The History of Nintendo 1889-1980* and *The History of Nintendo 1980-1991*, Triel-sur-Seine, France; London: Les Editions Pix'N Love, 2012.

20   Nintendo was perhaps the most extreme example of physical locking, taking countermeasures even against mechanical access to the hardware. After initially using standard Philips head screws to assemble its console, it later migrated to a proprietary screw head for the outer screws which held the console's case together. These special Nintendo 'Gamebit' screws required a Nintendo screwdriver to release – a screwdriver that was not available on the general market. In the absence of the screws, access to the inside of the Nintendo 64, for example, required the destruction of the screws with a power drill.

and advanced titles markedly heavier, owing to a denser array of ROM chips, which held the game program.[21] With ROM chips relatively expensive, in this terminal phase of cartridge distribution, gaming data was being purchased by the gram.

With the rise of the Playstation in the mid-1990s, the long decline into digital weightlessness had begun. Optical disks varied little in appearance, the same in form factor as the audio CD. Discs were a fully commoditized and disappointingly insubstantial medium – pressed at will from polycarbonate and aluminium, and holding only cents worth of intrinsic value, which clung desperately to the optical platter, only tens microns of ill-handling away from an unrecoverable scratch. The ever-increasing abstraction of the game from its medium of delivery, arguably heightened dissatisfaction with any delay in it reaching a PAL market Gone was the material dimension of the cartridge; a proprietary format, not interchangeable with mass market optical disks, and with a distinctive design and aesthetic of its own.

There was, by the end of the first Playstation age in the late 1990s, no more mystique about the physicality of gaming software. Interest in the game software as an object rapidly became confined to the arcane antiquarianism of retro-video game collectors.[22]

Geometry lockout had matched, for a short moment, a hybrid digital world, where information was digital, but had to be affixed to ROM chips for its survival and global dissemination. It travelled in bulk container ships and 747 cargo conversion holds, and was restricted by the costs of commercial shipping, not arbitrarily emplaced IP block ranges. Its encryption was a geometrical puzzle; an alteration in cartridge shape, and no more. At the time of the 16-bit consoles, especially the Megadrive, geo-locking was a spatial exercise – and its resolution could be found in spatial ingenuity. For those passionate enough to husband the safe travel of those bits through the geographic space of Japan to Australia, and to pilot the delicate final leg, through the micro-geographic shoals of occluded cartridge slot to unshielded cartridge port, the impediments imposed were merely those of the real geo-, not the stratified one prescribed by corporate entities.

References

Altice, Nathan. *I Am Error: The Nintendo Family Computer / Entertainment System Platform*, Cambridge, MA: MIT Press, 2015.

Baer, Ralph. *Videogames: In the Beginning, Springfield*, NJ: Rolenta, 2005.

Burkart, Patrick. *Pirate Politics: The New Information Policy Contests*, Cambridge, MA: MIT Press, 2014.

---

21 For a précis of ROM technology, its characteristics, and evolution over time, see note at Computer History Museum, 'Semiconductor Read-Only-Memory Chips Appear', available at http://www.computerhistory.org/semiconductor/timeline/1965-ROM.html; for further detail, see University of Michigan, 'ROM, EPROM, EEPROM', https://web.eecs.umich.edu/~prabal/teaching/eecs373-f10/readings/rom-eprom-eeprom-technology.pdf; Smithsonian Institution, 'The MOS Memory Market (1996)', available at http://smithsonianchips.si.edu/ice/cd/MEM96/SEC01.pdf.

22 The materiality of games and their conservation has only recently begun to emerge as a topic of academic inquiry, see notably Raiford Guins, *Game After: A Cultural Study of Video Game Afterlife*, Cambridge, MA: MIT Press, 2014.

Christophers, Brett. *Envisioning Media Power: On Capital and the Geographies of Television*, Plymouth: Lexington, 2009.

Christophers, Brett. 'Spaces of Media Capital', in Paul Adams et al. (eds), *The Ashgate Research Companion to Media Geography*, Surrey: Ashgate, 2014, 363-376.

Dataquest, 'Asian Semiconductor and Electronic Technology Service', report, 1991, http://archive. computerhistory.org/resources/access/text/2013/04/102723217-05-01-acc.pdf.

Dillon, Roberto. *The Golden Age of Video Games: The Birth of a Multibillion Dollar Industry*, Boca Raton, FL: Taylor & Francis, 2011.

Donovan, Tristan. *Replay: The History of Video Games Paperback*, East Sussex: Yellow Ant, 2010.

Gorges, Florent. *The History of Nintendo 1889-1980*, Triel-sur-Seine: Les Editions Pix'N Love, 2012.

Gorges, Florent. *The History of Nintendo 1980-1991*, Triel-sur-Seine: Les Editions Pix'N Love, 2012.

Harris, Blake. *Console Wars: Sega, Nintendo, and the Battle that Defined a Generation*, New York: HarperCollins, 2014.

Herman, Leonard. Phoenix: The Fall and Rise of Video Games, Springfield, NJ: Rolenta, 1997.

Johns, Adrian. *Piracy: The Intellectual Property Wars from Gutenberg to Gates*, Chicago: University of Chicago Press, 2011.

Kent, Steven. *The Ultimate History of Video Games: From Pong to Pokemon: The Story Behind the Craze That Touched Our Lives and Changed the World*, New York: Three Rivers, 2001.

Kohler, Chris. *Power-Up: How Japanese Video Games Gave the World an Extra Life*, Indianapolis, IN: Brady Games, 2004.

Lobato, Ramon. *Shadow Economies of Cinema: Mapping Informal Film Distribution*, London: British Film Institute, 2012.

Montfort, Nick. *Racing the Beam: The Atari Video Computer System*, Cambridge, MA: MIT Press, 2009.

Ogawa, Megumi. *Protection of Broadcasters' Rights*, Leiden: Brill, 2006.

Pettus, Sam. *Service Games: The Rise and Fall of SEGA: Enhanced Edition*, Seattle: CreateSpace, 2013.

Postigo, Hector. *The Digital Rights Movement: The Role of Technology in Subverting Digital Copyright*, Cambridge, MA: MIT Press, 2012.

Ryan, Jeff. *Super Mario: How Nintendo Conquered America*, London: Penguin, 2012.

Sheff, David and Andy Eddy. *Game Over Press Start To Continue*, Wilton, CT: Cyberactive Press, 1999.

Slater, Jim. *Modern Television Systems*, London: CRC Press / Longman, 1991.

'Semiconductor Read-Only-Memory Chips Appear', *Computer History Museum*, http://www.computerhistory.org/semiconductor/timeline/1965-ROM.html.

Integrated Circuit Engineering Corporation. 'The MOS Memory Market', report, 1996, http://smithsonianchips.si.edu/ice/cd/MEM96/SEC01.pdf.

Strangelove, Michael. *Post-TV: Piracy, Cord-Cutting, and the Future of Television*, Toronto: University of Toronto Press, 2015.

Stuart, Keith and Wall, Darren. *Sega Mega Drive/Genesis: Collected Works*, n.p: Read Only Memory, 2014.

Szczepaniak, S.M.G. *The Untold History of Japanese Game Developers*, n.s., 2014.

Vendel, Curt and Marty Goldberg. *Atari Inc.: Business is Fun*, Carmel, NY: Syzygy Press, 2012.

Wilkins, Christopher.*The Story of the Sinclair ZX Spectrum in Pixels*, n.p., Fusion Retro Books, 2014.

Wilkins, Christopher. *The History of Ocean Software*, n.p., Fusion Retro Books, 2014.

Wilkins, Christopher. *The Story of U.S. Gold*, n.p., Fusion Retro Books, 2015.

Wolf, Mark. *The Video Game Explosion: A History from Pong to PlayStation and Beyond*, Westport: Greenwood, 2007.

Wolf, Mark (ed.), *Before the Crash: Early Video Game History*, Detroit: Wayne State University Press, 2012.

PART II:
CIRCUMVENTION CASE STUDIES

The following chapters focus on ground-level internet circumvention practices – how people around the world negotiate different kinds of blocks, including both commercial geo-blocking and government censorship. Together, these chapters reveal that the use of VPNs, proxies, and other workarounds is now a global phenomenon, even though tools and habits vary from country to country.

Our comparison of nine countries – China, Australia, Turkey, Sweden, Malaysia, Brazil, Iran, Cuba and the United States – illuminates some of the continuities and specificities of global circumvention. As we will see, each region has its own mix of drivers and practices. In some parts of the world, circumvention is mostly driven by demand for first-release entertainment content. In other countries it is about gaining access to social networks or communication tools that have been blocked by the government. But in all cases, the use of circumvention software, apps and plugins changes the official geography of video access. The authors in this section tell richly detailed stories about these circumvention practices and discuss their implications for how digital media circulate today.

Sweden	92.5	
United States	87.4	
Australia	84.6	
Malaysia	67.5	
Brazil	57.6	
Turkey	51	
China	49.3	
Iran	39.4	
Cuba	30	

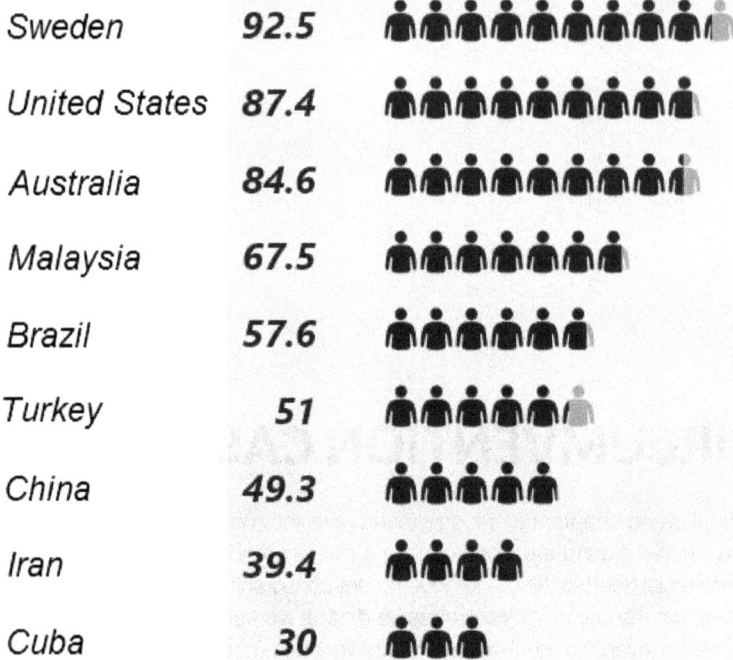

Figure 1. Average connection speed (Mbps). Data source: Akamai State of the Internet Report Q4 2014

Sweden	14.6	★★★★★★★★★★★★★★★
United States	11.1	★★★★★★★★★★★★☆
Australia	7.4	★★★★★★★☆
Turkey	5.8	★★★★★★
Malaysia	4.1	★★★★☆
China	3.4	★★★☆
Brazil	3	★★★

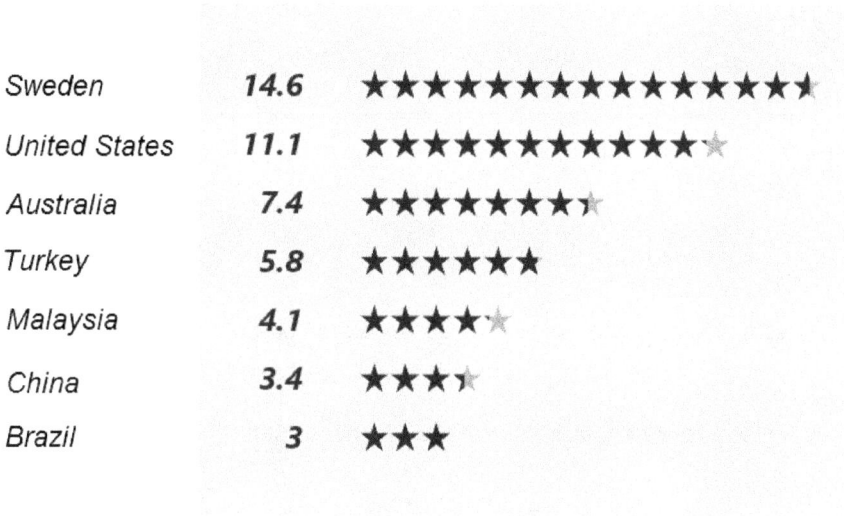

Figure 2. Internet users per 100 people. Data source: The World Bank

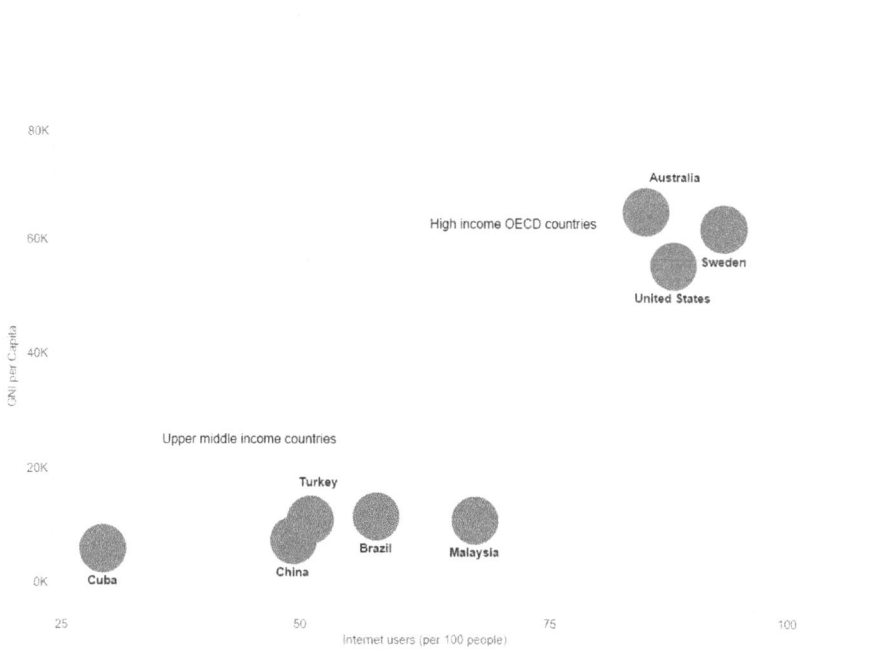

Figure 3. Income status of internet users. Data source: The World Bank.

CHINA: THE TECHNO-POLITICS OF THE WALL

JINYING LI

---

668 MILLION

total number of internet users in China

433 MILLION

estimated number of online video consumers in China

65,815

number of URLs that are currently blocked by the GFW

20%

proportion of Chinese internet users who use VPNs and proxies to bypass the GFW

'If you are arrested, your freedom curtailed, your posts deleted, these can all be cases of being 'walled." – Murong Xuecun, Writer, 2015

The Great Firewall (GFW) is one of the most sophisticated and effective Internet blocking projects, and it functions as a powerful instrument for censorship in China.[1] The existence of the "wall," as both a technological apparatus and a structure metaphor, is a symptomatic object of the global media network, shattering the myth of borderless global access and foregrounding the regulatory power of the nation-state.[2] But what makes the wall more meaningful is the practice of "wall-crossing" (*fanqiang*). As counterprotocols for tactical media, a series of tools and strategies based on VPNs and proxy servers have been developed by Chinese users to circumvent the Great Firewall and to access blocked media content.[3]

The battle over the GFW reveals the lived experience of (dis)connected global media flow that is marked by constant struggles between restriction and access. By investigating the GFW and the practices used to bypass it, this study aims not just to understand the GFW itself, but to interrogate the discursive meanings and political outcomes of technological knowledge, devices, and infrastructures that formed seemingly invisible, yet deeply prevalent

---

1   The term 'Great Firewall' was first and it was quickly adopted by Chinese people and media.
2   Jack L. Goldsmith and Tim Wu, *Who Controls the Internet?: Illusions of a Borderless World*, Oxford: Oxford University Press, 2008.
3   The notions of 'counterprotocols' and 'tactical media' are borrowed from: Alexander R. Galloway and Eugene Thacker, *The Exploit: A Theory of Networks*, Minneapolis: University of Minnesota Press, 2007; Rita Raley, *Tactical Media*, Minneapolis: University of Minnesota Press, 2009.

power struggles that affect identities, decisions, and activities. China's GFW provides an ideal case, because it was envisioned, designed, and operated with such a clear political purpose that the struggle against it would inevitably be implicated with political meanings. The techno-politics of the wall (and wall crossing), therefore, manifests the political fabrics that are embedded in the technical coding of even the most mundane activities in our ever-changing digital life.

Between the Wall and the Space: A Brief History

A wall, as an architectural structure, a metaphor, or an imaginary, always has certain political connotations that signify uneven power relations. The Great Wall, built at the dawn of a powerful Chinese empire, stood as a monument of hegemony for thousands of years. What makes this mundane object political, however, is not the wall itself, but the complex relation *between the wall and the space around it*, a relation that is marked by division, domination, containment, and control. In the case of China's Great Firewall, the space it seeks to divide, dominate, and control is obviously cyberspace, whose imagined "unruliness" pronounces both threat and vulnerability.

When computers and the internet were first introduced to China, they were seen as technological opportunities for economic growth and were highly promoted by the Chinese government. Since the early 1990s, China has invested significantly in network infrastructure, and its internet user base has expanded at exponential speed. By 2015, China had 668 million internet users, the largest number in the world, and it is moving toward a fast-growing information society with over 3.35 million websites and 250 million microbloggers (China's equivalent of Twitter).[4]

Amidst such an eye-catching cyber boom, one of the fastest growing areas is video consumption. Currently, there are 433 million Chinese online viewers. Demand for online videos is so strong that some describe Chinese cyberspace as an 'entertainment highway' instead of an 'information highway.'[5] The proliferation of video-sharing services, such as Youku, Tudou, Xunlei, LeTV, and Bilibili, further nurtured a dynamic video culture including cellphone movies, Flash animations, spoof videos, and amateur journalism.[6] What is missing from this vibrant cultural scene, however, is the world's most popular video-sharing platform, YouTube, which is blocked by China's Great Firewall. Also blocked are Vimeo, Facebook, Twitter, Google+, Blogspot, as well as many human rights and democracy-related websites, blogs, and forums.[7]

---

4   Data Source: China Internet Network Information Center (CNNIC), *The 36th Statistical Report on Internet Development in China*, 23 July 2015.
5   Guo Liang, 'Surveying Internet Usage and Its Impact in Seven Chinese Cities', Center for Social Development, *Chinese Academy of Social Sciences*, 2007.
6   Paola Voci, *China on Video: Smaller-Screen Realities*, London: Routledge, 2010.
7   The list of blocked websites and media platforms is constantly changing. Google, for instance, has been blocked and unblocked recurrently. For a real-time monitoring of the list of blocked websites, IPs, and webpages, see: https://en.greatfire.org.

The GFW was built at almost the same time as the space it sought to contain was dramatically expanding. Described as 'networked authoritarianism' or 'authoritarian informationalism', the Chinese government's intertwined efforts to foster and control information networks highlight the fundamental tension in post-Socialist China, which struggles between the economic reform toward free-market neoliberalism and tightening political coercion.[8] In 1996, a list of foreign websites was blocked in China for the first time. In 1997, the government issued the Computer Information and Internet Security Protection Management Regulation, a far-reaching law to dramatically tighten information control online. A comprehensive project was initiated in 1998 and launched in 2003 to systematically monitor, filter, and regulate internet traffic between China and the outside world. The GFW was soon recognized as the world's most sophisticated and ambitious system for information control.

The construction of the GFW was never officially announced or acknowledged. Its existence, however, is widely known, because its effects are constantly experienced by hundreds of millions internet users in China. Whenever they try to get onto YouTube or search for a 'sensitive word' (*mingan ci*), a page appears with the error message: '404 page not found'. The interface of blockage is so blatantly confrontational that Chinese users often characterize the GFW as an action instead of an object. Thus the 'wall' is sometimes spoken of as a verb and a blocked access attempt is described as being 'walled' (*beiqiang*). The ways in which a certain website can be 'walled' are diverse and comprehensive. These include DNS pollution, IP blocking, URL filtering, TCP packet inspection, and Man-on-the-side attack.[9]

It is widely believed that the purpose of the GFW is to block foreign content of a political nature – the kind of information sources that Min Jiang describes as "international deliberative spaces".[10] A closer look, however, reveals that many of the blocked sites are actually coming from inside China, which are nevertheless pushed outside because they deal with sensitive topics such as human rights, democracy, and even the GFW itself. For instance, Bullog.cn, a Chinese blogging site founded in Beijing, was shut down by the government in 2007, forcing the site to be moved to an international server which was then blocked by the GFW. Many popular blogs faced the same fate when the Chinese blogsphere was subjected to tightened control. Thus when people climb over the wall, what they often see is information about domestic affairs from domestic sources.[11] What the wall really achieves is not simply to stop outside content from coming in, but to purge out the unwanted information from inside. Therefore, by blocking video-sharing sites such as YouTube and Vimeo, what are in fact blocked are not videos from the U.S. but underground films, documentaries and citizens' reportage *from China*. The wall, by and large, is an effective weapon for

---

8   Rebecca MacKinnon, 'China's "Networked Authoritarianism"', *Journal of Democracy* 22. 2 (2011):
     32-46; Min Jiang, 'Authoritarian Informationalism: China's Approach to Internet Sovereignty', *SAIS
     Review* 30. 2 (2012): 71–89.

9   Daniel Anderson, 'Splinternet Behind the Great Firewall of China', *Queue* 10. 11 (November 2012):
     40-49.

10   Min Jiang, 'Authoritarian Deliberation on Chinese Internet', *Electronic Journal of Communication* 20.
     3-4 (2009).

11   Murong Xuecun, 'Scaling China's Great Firewall', *The New York Times*, 17 August 2015, http://www.
     nytimes.com/2015/08/18/opinion/murong-xuecun-scaling-chinas-great-firewall.html.

information abjection.

In China's enormous information control systems, the GFW is only a small component. But the public response to the GFW is far more pronounced, because its blockage of international portals is tremendously blunt, with entire services such as Google rendered inaccessible. Such bluntness in its denial of access results in a highly visible encounter with void and disconnection (e.g. the '404 Not Found' message), and thus makes the GFW an iconic symbol of network control. The symbolic meaning is highlighted by the popular nickname itself, which is less metaphorical than allegorical. The affective experience generated by the GFW resonates with the widespread feelings of entrapment, suppression, and control in people's daily life online and offline. Thus the experience with, and the imagination of, the 'wall' are often evoked to express the public anger and anxiety toward many different forms of suppression that go far beyond internet control. 'If you are arrested, your freedom curtailed, your posts deleted, these can also all be cases of being walled.'[12]

The construction of the GFW is both technical and discursive. It is not only a technological project but also a cultural and political one. Its formation has to be mapped in the broader landscape of Chinese popular media forms that have transformed dramatically in the past decades from state propaganda to commercial entertainment. A huge gap thus emerged between the market and content-controlled official media, a cultural void that has to be filled by illicit activities. In film culture, for instance, piracy created an alternative public sphere that functions as a powerful underground circuit to evade censorship.[13] In a similar fashion, an illicit practice was quickly developed and popularized among Chinese netizens to circumvent the Great Firewall and to create an alternative cultural space outside it.

Crossing the Wall

Ever since the GFW was built, there have been efforts to bypass it. Countless circumvention tools based on proxies, VPNs, and encryption technologies were developed and adopted. They are described as 'ladders' (*tizi*). Popular ladders include Tor (The Onion Router), FreeGate (a proxy network system), Ultrasurf (a freeware based on proxy servers and encryption protocols), I2P (the Invisible internet Project, a free, open-source program for pseudonymous information transfer), Psiphone (a combination system developed by the Citizen Lab at the University of Toronto), and GoAgent (a cross-platform software). Other new weapons are constantly emerging, including VPN Gate (a free public-minded VPN service), Lantern (a P2P network where users share bandwidth), Pritunl (a enterprise distributed VPN server), Shadowsocks (a socks5 server), FreeBrowser (a free internet browser for Android systems), and Fqrouter (a circumvention router for Android systems).

The battle between the wall and wall crossing is fierce and continuous, and all these tools have to be updated frequently in order to remain functional. New technological develop-

---

12   Xuecun, 'Scaling China's Great Firewall'.
13   Jinying Li, 'From "D-Buffs" to the "D-Generation": Piracy, Cinema, and an Alternative Public Sphere in Urban China', *International Journal of Communication* 6 (2012): 542-63.

ments such as cloud computing and IPv6 also pose challenges to the GFW and provide more ladders for wall crossing. Information about how to circumvent the GFW, where to download the tools, and how to use them is abundant on the internet, though some of this information is censored in China. Since many of these circumvention tools are free, open-source projects, they are often hosted at GitHub, a source code management network where programmers collaborate and share information. Most users obtain circumvention software through email or P2P file sharing, and the latter proves to be particular effective because of its highly distributed structure. Many local vendors even sell computers and cellphones with pre-installed circumvention programs.

Due to the underground nature of wall crossing, it is difficult to estimate how many Chinese users practice circumvention. There have been conflicting reports about the size and impact of the wall-crossing community. In 2014, Globalwebindex reported that there are 93 million Chinese VPN users, which amounts to 20% of total internet users in China and is the largest number in the world.[14] The actual impact of circumvention, however, cannot be simply measured by its popularity. Since the GFW has become so visible and ubiquitous, circumvention talk is also widespread in everyday life. Online popular culture is full of references to the GFW, mostly in the form of jokes or spoofs. The public awareness of, and the widespread antagonism toward, the GFW is reflected in the popular anger toward its claimed creator, Fang Binxing, the former president of Beijing University of Posts and Telecommunication who is widely known as the 'father of GFW'.[15] Fang's university website was often hacked by angry netizens and was once replaced with 'Angry Shoes,' a video game that imitates *Angry Birds* and features Fang as a villain to be attacked by flying shoes.

The Right to Look: Popular Video Cultures Inside and Outside the Wall

The impact of the wall and wall crossing is especially visible in Chinese video culture, because the government is particularly wary of photo- and video-sharing sites such as Flickr and YouTube.[16] This emphasis on visual culture continues the Chinese Communist Party's long-time belief in the propaganda function of images, which is manifested in its especially harsh censorship over cinema that remains the most tightly regulated medium in China. As moving images become increasingly digitized and net-based, the control over looking inevitably leads to tightened restriction of video-sharing platforms, especially when the proliferation of portable and affordable digital devices resulted in a flourish of amateur journalism that radically challenges official media. With the recent rise of mass demonstrations, dubbed 'public incidents' (*gonggong shijian*) in China, the images produced and shared by citizen journalists play an important role in recording, publicizing, and mobilizing such events. Thus, it is not accidental that the GFW's first blockage of YouTube in 2007 coincided with the

---

14   Globalwebindex, 'GWI Social Q3 2014: The Latest Social Networking Trends', 18 November 2014,
      https://www.globalwebindex.net/blog/social-q3-2014.
15   'Great Firewall Father Speaks Out', *Global Times*, 18 February 2011.
16   Howard W. French, 'Great Firewall of China Faces Online Rebels', *The New York Times*, 4 February
      2008, http://www.nytimes.com/2008/02/04/world/asia/04china.html.

aftermath of the mass protest in the city of Xiamen against the construction of a chemical plant. Cellphone videos recorded at the Xiamen protest were widely circulated on the internet, generating heated public debate about China's environmental problems. Months later, YouTube was walled.

The GFW's tight control over video access generated popular upheaval in Chinese cyberspace, which was largely shaped by the collective sentimentality of the so-called post-80s generation. Born in the 1980s when China just began its economic reform, the post-80s generation came of age amidst the skyrocket boom in both economy and popular media. They are the first generation to witness the spread of television, computers, and the internet in Chinese households, and thus became the first group of avid media consumers in China. Growing up in the age of globalization, this generation is also decidedly cosmopolitan. Their increasing desire for global media is the major force that drives the fierce battle against the GFW. This is also a generation who is most familiar with a wide variety of illicit digital practices, such as piracy, hacking, P2P file sharing, and jail breaking, which form a rich cultural and technological environment for practicing alternative media access against various forces of restriction.

The cultural sensitivity of the post-80s generation determines that their challenge to the GFW often takes the form of popular, lowbrow entertainment, including pornography. In fact, the crusade against pornography is frequently the official excuse to tighten censorship. To access to pornographic videos, therefore, often becomes the reason to breach the GFW. For instance, when Japanese porn star Aoi Sora encouraged her Chinese fans to follow her on Twitter, many did so despite Twitter being blocked. She was thus credited for 'having brought down China's Great Firewall.'[17] Sometimes, such a seemingly benign desire for obscenity can deliver quite subversive messages. In 2009, the Chinese government launched a dramatic 'anti-smut' campaign, whose true purpose however was to censor information about a pro-democratic online petition. Right in the middle of the campaign, an imaginary creature named 'Grass Mud Horse' (*cao ni ma*) became a huge internet phenomenon after a series of widely circulated online videos attracted millions of viewers. The videos feature cute images of an alpaca-like animal as the embodiment of the homophone of a sexually charged profane curse, which expresses public anger toward censorship in a hilarious manner. Although the videos were quickly banned in Chinese cyberspace (but can be accessed on YouTube), the phenomenon continued in countless internet memes, video games, toys, and even clothing lines that all referenced the lovely animal.

---

17   Katrien Jacobs, *People's Pornography: Sex and Surveillance on the Chinese Internet*, Intellect Books, 2012, p. 38.

Figure 1. The Grass Mud Horse became a popular expression of resistance to internet censorship. Credit: chums-dock (CC BY SA 2.0)

Equally provocative is the animation series *Kuang Kuang*, which was created by artist Pi San and his independent studio Huxiao Animation. The first installment of the series, *Bombing the School* (*Zha Xuexiao*), was released in 2008 on the Chinese video-sharing site Youku and became an instant hit that attracted millions of views. Combining youthful cuteness with rebellious violence, the video creates a dark, humorous metaphor of the oppressive social intuitions in China. Despite (or because of) its popularity, the video was banned from domestic sites and had to be re-posted on YouTube, requiring viewers to bypass the GFW to watch it. To avoid further trouble from the censors, subsequent videos in the *Kuang Kuang* series were divided into two groups: the seemingly benign ones were released on Chinese domestic sites for general viewers and the politically challenging ones were posted on YouTube for those who know how to cross the GFW. Such a practice reflects a popular strategy taken by Chinese artists and filmmakers who use the GFW (and wall crossing) as a shield from censorship. The GFW, in this regard, functions as the political division among different content, platforms, and target audiences.

The division between what is inside and outside the GFW is marked by the peculiar function of YouTube as an effective distribution channel for Chinese underground films and videos that are barred from domestic release. Widely regarded in China as a 'free' space beyond the control of censorship, YouTube has become a popular platform for Chinese independent filmmakers to publish those works that are considered 'sensitive', most of which are documentaries about political issues and historical subjects. Artist Ai Weiwei's critically claimed documentary *Disturbing the Peace* (*Lao Ma Ti Hua*, 2009) was primarily circulated through YouTube. Ai and his studio also established their own YouTube channel to distribute a series of documentaries that they produced as part of 'citizens' investigation' (*gongmin diaocha*), which probed China's human-rights abuse with in-depth reportage. Similarly, filmmaker Ai Xiaoming's investigative documentary series on the Sichuan earthquake and Hu Jie's historical documentaries on the Cultural Revolution all rely on YouTube as the crucial, if not the only, distribution platform. For Chinese filmmakers and audiences, to release, share, and consume these underground documentaries is to challenge the wall, the existence of which is both the pre-condition for and the obstacle to evade censorship. It is disconnection and blockage, instead of connection and access, that highlight the intermediary function of YouTube as a political platform.

The wall-crossing tools have also increasingly been used to access peer-to-peer file-sharing portals that recently became the new targets of the GFW. For the most part, the Chinese government expressed little concern with online piracy despite the continuous pressure from foreign rights-holders. But in recent years, websites for several major P2P networks established by fansubbing communities (dubbed *zimuzu* in Chinese) began to be blocked. One of the first fansub networks blocked by the GFW was doulan.net, run by a group of Chinese fans who translate, subtitle and share documentaries made by the Japanese TV network NHK. Some of these documentaries are about Chinese history and politics, which made many suspect that the true purpose of such blockage was less copyright protection than information censorship. In fact, P2P networks have long functioned as a powerful underground channel for cultural circulation that evades not only the corporate ownership of copyright but also state censorship of content. The GFW's blockage of P2P networks signals the government's growing effort to suppress this otherwise unruly domain that used to operate outside the system of culture control.

The Techno-Politics of the Wall and (Re)politicization of the Space

Neither YouTube or fansub is in itself political. Nor is the practice of wall crossing. In most cases, the GFW is bypassed simply to access apolitical content and services. However, the discursive formation of the wall, as well as the subsequent cultural imagination of it, inevitably politicize almost every notion and activity that interacts with it. As the wall becomes a symbol of political oppression, crossing the wall is thus taken as a practice of political activism regardless of individual purpose and motivation. The concentration of Chinese underground documentaries on YouTube, for example, suggests a popular imagination of a free, open space of political resistance outside the wall, despite the fact that this outside space is itself a discursive construction. Although YouTube fashions itself as a transparent, neutral, and apolitical service, its blockage by the GFW exposes the unseen struggle between access and restriction.[18] Similarly, we are now seeing a conscious gathering of like-minded Chinese activists on Twitter and Google+, the social networks blocked by the GFW and thus imagined as oppositional spaces. In fact, the most famous and widely followed Chinese Twitter accounts, such as Isaac Mao, Michael Anti, Hexie Farm, Rebel Pepper, and China Digital Time, all belong to well-known activists and dissidents, who took the social network as an organization platform for political resistance. For these activists, to access Twitter is to cross the wall, which is an action of political transgression.

---

18   On the politics of YouTube, see Tarleton Gillespie, 'The Politics of "Platforms"', *New Media & Society* 12. 3 (1 May, 2010): 347–64.

For those who are not engaged with political activism, the decision of whether, why, or how to circumvent the GFW is no less political, because the discursive formation of the wall has profoundly politicized almost all aspects of Chinese cyber life. We can see this in many technology-related online forums, most of which discuss wall-crossing tactics. One prominent example is the famous blogger Program Think (*biancheng suixiang*), who initially set up his blog mainly to discuss computer techniques. The blog took a radical turn in 2009 when its hosting site, BlogSpot (owned by Google), was blocked by the GFW. The blogger thus began to share and promote circumvention strategies, and posted in-depth political discussions on such issues as democracy, authoritarianism, corruption, and even revolution. The blog posts quickly became more political than technical.[19]

The politicization comes as a surprising turn after two decades of massive de-politicization in China since the Tiananmen Massacre in 1989. The daily encounter with the wall, I would argue, plays a significant role, because it discloses the hidden contradiction in the imaginary network that is supposed to promise a transparent, effortless, and limitless delivery of information. The network, managed by the principle of protocols, is as much an apparatus of control as a distributive platform.[20] The Great Firewall is precisely such a controlling apparatus based on protocols. As a structure and a metaphor, however, the wall makes what is invisible visible. It embodies the power of control in its structural function, graphic connotation, and cultural imagination. The wall enables a precious space for political struggle precisely because it opens up visible gaps and disconnections. As Alexander Galloway and Eugene Thacker argue: 'Protocological struggles do not center around changing existent technologies but instead involve discovering holes in existent technologies and projecting potential change through those holes.'[21] The wall generates those holes through missing links, blocked contents, and error messages. And that is where counterprotocols — the wall-crossing tactics — emerge and exploit, politicizing our mundane technological life of searching, browsing, and networking.

References:

Anderson, Daniel. 'Splinternet Behind the Great Firewall of China.' *Queue* 10, no. 11 (November 2012): 40-49.

French, Howard W. 'Great Firewall of China Faces Online Rebels', *The New York Times*, 4 February 2008, http://www.nytimes.com/2008/02/04/world/asia/04china.html.

Galloway, Alexander R. *Protocol: How Control Exists After Decentralization*. Cambridge, MA: MIT Press, 2004.

Galloway, Alexander R., and Eugene Thacker. *The Exploit: A Theory of Networks*. Minneapolis, Minn: University of Minnesota Press, 2007.

Gillespie, Tarleton. 'The Politics of "Platforms"', *New Media & Society* 12. 3 (2010): 347-64.

Globalwebindex. 'GWI Social Q3 2014: The Latest Social Networking Trends', 18 November 2014,

---

19   See: 'The Blog of Biancheng Suixiang', http://program-think.blogspot.com/.
20   Alexander R. Galloway, *Protocol: How Control Exists After Decentralization*, Cambridge, MA: MIT Press, 2004.
21   Galloway and Thacker, *The Exploit*, 81.

https://www.globalwebindex.net/blog/social-q3-2014.

Goldsmith, Jack L., and Tim Wu. *Who Controls the Internet?: Illusions of a Borderless World*, New York: Oxford University Press, 2008.

'Great Firewall Father Speaks Out'. *Global Times*, 18 February 2011.

Guo Liang. *Surveying Internet Usage and Its Impact in Seven Chinese Cities*, Center for Social Development, Chinese Academy of Social Sciences, 2007.

Jacobs, Katrien. *People's Pornography: Sex and Surveillance on the Chinese Internet*, Intellect Books, 2012.

Jiang, Min. 'Authoritarian Deliberation on Chinese Internet', *Electronic Journal of Communication* 20.3&4 (2009).

— — —. 'Authoritarian Informationalism: China's Approach to Internet Sovereignty', *SAIS Review* 30. 2 (2012): 71–89.

Li, Jinying. 'From "D-Buffs" to the "D-Generation": Piracy, Cinema, and an Alternative Public Sphere in Urban China', *International Journal of Communication* 6. 0 (April 12, 2012): 542–63.

MacKinnon, Rebecca. 'China's "Networked Authoritarianism"', *Journal of Democracy* 22. 2 (2011): 32–46.

Raley, Rita. *Tactical Media*. Minneapolis: University Of Minnesota Press, 2009.

The Blog of Biancheng Suixiang. http://program-think.blogspot.com/.

Tsui, Lokman. 'An Inadequate Metaphor: The Great Firewall and Chinese Internet Censorship', *Global Dialogue* 9. 1/2 (2007): 60–68.

Voci, Paola. *China on Video: Smaller-Screen Realities*. London: Routledge, 2010.

Xiao, Qiang. 'The Battle for the Chinese Internet', *Journal of Democracy* 22. 2 (2011): 47–61.

Xuecun, Murong. 'Scaling China's Great Firewall', *The New York Times*, 17 August, 2015, http://www.nytimes.com/2015/08/18/opinion/murong-xuecun-scaling-chinas-great-firewall.html.

AUSTRALIA: CIRCUMVENTION GOES MAINSTREAM

RAMON LOBATO AND JAMES MEESE

18%

proportion of Australians who use VPNs or proxies to access the internet

200,000

estimated number of unauthorised Netflix subscribers in Australia, in late 2014

$25-$134

Monthly cost of a Foxtel pay-TV subscription, in A$

$15-$20

Monthly cost of a US Netflix subscription and VPN, in A$

'You've all got VPNs anyway. All of you appear to be somewhere in Iowa when you go online I know that anyway, I won't go on.' – Australia's former Minister for Communications (and current Prime Minister), Malcolm Turnbull, in 2014

Over the last decade Australia has become an unlikely hotspot of circumvention activity. Frustrated by the high cost and slow delivery of first-release TV and movies from the United States – and by their own self-perceived status as 'second-class' media citizens – Australians have taken to offshore streaming with a singular enthusiasm, signing up for VPNs and proxy services and using them to access US Netflix, Hulu, HBO Now, and BBC iPlayer. Unlike many nations in the Asia-Pacific region, where circumvention has an overtly political dimension, the conversation in Australia has revolved substantially around access to entertainment rather than privacy, surveillance or censorship. Many Australians have acquired a working knowledge of circumvention tools simply because they were unable to watch episodes of their favourite television shows quickly and legally.

Take for example *Game of Thrones* and *House of Cards*, which have become massively popular in Australia thanks to unauthorised streaming and torrenting. When these shows first aired here they were only available as part of expensive packages with the pay-TV provider Foxtel. In the case of *Game of Thrones*, episodes were initially screened up to a week after their U.S. premiere (only later did they screen simultaneously, after a subscriber backlash). *House of Cards* was likewise locked to a pay-TV bundle, as Netflix was unavailable in Australia until 2015 and had sold the rights to Foxtel in the interim. Relatively few Australians watched these shows through the authorised channels, yet everyone seemed to have seen the latest episodes. How? The answer is directly related to the boom in popular circumvention, along with a longstanding national fondness for Bit Torrent. During the last few years Australian tech websites have been abuzz with tips and tricks on how to evade geoblocks; DNS routing services like Getflix and UnblockUS have attracted many Australian subscribers; and VPN brands like HideMyAss and Witopia have almost become household names. A complex informal apparatus for accessing digital content has become normalised among the early adopters and TV junkies that drive consumer technology adoption in Australia. In these circles, VPN- and proxy-enabled streaming has become a mainstream pastime – the polite alternative to Bit Torrent.

These early adopters are brazen about their circumvention. Most argue that they have a right to access content if it is not available legally and in a timely fashion, or if they feel they have to pay too much for it. The Australian conversation on circumvention has been firmly grounded in this discourse of audience rights. But there is more to the story, as in recent years the geoblocking and access questions have become inextricably linked to a wider set of policy debates concerning Australia's economic future and national self-image. As we will see, geoblocking and circumvention are evolving into first-order political issues, attracting the attention of parliamentarians, competition regulators, consumer groups and rights-holders, and overlapping with discussions around copyright protection, global governance, and tax evasion. In other words, they are trigger points for a wider conversation about Australia's place in the world.

Australian screen culture and the politics of distance

To understand the effects of geoblocking in Australia, we must first consider the national broadcast system and how it has evolved over time. There are three commercial free-to-air stations in Australia – Seven, Nine and Ten – and two public-service broadcasters – the ABC (Australian Broadcasting Corporation) and SBS (the Special Broadcasting Service, a multi-cultural broadcaster). Each of these free-to-air stations has additional digital multi-channels (ABC2, ABC3 and so on). Government-mandated quotas on commercial channels require at least 55% of prime-time programming to be locally produced, with the rest mostly imported from the US and UK.

As noted, Australia does not have a strong tradition of cable and satellite TV. There is only one pay-TV provider, Foxtel, which reaches around a third of Australian households and has long been struggling to grow its market share. Accustomed to free-to-air broadcasting, Australians are generally uncomfortable with the idea of direct payments for TV content.

Australian screen culture has also been strongly influenced by the nation's geography and politics. Australia is a huge and mostly uninhabited island, almost as big as Europe, but with a much smaller population (23 million). Its nearest neighbour is Papua New Guinea; New Zealand is over a thousand kilometres away. There is no tradition of cross-border satellite television here, as in Europe or the Middle East. A colonial broadcast model endures in the development of the national public-service broadcaster, the ABC (it was modelled on the BBC template, with news presenters trained to speak in the Queen's English, and BBC content featuring prominently on this station well into the twenty-first century). Australia's post-war turn towards the United States was reflected in our status as a high-margin English-language export market for American content.

Imported movies and TV shows are subject to long delays. As Jock Given, Rosemary Curtis and Marion McCutcheon note, 'it was common for Australians to wait 3-5 months to see US blockbusters in their cinemas'.[1] Television programs were just as slow to arrive, due to the U.S. premiere season occurring at the same time as the Australian summer holiday season. Local networks preferred to hold over this imported content until the official local ratings season started after the summer break. Consequently, delays of several months – and sometimes years – were common.

In the past this time-lag was not a huge problem. Australians had few other alternatives and were generally content to wait. But the internet has changed all that. Local audiences are hooked into global TV fandom in real-time through Twitter, internet forums and fan websites. They know what is happening in the US and refuse to wait for the latest episodes. Broadcasters have tried to reduce these delays where possible, with many shows now fast-tracked from the US. But these are the exceptions that prove the rule. In the current licensing and advertising environment Australian broadcasters simply cannot get content to air quickly enough to satisfy audiences, who turn to Bit Torrent and VPNs as a way around the time lag.

Making matters worse is the problem of pricing. Digital content is invariably more expensive in Australia than overseas when purchased through iTunes and other online services. According to the consumer group Choice, Australian viewers of *The Walking Dead*, 'will be paying up to 376% more than people watching the same show in the United Kingdom'.[2] This discrepancy, known colloquially as the 'Australia tax' has been a major topic of public discussion. Dissatisfaction about digital pricing has become a rallying cry for Australian early adopters who increasingly see themselves as 'second-class' media citizens, who are 'fed on a diet of geo-blocking, slow content delivery and price gouging'.[3] This adds fuel to the fire of consumer resentment, and provides a rhetorical justification for piracy and geo-hacking.

Geoblocking and Cultural Nationalism

By 2012 geoblocking had become a political issue. Sensing the mood of the public, Australian regulators were questioning the price-discrimination policies of U.S. tech companies and asking why our media and software products were more expensive than they needed to be. Opportunistic politicians started to see geoblocking as a popular issue, one that enabled

---

1   Jock Given, Rosemary Curtis and Marion McCutcheon, *Cinema in Australia: An Industry Profile*, Melbourne: The Swinburne Institute, 2012, p. 3.
2   Madison Cartwright, 'Australians pay more', *Choice*, 13 October 2014, https://www.choice.com.au/electronics-and-technology/internet/using-online-services/articles/digital-pricing-and-the-australia-tax.
3   Mark Gregory, 'Turnbull's piracy crackdown and the fate of VPNs', *Technology Spectator*, 21 April 2015, http://www.businessspectator.com.au/article/2015/4/21/technology/turnbulls-piracy-crackdown-and-fate-vpns.

a nationalist narrative (US-based multinationals ripping off Australians) to be fused with a free-market narrative (geoblocking as anti-competitive). In other words, it was a vote-winner. As Labor MP Ed Husic put it:

> For too long, businesses and consumers have asked: why does it sometimes cost up to 80 per cent more to simply download software in Australia compared to overseas… No one doubts that IT firms should be able to recover legitimate costs but the Australian consumer shouldn't shoulder an unfair share of the pricing load.[4]

The level of disquiet was such that the government announced a Parliamentary Inquiry into the 'Australia tax' in 2012. Its final report included some remarkable recommendations, including abolishing all parallel-import restrictions, amending the 1968 Copyright Act to allow lawful circumvention of geoblocking, and educating consumers about how to use VPNs effectively.[5] The report even floated the possibility, as an 'option of last resort', of a government ban on geoblocking. Although none of these recommendations have been actioned, the report was widely seen as tantamount to an official endorsement of circumvention. As a Choice representative said during the hearings, 'Look, if businesses want to set up virtual walls to make Australians pay higher prices, then we think Australians have every right to use legitimate means to climb those walls, to knock them down, to get around them'.[6]

At this point, it is worth noting that this strong political push for equitable pricing did not come out of nowhere. Australians have had to pay a higher price for cultural goods for much of the twentieth century. The country's geographic isolation means higher shipping costs, lower levels of competition, and, in many cases, price gouging by media companies and publishers. Many incumbents have also been protected by legislative bans on parallel-importing cheaper goods from overseas, keeping prices artificially high. While these parallel import bans have been partly dismantled since the 1990s – imports of CDs are now permitted, reducing what were previously 'exceptionally high' prices for recorded music[7] – protectionist measures remain in other sectors. There is still no broad provision to allow for the parallel importation of books into Australia, which means that in addition to being charged higher prices Australians have had to deal with the late publication of new releases and shops regularly running out of stock.[8] This history of geographic price discrimination is one reason why the practice of geoblocking carries such cultural resonance for Australian consumers.

---

4   See http://www.edhusic.com/it-pricing-inquiry-to-go-ahead/.
5   'At what cost? IT Pricing and the "Australia tax"', Australian House of Representatives Standing Committee on Infrastructure and Communications, The Parliament of the Commonwealth of Australia, 2013.
6   'Choice tells Australians to become digital smugglers', ABC Radio AM program, 23 March 2013, http://www.abc.net.au/news/2013-03-23/choice-tells-australians-to-become-digital/4590164.
7   David Richardson, 'Copyright and Monopoly Profits: Books, Records and Software', Current Issues Brief 15, 1996, The Parliament of Australia, http://www.aph.gov.au/About_Parliament/Parliamentary_ Departments/Parliamentary_Library/Publications_Archive/CIB/CIB9697/97cib15.
8   Books can be legally parallel imported in specific circumstances to fill market gaps. For example, if an order for a book is not filled within ninety days by the copyright holder or licensee.

Indeed, it is partly due to the historical weight of these debates around parallel importation that the issue of digital content availability has such traction in Australia. With government officials and consumer advocates singing from the same songbook, circumvention of geo-blocking has become a quasi-sanctioned practice. This state of affairs arguably reflects the inequities of digital media geography, with Australian consumers often facing significant pricing differentials for the same products and companies regularly providing little or no justification in response to complaints about the practice. But over time these pricing issues have unfortunately become intertwined with other discourses about foreign services and offshore 'competition', leading to a situation where many Australians now see themselves as victims of cultural globalization. A politics of resentment has taken hold, tinged with nationalist overtones. Its central figure: the ripped-off Aussie consumer.

The VPN Explosion

Renewed attention to the parallel-import issue has naturally drawn attention to geoblocking. Taking a cue from their elected representatives, Australians have recently begun to sign up for offshore streaming services in ever-greater numbers, using fake IDs and location-masking tools. In part this was due to more people using streaming services generally: internet speeds were rising, catch-up TV was catching on, and everyone was used to watching TV in their browsers. From here it was just a small step to hacking into BBC iPlayer, Netflix and Hulu.

One of the first indicators of a shift came in August 2011 when a national electronics retailer, Harvey Norman, caused a stir by selling a product package designed explicitly for geo-circumvention. The product in question was a set-top box – the McTivia – which came bundled with a VPN subscription. 'Stream direct from the USA!', promised the marketing material. '[T]ailor your home entertainment system to meet your lifestyle and gain access to a global library of previously geographically restricted media direct to your TV.' A minor scandal followed after the national newspaper *The Australian* picked up the story, and Harvey Norman insisted that it did not mean to promote geo-hacking.[9]

Detailed how-to guides also began to appear on Australia tech websites. Forums overflowed with tips about which VPN had the best download speeds or customer service. National newspapers buzzed with reports of 200,000 unauthorised Netflix subscribers in Australia. Tech journalists openly instructed their readers on the finer points of VPN and proxy use, proclaiming the benefits of browser plugins like MediaHint and Hola. On tech websites, such as Gizmodo, Whirlpool and ITNews, the discussion about circumvention was even more ubiquitous, and unapologetic.

This was the tip of the iceberg. By now, thousands of Australian households had taken up personal VPNs and proxies. In research we conducted during 2013 with Swinburne University's World Internet Project, a biannual telephone survey of 1000 Australian users,

---

9   Nic Christensen, 'Harvey Norman Mulls Next Move after Questions on Sale of McTivia', *The Australian*, 12 September 2011.

it emerged that 18% of Australian internet users use VPNs or proxies – a much higher figure than expected.[10] While some of this usage was business-related, it still represents a remarkably high level of familiarity with what were formerly obscure networking tools. A follow-up study by Essential Research in 2015 produced similar findings, suggesting that 16% of Australians have used VPNs or Tor.[11]

Australia's then-Communications Minister and current Prime Minister Malcolm Turnbull – a former internet entrepreneur known for his early-adopter habits – summed up the general mood when he addressed a crowd at a Govhack event in 2014. 'You've all got VPNs anyway,' he laughed. 'All of you appear to be somewhere in Iowa when you go online I know that anyway, I won't go on.' For a Minister to joke about mass-scale internet circumvention in this way would in other circumstances appear unusual. In Australia, it is now par for the course.

Governing Circumvention

Running through this debate about geoblocking are several unresolved legal and policy issues. One of these is the uncertain legal status of VPNs as circumvention tools.

There is no clear consensus as to whether or not using VPNs to access offshore content infringes Australian copyright law. When he was Communications Minister, Turnbull stated that circumventing geoblocking in order to access content was not illegal under the Australian Copyright Act – but rights-holder groups such as the Australian Copyright Council disagree.[12] Some media producers have even called for the government to legislate against unauthorized VPN use.[13] Legal scholar Nic Suzor has examined the issue, and concluded that VPN-enabled geo-circumvention is primarily a contractual issue between users and platforms, but that it 'might technically be an infringement of copyright under Australian law, and there is a small possibility that it might be a crime under Australian law as well'.[14] In other words, this is a grey area of the law.

This legal uncertainty is an issue because it is clouding the Australian public's understanding of VPNs, which can of course be used for many purposes unrelated to geo-evasion. In the

---

10   Ramon Lobato and Scott Ewing, 'Unlocking the Geoblock: Australians Embrace VPNs', *The Conversation*, October 2 2014, https://theconversation.com/unlocking-the-geoblock-australians-embrace-vpns-32373.

11   These usage levels are broadly in line with other early-adopter countries. In Sweden, for example, VPNs are used by 18% of the population. See Stefan Larsson et al, 'Law, Norms, Piracy and Online Anonymity: Practices of De-identification in the Global File Sharing Community', *Journal of Research in Interactive Marketing* 6.4 (2012): 260-280.

12   See information sheet G127v01, 'Geo-blocking, VPNs & Copyright', Australian Copyright Council, July 2015.

13   Nick Murray, the managing director of TV producer Cornell Jigsaw Zapruder argues that these tools inhibit the ability of these companies to sell the same content to different regions, which is how 'they make [their] money'. See http://mumbrella.com.au/cjz-boss-calls-for-a-clampdown-on-australians-using-vpns-to-access-content-287634

14   Nicolas Suzor, 'Using a VPN to Access Netflix: Is it Legal?', *NicSuzor.Net*, July 22, 2013, http://nic.suzor.net/2013/07/22/using-a-vpn-to-access-netflix-is-it-legal/.

wake of hacking scandals and daily reports of cybercrime, VPN use is being promoted by consumer and technology advocates as a way to stay safe online – an act of responsible cyber-citizenship. VPN use is also being recommended as an antidote to Australia's controversial metadata retention law, the Telecommunications (Interception and Access) Amendment (Data Retention) Act 2015, which has just come into effect. This law requires ISPs and telcos to retain logs of customer activity, NSA-style, for two years. Unsurprisingly there has been massive public backlash against this data retention regime, and VPN services are an appealing counter-measure. Savvy VPN companies such as PureVPN and IBVPN, now promote themselves to Australian users on this basis (see Figure 1).

Figure 1. Australia-specific VPN marketing. Source: http://www.ibvpn.com/australia-vpn-service/

Recent developments in copyright law also bear directly on VPNs. In June 2015 federal legislation was passed that gives judges the power to block access to pirate websites such as The Pirate Bay. While the law is expected to mostly target file-sharing and streaming sites, the initial wording of the law was vague and many consumer groups feared that websites for VPN services could be blocked too. In the end the government was forced to add an Explanatory Memorandum specifying that the blocking should not apply to VPNs 'that are promoted and used for legitimate purposes, or merely used to access legitimate copyright material distributed in a foreign geographic market'. But given that the marketing practices adopted by many VPNs are not always legitimate, there is still some ambiguity here. All this is happening at the same time that the Government is trying to introduce a new internet industry Code of Practice – a three-strikes graduated response scheme in which repeat offenders receive infringement notices. Like the metadata law, the three-strikes Code is likely to further increase demand for VPNs as an identity-masking tool for P2P users. In this complex game of whack-a-mole, public awareness of VPNs, proxies and other circumvention tools is always on the rise.

The Coming of Netflix

Another recent development is the launch in March 2015 of Netflix's Australian service. For the first time Australians can now access an authorised, local version of the service, which should in theory reduce the appeal of geo-hacking. However, due to existing licensing agreements and limited investment in local content acquisition, the local Netflix has a much smaller library. Only 1116 streaming titles were available at launch, compared to 7000 in the United States. This is a sore point for Australian consumers, and it has attracted a lot of media attention.

What does the arrival of Netflix mean for geoblocking and circumvention? There are two contrasting implications here. On the one hand, there is broad agreement that Netflix Australia has been a success: subscriber numbers have been strong and Australians for the first time seem happy to pay for TV. So in theory this should reduce both piracy and circumvention. On the other hand, widespread awareness of the catalogue disparity has stirred resentment and is fuelling a different kind of circumvention – a kind of transnational 'shopfront-hopping' by paid-up Netflix subscribers, which is considered to be a much more unthreatening act of middle-class consumer rebellion. So, just as one driver for VPN use disappears, another appears in its place. Consequently, it seems reasonable to assume that geo-circumvention activity will be a feature of Australian digital media consumption for some time to come.

The geoblocking issue has also become entwined with a sometimes heated debate about taxation. In May 2015 the former Australian treasurer, Joe Hockey, announced a 'Netflix tax' – a tax on offshore digital services operating in Australia, designed to bring foreign over-the-top services into line with local services that must by law charge a 10% Goods and Services Tax. This policy was designed to boost the national coffers while mollifying nervous Australian media moguls who have been clamouring for government protection against foreign streaming services (for example, Presto, owned by Foxtel and Seven West Media, and Stan, owned by Fairfax Media and FTA broadcaster Nine, already argue that Netflix's GST-free status constitutes an unfair commercial advantage). But the Netflix Tax had another political advantage for the government. It played neatly into the narrative that both sides of Australian politics have been pushing – that tax-dodging multinationals are ripping off Australian consumers and citizens.

Looking ahead, one issue to watch is the relationship between internet privacy and consumer advocacy. Historically, Australia does not have a strong tradition of constitutional privacy protections unlike Europe and the United States, and public discussion of surveillance and privacy is somewhat muted by comparison. Yet the rise of VPNs seems to constitute something of a turning point where privacy, anonymity and media consumption are now fused together as a public controversy for the first time. Many Australians already have a strong familiarity with the use of VPNs to torrent safely and avoid geoblocking, so it is likely that there will be some spill over into other privacy-related uses.

As we have seen in this chapter, in the wake of the Snowden revelations these practices now appear to be spreading beyond early adopters and geeks to include a certain subset of more mainstream users – exactly the same community who are the biggest fans of streaming and download media. Know-how relating to DIY internet privacy and anonymity circulates widely among these users. Here again, a link between consumption and citizenship is evident, as Australian consumers' impatient desire for the latest thing feeds directly into an understanding of digital citizenship. The end result is something quite unexpected: the mainstreaming of DIY privacy protection and anonymization as everyday practices among a substantial minority of the population.

References

'Choice tells Australians to become digital smugglers', ABC Radio *AM* program, 23 March 2013, http://www.abc.net.au/news/2013-03-23/choice-tells-australians-to-become-digital/4590164.

Australian Copyright Council, information sheet G127v01, 'Geo-blocking, VPNs & Copyright', July 2015.

Australian House of Representatives Standing Committee on Infrastructure and Communications. 'At what cost? IT Pricing and the "Australia tax"', The Parliament of the Commonwealth of Australia, 2013.

Cartwright, Madison. 'Australians pay more', *Choice*, 13 October 2014, https://www.choice.com.au/electronics-and-technology/internet/using-online-services/articles/digital-pricing-and-the-australia-tax.

Christensen, Nic. 'Harvey Norman Mulls Next Move after Questions on Sale of McTivia', *The Australian*, 12 September 2011.

Given, Jock, Rosemary Curtis and Marion McCutcheon. *Cinema in Australia: An Industry Profile*, Melbourne: The Swinburne Institute, 2012.

Gregory, Mark. 'Turnbull's piracy crackdown and the fate of VPNs', *Technology Spectator*, 21 April 2015, http://www.businessspectator.com.au/article/2015/4/21/technology/turnbulls-piracy-crackdown-and-fate-vpns.

Larsson, Stefan et al. 'Law, Norms, Piracy and Online Anonymity: Practices of De-identification in the Global File Sharing Community', *Journal of Research in Interactive Marketing* 6.4 (2012): 260-280.

Lobato, Ramon and Scott Ewing. 'Unlocking the Geoblock: Australians Embrace VPNs', *The Conversation*, October 2 2014, https://theconversation.com/unlocking-the-geoblock-australians-embrace-vpns-32373.

Richardson, David. 'Copyright and Monopoly Profits: Books, Records and Software', Current Issues Brief 15, 1996, The Parliament of Australia, http://www.aph.gov.au/About_Parliament/Parliamentary_Departments/Parliamentary_Library/Publications_Archive/CIB/CIB9697/97cib15.

Suzor, Nicolas. 'Using a VPN to Access Netflix: Is it Legal?', *NicSuzor.Net*, July 22, 2013, http://nic.suzor.net/2013/07/22/using-a-vpn-to-access-netflix-is-it-legal/.

TURKEY: COPING WITH INTERNET CENSORSHIP

ÇIGDEM BOZDAG

54%

Proportion of the Turkish population who have access to the internet

60TL (US$20)

Monthly cost for a 50/mbit fiber connection

94%

Proportion of mobile phone subscribers in Turkey

31%

Proportion of Turkish internet users who made online purchases in 2014

Figure 1. This image promoting DNS proxies circulated widely during the 2014 Twitter ban. Translation: 'DNS - let your bird sing' (Author unknown)

In recent years the acronyms DNS and VPN have entered into the everyday vocabulary of Turkish internet users. Since 2007, when Law No. 5651 was passed giving Turkish authorities unprecedented regulatory powers over the internet, thousands of websites including YouTube and Twitter have been blocked. Most internet users became aware of this issue after YouTube was blocked sporadically from 2007 to 2010. During this period, users started to look for other ways to access the site and started using alternative DNS providers as a solution. At this time, it was easy to find hundreds of articles, tutorials and posts in Turkish about how to change your DNS settings and access blocked websites through a simple online search. However, when Twitter and YouTube were blocked (again) in March 2014, the most commonly used DNS providers were also blocked. This in turn has prompted many Turkish internet users to take up VPN services that allow them access to banned websites.

Media freedom has always been a problematic issue in Turkey. Freedom of expression is restricted by laws that include quite broad definitions of crimes such as 'defamation of Atatürk', 'threats against the unity of the state', 'threats against national security' or 'defamation of religion'. Although communication rights improved in the early 2000s under the AKP (Justice and Development Party), the situation seems to have worsened in recent years, especially after the 2013 Gezi protests when hundreds of thousands of people took to the streets in Istanbul against the Erdoğan government. Since then, the government has attempted to put pressure on mass media outlets and introduce stricter control measures for online content. A change to the law in 2014 enabled the blocking of websites within 24 hours, in the absence of a court order, by the Telecommunications Communication Presidency and the Ministry of Transport, Maritime Affairs and Communication. This leads to the arbitrary blocking of many websites in Turkey that are critical of government policies.

Given this political situation in Turkey, VPN, DNS and proxy services have become important tools to circumvent censorship and access content. In this sense, circumvention practices in Turkey have evolved in response to local political conditions. The key issue here is access to blocked social networking and video sites, especially YouTube and Twitter. Using VPNs to access commercial streaming sites like Netflix is not popular – partly because Turks have long used P2P networks and, more recently, illegal streaming sites to access TV content, films and music. Piracy became the norm for consuming video content in Turkey long before legal streaming services were available. In other words, the online video culture in Turkey is marked on the one hand by internet censorship, and pirate consumption of videos on the other.

Internet Use and Video Consumption in Turkey

Although Turkey is one of the world's fastest growing countries in terms of internet adoption, the digital divide is still a crucial issue to consider. According to the Statistical Institute of Turkey (TUIK), only 54% of Turks are online and only 45% of the population uses the internet regularly, at least once a week.[1] In general, young people go online much more than older people, men much more than women, and people in urban areas much more than in rural areas. However, in recent years overall internet adoption has increased tremendously in all population groups, especially through mobile internet subscriptions.

Looking at people's reasons for using the internet, we can say that social media – including Facebook, YouTube and Twitter – is a major driver. Facebook is the third most visited website in Turkey, and a majority of the population are Facebook users. According to TUIK, 67% of users look for information about goods and services when they go online and 59% use the internet to download games, images, films or music.[2]

Turkey, with its growing economy and young population (the average age is 30), is considered a promising market for internet services and ICTs generally. Digital technology is of growing importance to the economy more generally, and more and more online shops and services are emerging. More than a quarter of Turks use online shopping services, and the

1   TUIK, 22 August 2014, http://www.turkstat.gov.tr/PreHaberBultenleri.do?id=16198.
2   TUIK, 22 August 2014, http://www.turkstat.gov.tr/PreHaberBultenleri.do?id=16198.

number is growing steadily.[3]

Watching and downloading videos is one of the most common internet activities of the Turkish users. Video streaming makes up a growing proportion of overall internet traffic, especially among mobile users. YouTube, the fourth most visited website in Turkey, is far and away the most popular video service, followed by DailyMotion and various other local and international sites including 59Saniye, İzlesene, Vimeo and UzmanTV. Unlike the other video portals, UzmanTV is a professional video site featuring expert advice on topics such as beauty and health. Facebook and newspaper websites such as Hurriyet and Milliyet are also increasingly used for streaming videos.

Besides video platforms such as YouTube, İzlesene or DailyMotion, there are many illegal streaming websites that offer links to Turkish and foreign TV series. These 'series websites' often use Russian or Asian video platforms such as VK that are more difficult to control through national regulation. They even offer subtitles for foreign content. Most of these offshore video services target the Turkish diaspora as well as viewers in Turkey. Websites such as Canlidizi.tv or Dizist.com are popular among Turks living in Germany, home to the largest Turkish expatriate community, and in the United States. Some of these series websites focus on Turkish content, while others concentrate on subtitled foreign series. There are also similar illegal streaming services for watching movies, and these are quite popular in Turkey. FullOnlineFilmİzle and HDFilmiFullizle are two examples – both are among the 100 most visited websites in Turkey.

Legal streaming alternatives are starting to emerge. Examples include Tivibu and Tvyo, which began operation in 2010 and in 2012 respectively. Turkish TV channels have also started to provide streaming content via their own websites, after a late start. User numbers for these legal services are increasing. However, offshore video services such as Netflix and Hulu are not yet very popular in Turkey. While some early adopters have taken up offshore streaming – as can be seen in discussions in Turkish tech blogs and forums such as DonanimHaber – most Turkish internet users are used to accessing series and videos for free and are not ready to pay for streaming services.

One example for this was the popular TV series *Ulan İstanbul*, which was cancelled by the Kanal D channel in 2015. Following a backlash by fans, the producers decided to offer the series online via a pay-per-view model. Although more than a million people watched the first online-only episode of the series, which was available for free, the subsequent episodes could not keep up with the series' former success and *Ulan İstanbul* was cancelled. This again shows that although Turkish internet users are increasingly paying for online services and buying products online, paying for on-demand videos or streaming services is still not a common practice.

---

3   Boston Consulting Group, Türkiye'de Internet Ekonomisi Raporu, 2013, p. 5.

Internet Censorship, Circumvention and Resistance Practices

Internet regulation in Turkey was introduced in the early 2000s as online content became bound to the RTUK law (2002), which regulated broadcasting in Turkey. Prior to this, various websites in Turkey had been blocked due to their critical content. The Telecommunications Communication Presidency (TIB), which still continues to be responsible for the regulation and control of online content, was founded in 2005.

The first law in Turkey that focused directly on the regulation of online content – Law No. 5651 on the Regulation of Publications on the Internet and Suppression of Crimes Committed by means of Such Publications ('Law No. 5651') – was passed in 2007. This law originally was drafted to define and regulate cybercrime. However, the enacted law had an expanded scope, and included vague statements that pave the way for arbitrary political censorship of media content as noted in the previous section. For example, article 8 defined '[encouraging] suicide, sexual abuse of children, facilitating the usage of drugs and stimulants, provision of materials being dangerous for the health, vulgarity, prostitution, providing area and opportunity for gambling, crimes indicated in the Law about the Crimes Committed Against Atatürk'[4] as crimes. Accordingly, entire websites could be banned for allegedly violating the principles and reforms of Atatürk – as was the case with the first blocking of YouTube in 2007 – or for making alleged threats to Turkey's independence. Given the vague wording of the law, almost anything critical can be considered as a violation of Atatürk's reforms or as a threat to Turkey's independence. This problematic article of the law was also taken to the European Human Rights Court in 2012, which found the law incompatible with article 10 of the European Convention on Human Rights.[5]

In 2011 the government attempted to introduce a new law that would make internet filtering mandatory for all users in Turkey. The draft law provoked a passionate reaction, mobilizing not only activists and NGOs but also regular users of the internet, who are not necessarily politically active. Large protests were organized under the slogan 'Don't touch my internet'. Over half a million people participated in the campaign, which included both online and offline activism. This was one of the most successful internet freedom campaigns in Turkey to date, and it forced the government to change the draft law. The use of filters became voluntary, not mandatory.

Another controversial change in Turkish internet law took place in 2014, when Law No. 5651 was changed to enable URL-based blocking of websites. Fines for crimes defined in this law also increased.[6] Furthermore, the new law authorized TIB and the Ministry of Transport,

---

4   Banu Terkan and Nurullah Terkan, 'Analysis of the Political Discourses of the Ruling and Opposition Parties Regarding the New Regulations in the Internet Law in Turkey', Proceedings of the 13th International Academic Conference, Antibes, 2014, p. 552.
5   Yaman Akdeniz and Kerem Altıparmak, 'AİHM Kararı: 5651 Sayılı Yasa AİHS'e Aykırı', Bianet, 19 December 2012, http://bianet.org/bianet/ifade-ozgurlugu/142923-aihm-karari-5651-sayili-yasa-aihse-aykiri.
6   Yaman Akdeniz and Kerem Altıparmak, '5651 sayılı Kanunun Değişiklik Tasarısının Getirdiği Değişiklikler Üzerine Bir Değerlendirme', Cyber Rights, 2014, p. 14, http://cyber-rights.org.tr/docs/5651_Tasari_

Maritime Affairs and Communication to block websites within 24 hours after a takedown request – without a court order.[7] The law was passed in February 2014, however, the article giving the Ministry the right to block websites was found to be unconstitutional and was removed. Yet, another omnibus bill that was passed in the beginning of 2015 that put this article back on the table, and this time it was passed by the parliament.

The amended Law No. 5651 contained a new article about the protection of personal rights and privacy of individuals, but once again these terms are vaguely defined. This leaves the TIB, the Ministry and the courts with a lot of flexibility as to what can be considered a violation. According to the new law, individuals can directly apply to the TIB, which can decide to block websites as a precaution before a court order has been granted. These extrajudicial blocks have been criticized as unlawful, since TIB and the Ministry might block websites without a court order for quite long periods.

These changes provoked a strong reaction on Twitter, Facebook and Eksisozluk, a widely used dictionary-like user-generated website in Turkey. However, not as many people participated as in the 'Don't touch my internet' mobilization of 2011. One reason behind for this is the fallout from the Gezi protests, which saw escalated police violence. Another reason is that people were more interested in the local election campaigns that also took place in March 2104.

In March 2014 – a month after this new law was passed, and shortly before the local elections – Twitter was suddenly blocked again for two weeks (20 March to 3 April). The purported reason for this was claims about violations of personal rights and privacy of individuals, who applied to TIB. Shortly after, YouTube was also blocked, this time for more than two months (27 March to 29 May). The official explanation this time was that the YouTube block was a response to a user uploading voice recordings from a secret government meeting, in which officials discussed a military intervention in Syria. The YouTube video containing these voice recordings was said to reveal state secrets and as such was considered a threat to the national security of Turkey. Once again, this prompted massive reactions on Facebook, Twitter and Eksisozluk, with people united around hashtags such as #direntwitter (resist Twitter) and #direnyoutube (resist Youtube). This was a clear reference to the Gezi protests, where the hashtag #direngezi (resist Gezi) became a symbol of the protest.

As was also the case in Gezi, people's online protests were full of irony and humour. This can be considered a form of 'passive resistance', putting the legitimacy of government discourses about the need for site blocks into question.[8] This time, despite a strong reaction online, there were only small street protests and almost no organized and long-lasting campaign

---

Rapor.pdf.

7   Yaman Akdeniz and Kerem Altıparmak, '5651 sayılı Kanunun Değişiklik Tasarısının Getirdiği Değişiklikler Üzerine Bir Değerlendirme', *Cyber Rights*, 2014, p.14, http://cyber-rights.org.tr/docs/5651_Tasari_ Rapor.pdf.

8   Çağrı Yalkın, Finola Kerrigan and Dirk vom Lehn, 'Legitimisation of the Role of the Nation State: Understanding of and Reactions to Internet Censorship in Turkey', *New Media and Society* 16 (2014): 271.

against the blocks. The online protests decreased over time, although some activist groups and politicians continued to speak about the matter.

The most common form of internet resistance in Turkey is the use of software tools to access blocked websites. Until 2014, most users preferred alternative and free DNS providers outside of Turkey, such as Google DNS and OpenDNS. Countless websites provided advice on how to change DNS settings to get around the government blocks, and users quickly became familiar with these tactics. This increased again after YouTube and Twitter were blocked in March 2014, as people searched online for information about changing DNS settings. This can be seen in Table 1 below, which shows the use of the words DNS, VPN and *sansür* (censorship) on Twitter during the first days of the blocks in Turkey.

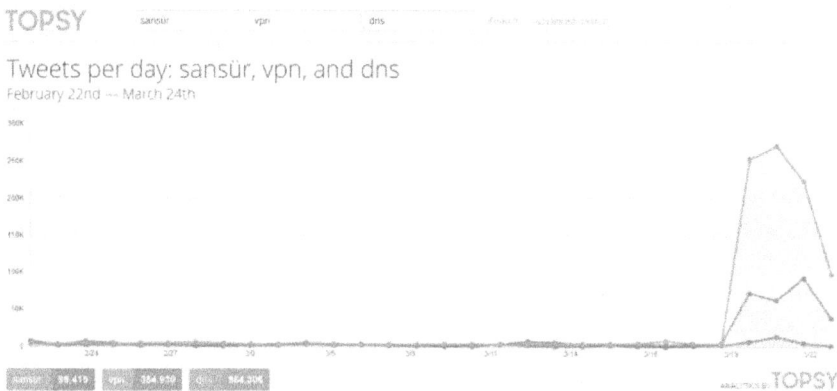

Figure 2. During the March 2014 Twitter ban, a global search of tweets shows that 'VPN' and 'DNS' as well the Turkish word for censorship were prominent terms

On the second day of the Twitter ban in March 2014, access to commonly used DNS providers was also blocked from within Turkey. This was a turning point for Turkish internet users, and many of them became aware of VPN services for the first time. As can be seen in the Twitter statistics above, the word VPN suddenly entered into online conversation. During this period two popular free VPN services, Hotspot Shield and TunnelBear, removed the usual download limits for their Turkish customers, to support their circumvention practices against censorship. These apps were downloaded by hundreds of thousands of people in a couple of hours after the Twitter ban. Other VPN services such as Zenmate or VPNTraffic also became very popular within a short period of time. The popularity of VPN services for circumvention practices of Turkish audiences can be seen plainly in the marketing strategies of services like Torguard, which promotes its product to Turkish users as a tool to "unblock Twitter". Another tool used for circumvention was the Tor browser. It appears that the combined effect of these tools was successful overall, since the number of Tweets in Turkish did not decrease but actually increased during the first days of the 2014 Twitter ban.

Within a few weeks both Twitter and Youtube were unblocked following a decision by Turkey's constitutional court. The lawyers Yaman Akdeniz and Kerem Altıparmak – internet freedom campaigners and NGO activists – had petitioned the court on the basis that banning websites was a violation of the right to freedom of expression. The constitutional court decided in their favor and ordered the blocks to be lifted. Although this decision can be seen as a positive step, many other websites are still blocked in Turkey; in fact, the total number of blocked websites is increasing. For example, in the aftermath of the June 2015 general elections, when the ceasefire between the PKK and the Turkish state was violated, critical websites such as Sendika, ÖzgürGündem and DagMedya were blocked for being pro-PKK.

Unfortunately, there is no transparency about which websites are currently being blocked. However, activist groups are working to compile public lists of these blocked websites. One example is the anonymous collective behind the Engelli Web ('Blocked Web') project. According to their research, the most commonly blocked category of websites contain "obscene" content. These are not only pornographic websites, but for example also websites that contain any sort of nudity or homosexual content. Among these websites there is an increasing number of video and video series sites. Then there are the sites blocked for political reasons – for example, pro-Kurdish websites such as Firat News or Yeni Özgür Politika According to Engelli Web, more than 80,000 websites are blocked as of May 2015.[9]

Other activist groups in Turkey, such as Alternatif Bilisim Dernegi, the Pirate Party (Korsan Parti) and Internet Derneği (Inetd), focus on ICTs and internet freedom. These groups actively campaigns against internet censorship, mount legal challenges, and organize events to raise awareness. While marginal to national politics, they are increasingly popular among young people.

Prosecution of individual internet users for posting material in online forums has increased in recent years. These cases are again based on definitions of crime that refer to 'defamation of religion', 'violation of personal rights' and so on. Some of these cases are legitimate, but many of them seem to be simply attempts to silence anti-government voices. Although website blocks have little effect in terms of curtailing online expression (since people can always get around these blocks), the threat of court cases and imprisonment may be more effective in silencing dissent.

Conclusion: Circumvention as a Solution to Internet Censorship?

As the preceding discussion shows, over the last decade circumvention activity and online rights discourses have become widespread in Turkey. While some of this activity is entertainment-related, the main driver of circumvention is not the geoblocked commercial video streaming services but the country's internet censorship system.

Of course, people can always circumvent these IP-based blocks by using alternative DNS settings or VPN services. Blocking has been ineffective in reducing traffic to banned sites, and may even increase it. In this sense the blocking of the websites remains a rather symbolic act on the part of the government. First and foremost, it is a tool for intimidation and

---

9   Engelli Web, http://engelliweb.com/istatistikler/numbering.xml.

delegitimization. Combined with court cases against individuals on the basis of their posts online, these have long-term effects as people start to self-censor their online communication. Second, these blocks are a demonstration of power to the AKP's own voters. As Twitter was blocked shortly before the local elections in March 2014, Erdogan made this part of his political campaign by saying that 'they (AKP) were going to root out Twitter', thus signaling his power to take on a global internet actor. Third, through website blocking the government is forcing big internet companies like Twitter to be more cooperative in terms of removing content. Twitter representatives visited TIB a couple of times after the ban in 2014, however the content of the meetings was never made public. Many Tweets and Twitter accounts have been removed since then at the request of the TIB. Again these blocked accounts and tweets are not made public by Twitter.

Even the government is aware of the fact that they cannot completely ban websites. Erdogan himself argued that everybody, including himself, can access YouTube during the ban in 2009. Many state officials continued to use Twitter during the 2014 ban. Yet, this picture might change since there are also attempts to increase the level of control on both a legal and technological level. As we have seen, new laws are making it easier to block websites without a court order, and the government is investing in more sophisticated blocking technologies.

As the government extends internet regulation, people are looking for new technological workarounds. This was evident in March 2014, when the most used alternative DNS providers could not be used and people moved to alternative VPN services. These tools enable Turkish internet users to individually cope with internet censorship through circumvention, but not necessarily to fight it. Given the fast-changing political environment in Turkey, the issue of internet censorship seems to only gain priority when bigger websites such as Twitter and YouTube are being blocked. However, internet censorship in Turkey is an ongoing issue. Campaigns like 'Don't touch my internet' in 2011 showed the power of a well-organized protest, in which different actors from across the political spectrum come together. In the face of increasing government control, organizing well-networked, sustainable and effective action against internet censorship seems more important than ever in Turkey.

References

Akdeniz, Yaman and Kerem Altıparmak. 'AİHM Kararı: 5651 Sayılı Yasa AİHS'e Aykırı', *Bianet*, 19 December 2012, http://bianet.org/bianet/ifade-ozgurlugu/142923-aihm-karari-5651-sayili-yasa-aihs-e-aykiri.

Boston Consulting Group. Türkiye'de Internet Ekonomisi Raporu, 2013, http://www.turkiye-e-konomi.com/Turkey-Online-Turkish.pdf.

Manav, Volkan. 'Türkiye'den Netflix Izlemek Mümkün Olabilir mi?', *Teknoloji Oku,* 12 February 2015, http://www.teknolojioku.com/haber/turkiyeden-netflix-izlemek-mumkun-olabilir-mi-26053.html.

Terkan, Banu and Nurullah Terkan. 'Analysis of the Political Discourses of the Ruling and Opposition Parties Regarding the New Regulations in the Internet Law in Turkey', Proceedings of the 13th International Academic Conference, Antibes, 2014.

TUİK. 22 August 2014, http://www.turkstat.gov.tr/PreHaberBultenleri.do?id=16198.

Yalkın, Çağrı, Finola Kerrigan and Dirk vom Lehn. 'Legitimisation of the Role of the Nation State: Understanding of and Reactions to Internet Censorship in Turkey', *New Media and Society* 16 (2014): 271-288.

Yaman Akdeniz and Kerem Altıparmak. '5651 sayılı Kanunun Değişiklik Tasarısının Getirdiği Değişik-likler Üzerine Bir Değerlendirme', online report, *Cyber Rights,* 2014, http://cyber-rights.org.tr/docs/5651_Tasari_Rapor.pdf.

SWEDEN: CIRCUMVENTION AND THE QUEST FOR PRIVACY

CHRIS BAUMANN

97%

Proportion of Swedes aged 16-54 who have access to the internet

SEK 199

Monthly cost for a true fiber connection (100 Mbit/s or more)

85%

Proportion of Swedish internet users who made online purchases in 2014

14%

Proportion of Swedish internet users who paid for a video streaming service in 2014

'The Nordic countries constitute one of the most advanced markets for new services and technologies, and particularly Sweden...both for its high broadband speeds and its people who tend to be early adopters.'[1] *—
Reed Hastings, Netflix CEO and co-founder, in 2013*

*'We believe that the time is ripe for everyone to start using VPN services'
— Jon Karlung, CEO of the Swedish ISP Bahnhof, in 2014*

In mid-October 2012, Netflix flew its top three executives, co-founder and CEO Reed Hastings, Chief Product Officer Neil Hunt, and Chief Content Officer Ted Sarandos over to Sweden to have cocktails with a group of journalists at an upscale bar in the heart of Stockholm. Netflix had just launched its streaming service in the small Scandinavian country and, for all intents and purposes, needed the promotional power only their senior staff could provide. The company had announced its plans to launch in Sweden and some of the other Nordic countries only a few months before, on 15 August. Later that day, Time Warner informed the press that it would also launch a subscription-based video streaming service, HBO Nordic, in the same region sometime in the fall of 2012. All of a sudden, Sweden, a country of less than ten million people located in the periphery of Europe, was set to be host to two of the biggest names in streaming video. By the end of the year, both platforms were up and running. As time passed, however, it became clear that neither Netflix nor HBO Nordic were able to dominate online video in Sweden. Both of them launched into an oversaturated media landscape, with plenty of streaming video options, authorized and unauthorized, already competing for the viewer's attention.

While this overprovision of streaming video services has managed to crush the financial hopes of Netflix and Time Warner executives alike, it has, together with certain socio-technical and legal preconditions, contributed considerably to turning Sweden into something of a streamer's paradise. Yet, as I will show in this chapter, not everything is rosy for Swedish internet users. With the Swedish government trying to negotiate between its political duties within the European Union and its cyberlibertarian national politics that have made the country a haven for internet users, many Swedes have turned to VPN services to circumvent politically motivated data retention practices, and protect their privacy.

Video Streaming Platforms in Sweden

The Swedish media landscape is host to a plethora of local and offshore video streaming platforms. Viewers can choose between video streaming options from public service and commercial broadcasters, pay TV operators, and telecommunications companies alongside subscription-based, transactional, and advertising-supported streaming services, and a growing number of unauthorized alternatives.

Local video streaming platforms are predominantly in the hands of four media companies that dominate the Swedish television market: the public service broadcaster Sveriges Television, as well as its commercial counterparts Modern Times Group, TV4 Group, and SBS Discovery Media. All of these companies provide catch up TV services in addition to their free-to-air offerings, making previously broadcast programs available to stream for a limited time. Most notable here are SVT Play, TV3 Play, TV4 Play, as well as Kanal 5 Play. In addition to these free services, the major commercial networks also offer subscription-based video streaming platforms. These include ad-free versions of certain catch up TV services (TV4 Play Premium or Kanal 5 Play Premium), comprehensive online extensions to traditional pay TV services, such as Viaplay or C More Play, as well as standalone products like the movie and television series streaming platform Filmnet. Furthermore, viewers have the possibility to subscribe to aggregator streaming services such as Magine TV or Telia Play Plus, which package content from a number of public service and commercial broadcasters, as well as pay TV operators. Finally, there are transactional video streaming platforms, such as SF Anytime, Headweb, film2home, or Plejmo, that allow viewers to purchase movies and television shows, or rent them for a limited time (usually 48 hours).

A number of offshore video streaming platforms, predominantly from the United States, join these Swedish providers. The two services dominating the North American video streaming market, Netflix and YouTube, are present in Sweden as well.[1] Both of these services have a very similar look and feel in Sweden compared to their home market. However, the same

1   Todd Spangler, 'Netflix Streaming Eats Up 35% of Downstream Internet Traffic: Study', *Variety*, 20 November 2014, http://variety.com/2014/digital/news/netflix-streaming-eats-up-35-of-downstream-internet-bandwidth-usage-study-1201360914/.

cannot be said about their content libraries. YouTube is primarily a platform for user-generated and corporately sponsored content and is able to offer the great majority of content uploaded to its servers also in Sweden. In contrast, Netflix, as a premium subscription service, maintains different content libraries in its home country and the various international markets it operates, subject to varying license agreements. Swedish viewers also have the option to subscribe to Time Warner's HBO Nordic, a standalone video streaming service that offers access to the entire HBO library, including the company's latest television episodes twenty-four hours after they have been broadcast in the United States.

Given this abundance of local and offshore platforms, it is maybe surprising that YouTube and Netflix alone are responsible for more than half of the overall consumption of legal streaming video in Sweden.[2] In a country of just over 8.7 million internet users YouTube accounts for 1.3 million viewers every day.[3] Netflix falls behind with 465,000 daily viewers; however, with this number still has a lead in the Swedish subscription video streaming market, beating local and offshore competitors in this category, including Viaplay (198,000), TV4 Play Premium (60,000), HBO Nordic (34,000), and C More Play (17,000).[4] In the free catch up TV market, Sveriges Television, which was the first Swedish broadcaster to establish a video streaming service, has a commanding lead over its commercial competitors with 57 percent of all video streams coming through its SVT Play platform.[5]

In addition to the many authorized local and offshore video streaming options, there are an increasing number of unauthorized services competing for the attention of Swedish viewers. Probably the most visible of them is Swefilmer, a website that provides free access to pirated copies of thousands of movies and television shows hosted on a small server farm in Russia.[6] What makes the platform stand out is its attempt to appeal to a local audience. Besides offering the latest Hollywood content, Swefilmer makes a substantial amount of Swedish productions available to stream. Many of the video files come with Swedish subtitles hardcoded into them, and the website's interface is only available in Swedish. What differentiates the platform even further is the fact that it operates in a legal gray zone. Curiously, watching a video stream is an extralegal activity in Sweden, as the visitor of a website cannot necessarily be certain if the material he/she watches was obtained rightfully or not. For these reasons, Swefilmer has attracted considerable public attention, and copycat websites such as Dreamfilm, Swesub.tv, and Sweflix have imitated its model.[7] A further unauthorized video streaming alternative is Popcorn Time, a downloadable open source BitTorrent client with integrated media player, whose polished user interface recalls commercial platforms like Netflix or HBO Nordic. As opposed to gray services such as Swefilmer, however, Popcorn Time's reliance on BitTorrent technology means that the viewer is likely to break local law when using the software, as it is illegal to upload copyrighted material in Sweden.

2   Mediavision, *TV-insikt Q3 2014*, Stockholm, 2014.
3   Olle Findahl, *Svenskarna och internet 2014*, Stockholm, 2014.
4   MMS, *Trend och Tema 2014:4*, Stockholm, 2015.
5   MMS, *Årsrapport 2014 för TV och Webb-TV*, Stockholm, 2015.
6   Tobias Brandel, 'Svensk illegal streaming växer snabbt', *Svenska Dagbladet*, 29 April 2013, http://www.svd.se/nyheter/inrikes/svensk-illegal-streaming-vaxer-snabbt_8129082.svd.
7   In 2012, 'swefilmer' was the third-most searched term on google.se, according to Google Trends.

High Speeds/Low Spending

Arguably the most important reason for this overprovision of video streaming services in Sweden is the country's unique internet infrastructure. The internet did not spread particularly fast in Sweden during the 1990s, at least not compared to a country like the United States where it was originally conceived. However, whereas both broadband penetration and speeds have leveled out in many OECD countries, they continue to increase in Sweden. The Scandinavian country ranks third in the World Economic Forum's Network Readiness Index for 2014 with its 'world-class, affordable ICT infrastructure' and 'one of the highest technological and non-technological innovation performances in the world'.[8] Today, 91 percent of the Swedish population have access to the internet, a number that increases to a staggering 97 percent in the age group 16 to 54.[9] Broadband is available in 88 percent of Swedish households, with 61 percent of homes and enterprises having access to downstream connections of at least 100 Mbit/s.[10] Yet, despite these numbers, prices for fixed broadband remain comparatively low in Sweden. With true fiber connections costing from SEK 199 per month, the country ranks third cheapest globally for internet connections of 100 Mbit/s or more.[11]

It is predominantly because of this promising infrastructural arrangement that major U.S. media companies such as Netflix and Time Warner have expanded into the small Scandinavian country in the first place. In several interviews with the local press, Netflix executives were quick to point out the country's unique socio-technical conditions for the dissemination of digital media. Speaking to a handful of journalists on the eve of Netflix's Swedish launch, CEO Reed Hastings noted that '[t]he Nordic countries constitute one of the most advanced markets for new services and technologies, and particularly Sweden…both for its high broadband speeds and its people who tend to be early adopters.'[12] Chief Product Officer Neil Hunt seemed to agree with the remarks, adding that the company found the country's internet infrastructure to be much better than anywhere else they had previously been. For Time Warner, too, Sweden continues to play a significant role. In 2012 the decision to make HBO's entire library available to stream as a standalone subscription service under the moniker of HBO Nordic raised many eyebrows in Sweden, and abroad.[13] However, in light of the company's recent announcement to launch its HBO Now video streaming service — essentially a carbon copy of HBO Nordic destined for the U.S. market — it can be argued that the Nordic countries, and Sweden in particular, served as a test market for the media giant, and a convenient way to quietly launch their new flagship video streaming product.

---

8   World Economic Forum, *The Global Information Technology Report 2014*, Geneva, 2014.

9   Statistiska Centralbyrån, *Privatpersoners användning av datorer och internet 2014*, Stockholm, 2014.

10   Findahl, *Svenskarna och internet 2014*; PTS, *PTS bredbandskartläggning 2014: En geografisk översikt av bredbandstillgången i Sverige*, Stockholm, 2014.

11   PTS, *PTS prisrapport 2014: Prisutvecklingen på mobiltelefoni och bredband*, Stockholm, 2014.

12   Mats Lewan, 'Netflix: Därför valde vi Sverige', *NyTeknik*, 16 October 2012, http://www.nyteknik.se/nyheter/it_telekom/tv/article3560911.ece.

13   In addition to Sweden, HBO Nordic is also available in Norway, Denmark, and Finland.

As promising as this arrangement appears from a corporate perspective, however, it has surprisingly not resulted in any sizable consumer spending on subscription or transaction-based video streaming services. Swedes are generally open towards making their purchases online, with 85 percent of internet users regularly buying and paying for items or services via the internet.[14] Yet, whereas purchases of home electronics or clothes over the internet have surged in recent years, sales of digital media have not contributed nearly as much.[15] The numbers are somewhat improving in the music sector, where the Swedish company Spotify has helped to increase the number of users paying for music online from 15 percent in 2011 to 38 percent in 2014. In the online video sector, however, consumer spending is considerably lower as the great majority of content is still accessed for free. Only 14 percent of all Swedish internet users subscribed to a video streaming service in 2014.[16] The reasons behind this comparatively low spending on online video in Sweden are complex, with unauthorized streaming services such as Swefilmer, or peer-to-peer file sharing facilitated through third-party platforms like Popcorn Time or The Pirate Bay certainly contributing to this phenomenon. Yet, as Patrick Vonderau has demonstrated, pirating alone fails to explain why revenues generated through legal online video platforms remain so low.[17] Rather, we should be looking at the overprovision of free video services in Sweden, including the many free catch up TV services and the immensely popular YouTube, alongside easy-to-access unauthorized platforms like Swefilmer and Popcorn Time, if we want to begin to understand this development.

Privacy Matters

Given Sweden's comparatively strong digital infrastructure and historically laissez-faire approach towards internet use and censorship, it is easy to see why the country is often described as the prototypical cyberlibertarian information economy. It should not come as a surprise, then, that Sweden was always decidedly reluctant about the 2006 EU Data Retention Directive, which required EU member states to store citizens' telecommunications data, for up to two years. In 2010, The European Court of Justice (ECJ) ruled that Sweden had to follow the other member states and implement the directive. However, it was not until the spring of 2012 that the Swedish government gave in and adopted measures transposing the directive into local legislation. Yet, this collection of Swedish call records and internet metadata would only last for two years. In April 2014 the ECJ had a change of heart and declared the Data Retention Directive invalid, describing it as a 'serious interference with the fundamental rights to respect for private life and to the protection of personal data.'[18] Following the ruling, the Swedish Post and Telecom Authority (*Post- och telestyrelsen*) was quick to give Swedish telcos and ISPs the go ahead to stop collecting customer data. All

---

14   Findahl, *Svenskarna och internet 2014*.
15   PostNord, Svensk Digital Handel, and HUI Research, *E-barometern 2014*, Stockholm, 2014.
16   Findahl, *Svenskarna och internet 2014*.
17   Patrick Vonderau, 'Beyond Piracy: Understanding Digital Markets', in Jennifer Holt and Kevin Sanson (eds) *Connected Viewing: Selling, Streaming, and Sharing Media in the Digital Age*, New York and London: Routledge, 2014, pp. 99-123.
18   Court of Justice of the European Union, Press release 54/14, 8 April 2014, http://curia.europa.eu/jcms/upload/docs/application/pdf/2014-04/cp140054en.pdf.

of the major companies obliged without hesitation, with some of them going as far as to delete all old customer records.[19] The pause on data retention in Sweden was to be brief, however, as in another ruling in October 2014, Swedish communications companies were ordered to start collecting customer metadata yet again.[20]

The drama around data retention in Sweden reflects the country's efforts to negotiate between its political duties within a European context and its libertarian digital politics that have made it a haven for internet users. In recent years, many Swedish internet users have turned to VPN services to protect their privacy and avoid the crossfire between authorities and ISPs. Curiously, in their quest for privacy Swedish internet users are even supported by some of the companies that are supposed to collect data about them. In trying to avoid a fine of 5 million Swedish Kronor for its refusal to comply with local data retention rules, the Swedish ISP Bahnhof decided to offer a free VPN service to all of its customers the day it had to resume storing metadata.[21] Explaining the somewhat surprising move, Bahnhof CEO Jon Karlung said: 'The European Court of Justice has ruled that it is a human right to not have your internet traffic monitored. We therefore believe that the time is ripe for everyone to start using VPN services.'[22] In Sweden, the EU Data Retention Directive was never applied to VPN providers under the local implementation of the law. Therefore, by providing their customers with a free VPN service Bahnhof managed to find a loophole that enables the company to comply with EU and local law, and assure the privacy of their customers at the same time.

Anonine

VPN services make highly effective tools for hiding the identity of internet users. In Sweden, they predominantly act as efficient, and most importantly, legal, vehicles for circumventing politically motivated data retention practices. It is primarily thanks to the legal status of VPN services that Sweden has emerged as a home to a number of local VPN providers. One particularly successful example is Anonine, a Swedish premium VPN provider established in 2009. Anonine started out as a niche service, offering both Point-to-Point Tunneling Protocol (PPTP) and OpenVPN solutions through a handful of servers based in Sweden. In recent years, and certainly influenced by the implementation of the Data Retention Directive in Sweden in early 2012, Anonine's customer base grew so large that the company had to expand its servers considerably. Today, Anonine operates servers in more than a dozen international locations, and ranks as one of the most popular VPN services in Sweden.

19   Liam Tung, 'Four of Sweden's Telcos Stop Storing Customer Data after EU retention Directive
      Overthrown,' *ZDNet*, 11 April 2014, http://www.zdnet.com/article/four-of-swedens-telcos-stop-
      storing-customer-data-after-eu-retention-directive-overthrown/.
20   Förvaltningsrätten i Stockholm, http://www.forvaltningsrattenistockholm.domstol.se/Domstolar/
      lansrattenistockholm/Pressmeddelande/14891-14.pdf. rvaltningsrätten i Stockholm, in Sweden 1
      reason for VPN usenother ting customer data, with Bahnhof g customers' Court of Jus
21   Oscar Schwartz, 'LEX Integrity', *5th of July Foundation*, 16 November 2014, https://5july.
      org/2014/11/16/lex-integrity/.
22   Jon Karlung, 'Bahnhof aktiverar "plan B": erbjuder fri anonymisering', *Bahnhof*, 16 November 2014,
      https://www.bahnhof.se/press/press-releases/2014/11/16/bahnhof-aktiverar-plan-b-erbjuder-fri-
      anonymisering.

Given the uncertainty of many Swedish internet users about the collection of metadata, it is not surprising that privacy concerns turn out to be the main driver for VPN usage in Sweden. On Flashback — the biggest Swedish-speaking internet forum with around one million registered members — the six hundred or so threads dealing with VPN use often revolve around privacy concerns. In the lengthy thread dedicated to Anonine, one user responds to a question about the level of security provided by Anonine's different VPN solutions as follows:

> Well, in general PPTP is better than using nothing. However, if you are very serious about your security you should only use an OpenVPN solution with good encryption. I do use PPTP, but only if I want to protect myself from my ISP or the idiots at Wayne's Coffee [a Swedish coffee house chain]. If there is a bigger threat, then I turn to OpenVPN.[23]

Here, the use of a VPN service is justified out of fear that someone's internet activity could become uncovered — with anyone, from customers in a coffee shop, to an internet service provider, or even bigger threats (possibly the government?), a potential security risk.

Anonine is all too aware of the privacy concerns of its customers. The company's website is a gray and somewhat generic looking home page listing some of the key features of the service (Fig. 1). It is not until we look at the top right corner of the page that we notice a bright red button warning us: 'You are not anonymous!' Speaking directly at us, the internet users, the site makes a point of highlighting the danger of our behavior, namely surfing the web carelessly without the security only a VPN service can provide. Upon further inspection of Anonine's web presence, we notice that the first page alone makes mention of the word 'anonymous' five times (not counting the company's name, which is a wordplay on *anonym*, the Swedish version of *anonymous*), in addition to multiple uses of related terms like 'safe' or 'secure.' This, of course, is hardly a coincidence.

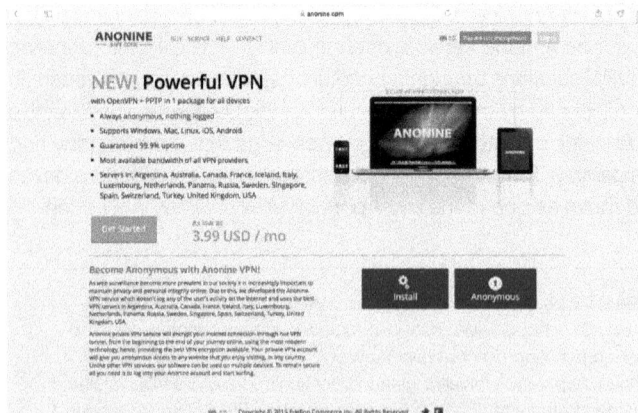

Figure 1. The website of Anonine, a popular Swedish VPN provider

---

23   BeatriceAsk, 'Den stora frågetråden om VPN-tjänsten Anonine! [Sammanfogad]', *Flashback,* 20 April 2012, https://www.flashback.org/p36938188#p36938188.

Another reason for Anonine's popularity among Swedish internet users is the company's "local" brand. Swedes tend to be loyal to homegrown services, as evident by the immense popularity of Spotify and Swefilmer, and Anonine proves that even in the competitive VPN field marketing a product as a local alternative can prove beneficial. Despite being registered in the Seychelles, Anonine very much feels like a local service with a website available in Swedish and English, and customer support provided in both languages. Furthermore, the service offers its clients to use local payment options, such as Payson (a Swedish alternative to PayPal) and Cellsynt (mobile payment via SMS and telephone), in addition to the more conventional credit card options. These might seem like small touches to some, but to a dedicated community of technology-savvy Swedish internet users discussing the ins and outs of different VPN services on an online forum, they can make all the difference.

Conclusion

Sweden is one of the most convenient places to stream online video. The country's media landscape is host to a plethora of streaming platforms, offering viewers a sumptuous mix of local and offshore, free and premium, as well as authorized and unauthorized alternatives. Further, thanks to one of the best ICT infrastructures in the world, high-profile players like Netflix and Time Warner (HBO) have been drawn to the small Scandinavian country, making available a considerable amount of premium content. At the same time, viewers who either do not want or cannot pay for this kind of content have the possibility to use gray video streaming platforms like Swefilmer, which despite providing free access to pirated copies of thousands of movies and television shows can be used legally.

Given this overprovision of local and offshore video streaming alternatives, geoblocking does not impact the online viewing experience in Sweden noticeably. Yet, much like in many of the countries studied in this book, circumvention tools are an important aspect of online culture. VPN services, which in other countries might be used for geoblocking circumvention purposes, are important tools for Swedish internet users to bypass government data retention. There are reports of Sweden being implicated in mass surveillance practices, based on documents provided by the NSA whistleblower Edward Snowden in the summer of 2013.[24] Consequently, privacy remains high on the agenda for many internet users who have become accustomed to a country famed for its libertarian digital politics. Companies providing VPN services like Anonine surely will not complain about Swedish internet users' quest for privacy.

The author wishes to thank Patrick Vonderau for helpful suggestions.

References

BeatriceAsk. 'Den Stora Frågetråden om VPN-tjänsten Anonine! [Sammanfogad]', *Flashback,* 20 April 2012. https://www.flashback.org/p36938188#p36938188.

Bie, Nanok. 'Strömmande Film ökar när Nedladdning Minskar', *SVT Nyheter*, 20 March 2013, http://

---

24   Privacy International, *The Right to Privacy in Sweden. Stakeholder Report: 21st Session, Sweden,* London, 2014.

www.svt.se/nyheter/inrikes/strommande-film-okar-nar-nedladdning-minskar.

Brandel, Tobias. 'Svensk Illegal Streaming Växer Snabbt', *Svenska Dagbladet*, 29 April 2013, http://www.svd.se/nyheter/inrikes/svensk-illegal-streaming-vaxer-snabbt_8129082.svd.

Court of Justice of the European Union. http://curia.europa.eu/jcms/upload/docs/application/pdf/2014-04/cp140054en.pdf.

Findahl, Olle. *Svenskarna och Internet 2014,* Stockholm, 2014.

Flashback. https://www.flashback.org/.

_____. 'Den Bästa Appen för att Surfa Anonymt Med iPhone? (proxy/VPN)', https://www.flashback.org/t2516629.

_____. 'Den Stora Frågetraden om VPN-tjänsten Anonine! [Sammanfogad]', https://www.flashback.org/t926057.

_____. 'Hur Anonymt är VPN Över Wifi, När det Kommer till Kritan', https://www.flashback.org/t2449802.

Förvaltningsrätten i Stockholm. http://www.forvaltningsrattenistockholm.domstol.se/ Domstolar/lan-srattenistockholm/Pressmeddelande/14891-14.pdf.

Google Trends. https://www.google.com/trends/topcharts#vm=cat&geo=SE&date=2012&cid.

Karlung, Jon. 'Bahnhof aktiverar "plan B": erbjuder fri anonymisering.' *Bahnhof*. 16 November 2014. https://www.bahnhof.se/press/press-releases/2014/11/16/bahnhof-aktiverar-plan-b-erbjuder-fri-anonymisering.

Lewan, Mats. 'Netflix: Därför valde vi Sverige', *NyTeknik*, 16 October 2012, http://www.nyteknik.se/nyheter/it_telekom/tv/article3560911.ece.

Mediavision. *TV-insikt Q3 2014*, Stockholm, 2014.

MMS. Årsrapport 2014 för TV och Webb-TV, Stockholm, 2015.

MMS. *Trend och Tema 2014:4*, Stockholm, 2015.

Muskelknutt. 'Den stora frågetråden om VPN-tjänsten Anonine! [Sammanfogad]', *Flashback*, 13 May 2012, https://www.flashback.org/p37334359#p37334359.

PostNord, Svensk Digital Handel, and HUI Research, *E-barometern 2014*, Stockholm, 2014.

Privacy International. The Right to Privacy in Sweden, Stakeholder Report: 21st Session, Sweden, London, 2014.

PTS. PTS bredbandskartläggning 2014: En geografisk översikt av bredbandstillgången i Sverige, Stockholm, 2014.

_____. PTS prisrapport 2014: Prisutvecklingen på mobiltelefoni och bredband, Stockholm, 2014.

Schwartz, Oscar. 'LEX Integrity', *5th of July Foundation*, 16 November 2014, https://5july.org/2014/11/16/lex-integrity/.

Spangler, Todd. 'Netflix Streaming Eats Up 35% of Downstream Internet Traffic: Study', *Variety*, 20 November 2014, http://variety.com/2014/digital/news/netflix-streaming-eats-up-35-of-downstream-internet-bandwidth-usage-study-1201360914/.

Statiska Centralbyrån. *Privatpersoners användning av datorer och internet 2014*, Stockholm, 2014.

Szalai, Georg. 'HBO Unveils Scandinavian Joint Venture as Netflix Also Plans Nordic Launch', *The Hollywood Reporter*, 15 August 2012, http://www.hollywoodreporter.com/news/hbo-nordic-joint-venture-netflix-scandinavia-382920.

Tung, Liam. 'Four of Sweden's Telcos Stop Storing Customer Data after EU Retention Directive Overthrown', *ZDNet*, 11 April 2014, http://www.zdnet.com/article/four-of-swedens-telcos-stop-storing-customer-data-after-eu-retention-directive-overthrown/.

Vonderau, Patrick. 'Beyond Piracy: Understanding Digital Markets', in Jennifer Holt and Kevin Sanson (eds.) *Connected Viewing: Selling, Streaming, & Sharing Media in the Digital Age*, New York and London: Routledge, 2014, pp. 99-123.

World Economic Forum. The Global Information Technology Report 2014, Geneva, 2014.

MALAYSIA: GLOBAL BINGE-VIEWING IN A RESTRICTIVE STATE

SANDRA HANCHARD

80%

Proportion of Malaysian internet users who stream or download video at least once a month[1]

5.48 MBPS

Average internet speed[2]

140%

Mobile penetration rate, of which 35% are smartphones[3]

RM8 (US$1.86)

Monthly cost of an iFlix annual subscription

'Flix will fight entertainment piracy and provide an entirely new and legitimate way for the region's hundreds of millions of internet users to enjoy their favourite films and television shows.' -Press release from Catcha Group's iFlix, March 2015.[4]

Internet circumvention practices in Malaysia are driven by two factors – the desire for global video content, and the need to avoid surveillance by local authorities. The population's growing interest in digital security and privacy skills are transferrable for both entertainment and political purposes.

Malaysia is a middle-income country with a growing appetite for digital technology. The

---

1   Kenneth Wong, 'Ad:tech Roadshow Kuala Lumpur 2014' (Malaysia Digital Association, 2014), http://www.adtechkl.com/images/ppt/mda_kenneth_wong.pdf. Data source: Nielsen.
2   Christina Chin, 'Speed Slower than Vietnam and Cambodia', *The Star Online*, 2014, http://www.thestar.com.my/News/Nation/2014/05/04/Our-Internet-not-so-broadband-after-all-Speed-slower-than-Vietnam-and-Cambodia/.
3   ecommerceMilo, 'With 140% Mobile Penetration, Malaysia has 10M Smartphone Users', *e27*, 5 March 2014, http://e27.co/140-mobile-penetration-malaysia-10m-smartphone-users/.
4   A. Asohan, 'Netflix-type Wars: Grove's Catcha Takes on Singtel's Hooq with iflix', *Digital News Asia*, 10 March 2015, https://www.digitalnewsasia.com/startups/netflix-type-wars-grove-catcha-takes-on-singtel-hooq-with-iflix.

goal of reaching the status of a developed nation by 2020, in terms of technology adoption and literacy, is part of Malaysia's national narrative. In the mid-1990s, the Malaysian government called for a move towards a knowledge-based economy in line with Vision 2020, a cornerstone policy of former Prime Minister Mahathir Mohamad. The 'democratic' use of the internet was seen as a key means for ensuring economic prosperity for all. The legacy of this macro policy has shaped internet-driven economies and startup cultures in urban centres. Access to the internet is steady at 67 percent of the population in 2014, representing more than 20 million users (although connection speeds are comparatively slow for the Southeast Asian region).[5] Through smartphone ownership, combined with free public wi-fi and relatively affordable data plans (for middle-income users), a substantial portion of Malaysian users have the opportunity to create and view media-rich content while 'on the go'. In Kuala Lumpur, netizens have access to a burgeoning number of co-working hacker spaces, wi-fi enabled cafés and tech meet-ups. Local movie streaming services such as iFlix are also starting to appear, giving Malaysian binge viewers yet another path to the high-quality productions they desire.

This burgeoning internet culture sits uncomfortably with the country's restrictive policies on media regulation and political expression. Malaysians face greater constraints in online consumption and sharing, with restrictions on freedom of speech through the legacy of colonial laws such as the Sedition Act. This directly affects user-generated content which is often political in nature. Therefore, circumvention tools such as VPNs and proxies have a dual function in this context, enabling anonymous and unfiltered participation in online political discussions while also opening up greater access to foreign digital media content.

Alternative Paths to Global Video Content

Malaysians' exposure to global media flows has fuelled a desire for 24/7 access to on-demand video. In 2014, Malaysians spent on average 6 hours a week watching online videos, compared to 10 hours on television.[6] Global platforms for video sharing (YouTube, Facebook, Vimeo, Youku, Tudou), rather than local services, dominate Malaysian consumption.

Malaysians often use YouTube to view full-length movies, whether serialised or published with advertisements. Services such as Netflix and Hulu have become popular among those Malaysians who have the technical expertise and disposable income for a VPN subscription. These activities are fuelled by the slow delivery of first-release movies and TV shows to Malaysia – a source of frustration for users. Malaysia's largest online community, Lowyat.net contains hundreds of forums on movies filled with complaints about international content windowing and time delays. As one user put it around Oscars season, 'They never release these movie internationally or did they exclude malaysia from their marketing plans delib-

---

5   Internet World Stats, 'Asia Internet Usage Stats Facebook and Population Statistics', http://www.
     internetworldstats.com/stats3.htm.
6   Kenneth Wong, '2014 Malaysia Digital Media Landscape', presentation at ad:tech Roadshow Kuala
     Lumpur, 2014, http://www.adtechkl.com/images/ppt/mda_kenneth_wong.pdf. Data sourced from
     comScore and Nielsen.

erately? Because malaysia hub of movie pirates?'[7] Lowyat.net also features boards where users share advice and tips related to circumvention.

Local streaming startup iFlix launched in Malaysia and the Philippines in May 2015, as an equivalent service to Netflix. Regionally, iFlix competes with Singapore-based Singtel's new VOD service, Hooq. At the helm of iFlix is the entrepreneur Patrick Grove, who estimates that 90 percent of households in ASEAN households consume pirated content.[8] Grove believes highly-quality American content is keenly sought after by Southeast Asian consumers, and that there is space in the market for a local streaming service as an alternative to torrents (which may be affected by viruses or malware). Based on an analysis of the content that has been released on iFlix so far, they do not appear to be strictly following Malaysian censorship restrictions. This of course could change as a result of greater scrutiny by the authorities if there is mainstream adoption of iFlix.

Figure 1. iFlix launched in Malaysia and Philippines in May 2015, as an equivalent service to Netflix. It provides access to both global and local content, including well-loved Malaysian film genres

Malaysian users are not just looking for shows from Hollywood. There is strong demand for movies and dramas from wider Asia, in particular Korea, Hong Kong, China, Japan and Thailand. There is also a taste for local popular genres, especially Bahasa-language horror and ghost dramas, as well as independent cinema. MovieGoGo, a startup which organises screenings of movies no longer in distribution based on online votes by enthusiasts, recently facilitated the theatrical re-release of the acclaimed Malaysian film *Sepet* by Yasmin Ahmad, loved by many Malaysians as a major work of national cinema. The gala event, ten years after the original release date, was well-attended by movie lovers and original cast members. A series of Malaysian documentaries on iconic Malaysian film celebrities, including Siti Nurhaliza and P. Ramlee, was published on iFlix to coincide with Merdeka Day celebrations (national independence from British colonial rule) in August 2015. Locally-produced content dominated the top 'viral' videos in Malaysia on YouTube in 2014.[9]

7   https://forum.lowyat.net/topic/905692/all.
8   Daniel Tay, 'iFlix brings Hollywood to Southeast Asia', *Tech In Asia*, 2015, https://www.techinasia.com/iflix-brings-hollywood-to-southeast-asia/.
9   The Malay Mail Online, '"Rewind" the Year — YouTube Recaps 2014's Top Videos', *The Malay Mail Online*, 2014, http://www.themalaymailonline.com/malaysia/article/rewind-the-year-youtube-recaps-2014s-top-videos.

Malaysian telcos have been actively promoting digital video consumption, with a number of on-demand multi-screen services available, including HyppTV Everywhere, Astro-On-The-Go, 1MalaysiaIPTV and Tonton. These and other subscription services are growing in popularity, supported by the availability of relatively affordable streaming devices such as Google's Chromecast (launched in Malaysia by the local telco giant Maxis), Apple TV and Roku. One of the motivations for telcos to promote video services is to encourage users to increase their data limit. In fact, the national government-owned ISP, Telekom Malaysia promotes the fact that users can download movies and music quickly through their services, even though this type of content cannot be downloaded legally in Malaysia. There is also increasing interest among users in routers and mobile devices (Android in particular) with pre-installed VPNs.

The VPN market is still maturing in Malaysia. VPNs usually require a credit card which can be a barrier to Malaysian students, typically the biggest media consumers. Su Gim Goh, Asia Pacific Security Advisor for F-Secure, a Finnish IT security firm with offices in Kuala Lumpur, says that demand for VPNs in Malaysia is not as high in Europe and developed countries. F-Secure offers their VPN, Freedome, for download on mobile app stores. Freedome is marketed to consumers based on ease of use, access to geoblocked content and privacy.

Currently, VPN use is a legal grey area in Malaysia. Downloading content illegally from global networks effectively has no ramifications for users in Malaysia because copyright infringement is not heavily policed. However, current practices of VPN-enabled offshore streaming could have greater legal ramifications in the future with the introduction of the U.S. Trans-Pacific Partnership (TPP) trade agreement. In Malaysia, as in other nations, the TPP has been widely criticised by civil society activists. Khairil Yusof and Ng Swee Meng of Sinar Project, a Malaysian non-governmental organization (NGO) that advocates for government transparency, say that acceptance of the TPP in Malaysia would not guarantee better digital content for Malaysians. Sinar Project notes that even if Malaysians could access global TV content legally, there would be no guarantee users would get the content they want, given stricter censorship rules in Malaysia.

Privacy Concerns and Circumventing Surveillance

These audience practices should be understood in the context of Malaysia's politically restrictive environment. Despite a programme of economic empowerment in the 1990s by the Government, the Malaysian state can still be described as authoritarian. As a result, Malaysian internet users are increasingly cautious about what they say online, and what video content they post on social media – especially given the high degree of connectedness within and between social networks. An increasing awareness of being 'watched' by authorities online is in tension with traditional communal values influencing tendencies to chat openly, at least in social contexts.

The internet once offered a compelling 'democratic' space, through the MSC Bill of Guarantees, for Malaysians to access content 'free' from state censorship. In contrast, the traditional press and broadcasting industries are tightly controlled and censored by the government. The Printing Presses and Publications Act (1984), which regulates the press, and the Communications and Multimedia Act (1998), which applies to broadcast and online media, directly empower ministers to determine who can own and operate media companies. As a result there is a concentration in ownership and alignment of outlets with political parties. In the television industry for example, the major media conglomerate, Media Prima owns all the major private stations. Media Prima is also linked to the political group, United Malaysia Nasional Organisation (UMNO).

Recent legislative attempts to curtail freedom of expression online have been condemned by internet freedom activists. Khairil Yusof, of Sinar Project, wryly muses that the current climate has created an internet where it is only safe in Malaysia to post videos of 'cute kittens'.[10] Amendments to the Evidence Act in 2012 mean that all internet users, ISPs and wi-fi providers are liable for content posted through their registered networks.[11] The Sedition Act – purportedly used by the Malaysian Government to temper hostility between the major ethnic groups, Malay, Chinese and Indian – has also been widely used to curtail legitimate political dissent. In 2015, amendments were made to the Sedition Act which could block social media platforms as publishers, and which increased penalties for users who post 'seditious' content. Malaysian technology consultant Keith Rozario says that with the Prevention of Terrorism Act (POTA) passed in 2015, the authorities have granted broad powers to intercept and store the communications of millions of Malaysians.

VPNs in Malaysia are increasingly marketing their services with reference to security and surveillance. Hide.me, a fast-growing Malaysian-based VPN, promises that with their encrypted tunnel 'you're safe to say and do what you want on the internet'. Su Gim Goh of F-Secure stresses that Malaysians should be more concerned with how their personal activity can be tracked, given the sensitivity of data being collected through high mobile usage. While there are choices in local and global VPNs available, Malaysians often wish to opt for global providers, out of concerns that local services, such as BolehVPN, might be subject to government data requests.

Advocacy initiatives around privacy and circumvention are developing in Malaysia. A niche cyberactivist culture has emerged, comprised of both hackers and journalists. NGOs such as Sinar Project recognise there is a pressing need to educate the wider public, beyond binge video viewers, about circumvention tools and services, and started running a Digital Security and Privacy education workshop in August 2015. This workshop was designed for at-risk users in Malaysia, including LGBT people, religious groups, activists and journalists. Nearly half of the attendees at the first workshop were journalists, who were interested in practical steps for identity protection. Topics covered included threat modelling, metadata, and suspected government surveillance and interception techniques. Users were advised to

10   Su-lyn Boo and Shaun Tan, 'With Revised Sedition Act, Only "Cute Kittens" Left on Social Media', *The Malay Mail Online*, 10 April 2015, http://www.themalaymailonline.com/malaysia/article/with-revised-sedition-act-only-cute-kittens-left-on-social-media.

11   A. Asohan, 'Govt Stealthily Gazettes Evidence Act Amendment, Law is Now in Operation', *Digital News Asia*, 8 August 2012, http://www.digitalnewsasia.com/digital-economy/govt-stealthily-gazettes-evidence-act-amendment-law-is-now-in-operation.

protect their online identity through password management, encryption, fake names, VPNs, Tails and Tor, amongst other approaches. One tactic suggested for citizens posting content that might be deemed seditious was to re-circulate content as widely as possible, to make it impractical for authorities to enforce charges on any one person.

Digital security and privacy practices are increasingly relevant where the Malaysian middle-class has become politically mobilised. There is widespread dissatisfaction with the Malaysian Government over allegations of corruption, especially in the wake of the recent scandal involving 1Malaysia Development Berhad (1MDB), an economic development company owned by the Government, in which $700 million in public funds were allegedly diverted to the bank account of Prime Minister Najib Razak.[12] Digital security skills were particularly relevant for the *Bersih* 4 protests, a movement which called for a 'clean' and transparent Government, over the Merdeka national holiday weekend in August 2015. The city was filled with hundreds of thousands of yellow t-shirts (a symbol for *Bersih*), with many protesters opting to sleep on the streets over the weekend. Users expressed fears about 'signal blocking' by authorities on apps such as Firechat, which was used for organising meeting points, sharing reliable up-to-date information and sharing user videos of the protest. The online news website Malaysiakini launched their Prime app to coincide with the rally, and this was officially adopted by the organizers of *Bersih* 4.

Futures of Online Consumption and Sharing in Malaysia

Malaysians users are resourceful; they will adopt practices required to access and post media content unhindered. Circumvention skills for gaining access to entertainment content are now being transferred for other uses, including to avoid penalties for posting politically sensitive content. Malaysia's large middle-class, which generally enjoys access to higher education, is a significant force to contend with for both commercial entities that attempt to control content distribution through geoblocking and government authorities that attempt to curtail dissenting user-generated content. Debates about access to global entertainment and politically sensitive local content continue, alongside parallel debates about the ethics and legality of consumption and circumvention. While competing services such as iFlix and Hooq will make it easier for Malaysians to access global content, especially from the United States and Korea, the production of local content may see stronger support with platforms committed to serving Malaysian films, dramas and documentaries. We are likely to see further cultural nuances of sharing content openly and privately, as Malaysians gain a greater appreciation of who may be watching them.

Postscript

On 6 January, 2016, Netflix announced that it would be adding more than 130 countries to their global services, including Malaysia. Many users on social media in Malaysia were excited by the launch, while aware of the large price difference between iFlix and Netflix

---

12   The Wall Street Journal, 'Scandal in Malaysia', 5 July 2015, http://www.wsj.com/articles/scandal-in-malaysia-1436113149.

(RM8 and RM33-RM51 resepctively). Some users said they would need to invest in a VPN service to access titles only available in the U.S. Netflix catalogue; others were concerned that access to content would still be censored in Malaysia. Some users said they would use both services, so they could continue to access Asian-oriented content on iFlix.

Acknowledgements

The author wishes to thank Khairil Yusof and Ng Swee Meng of Sinar Project; Su Gim Goh, Security Advisor for F-Secure; Keith Rozario, Technology Consultant; and Alan Chong, Founder of MovieGoGo, for their insightful comments.

References

Asohan, A. 'Govt Stealthily Gazettes Evidence Act Amendment, Law is Now in Operation', *Digital News Asia*, 8 August 2012, http://www.digitalnewsasia.com/digital-economy/govt-stealthily-ga-zettes-evidence-act-amendment-law-is-now-in-operation.

_____ 'Netflix-type Wars: Grove's Catcha Takes on Singtel's Hooq with iflix', *Digital News Asia*, 10 March 2015, https://www.digitalnewsasia.com/startups/netflix-type-wars-grove-catcha-takes-on-singtel-hooq-with-iflix.

Boo, Su-lyn and Shaun Tan. 'With Revised Sedition Act, Only "Cute Kittens" Left on Social Media', *The Malay Mail Online*, 10 April 2015, http://www.themalaymailonline.com/malaysia/article/with-re-vised-sedition-act-only-cute-kittens-left-on-social-media.

ecommerceMilo. 'With 140% Mobile Penetration, Malaysia has 10M Smartphone Users", *e27*, 5 March 2014,e27 http://e27.co/140-mobile-penetration-malaysia-10m-smartphone-users/.

Internet World Stats. 'Asia Internet Usage Stats Facebook and Population Statistics', 30 June 2015, http://www.internetworldstats.com/stats3.htm.

The Malay Mail Online. '"Rewind" the Year — YouTube Recaps 2014's Top Videos,' 10 December 2014, http://www.themalaymailonline.com/malaysia/article/rewind-the-year-youtube-recaps-2014s-top-videos.

The Star Online. 'Rais: Malaysia Will Stop Access to "Innocence of Muslims" Film', 1 June 2013, http://www.thestar.com.my/News/Nation/2012/09/15/Rais-Malaysia-will-stop-access-to-Innocence-of-Muslims-film/.

Tay, Daniel. 'iFlix Brings Hollywood to Southeast Asia', *Tech In Asia*, 10 March 2015, https://www.techinasia.com/iflix-brings-hollywood-to-southeast-asia/.

The Wall Street Journal, 'Scandal in Malaysia', 5 July 2015, http://www.wsj.com/articles/scan-dal-in-malaysia-1436113149.

Wong, Kenneth. '2014 Malaysia Digital Media Landscape', presentation at ad:tech Roadshow Kuala Lumpur. Data sourced from comScore and Nielsen, http://www.adtechkl.com/images/ppt/mda_ken-neth_wong.pdf.

BRAZIL: NETFLIX, VPNS AND THE 'PAYING' PIRATES

VANESSA MENDES MOREIRA DE SA

60%

Proportion of the total population in Brazil that has access to the internet

37TH

Netflix is the 37th most visited website in Brazil (Alexa ranking)

2.2 MILLION

Estimated number of subscribers to Netflix Brazil

38%

Proportion of VPN users from Brazil who have accessed the US Netflix in December 2014

From late 2014, the 'news' that Netflix had started to block anonymous or unidentified IP addresses spread all over the internet. The overall reaction from Brazilians who used location-masking practices presented similarities to the universal five stages of loss and grief[1]:

1. Denial and Isolation:

'I use 'Hola' to see the American Netflix. If Netflix decides to block me, I will go back to Torrents and Netflix will lose a customer'.

2. Anger:

'Media corporations are stupid and greedy. People will go back to Torrents!'

3. Bargaining:

'If I only have access to half the catalogue, I should only have to pay for half the catalogue. It should be my right to access what I want and the way I want'.

---

1   The quotes have been translated from Portuguese to English, edited and de-identified. Sources: Rafael Silva, 'Netflix Bloqueia Acesso de Assinantes Usando VPNs [Netflix Block Access to VPN Subscribers]', *Tecnoblog*, December 2014, https://tecnoblog.net/172153/netflix-bloqueio-acesso-vpn/ and Gabriel Garcia, 'Netflix Bloqueia Usuários que Burlam Restrição Geográfica [Netflix Block Users Who Circumvent Geographic Restriction]', *Abril*, 4 January 2015, http://info.abril.com.br/noticias/internet/2015/01/netflix-bloqueia-usuarios-que-burlam-restricao-geografica.shtml.

4. Depression:

'Why are they imposing such limitations? I use VPN to practice my English' [Netflix Brazil does not offer subtitles in English yet].

5. Acceptance:

'That's the way things work and they won't change. However, it is a setback, and it is against the reality of globalization.'

Netflix is the 37th most visited website in Brazil.[2] It arrived in 2011, and with over two million subscribers in 2015, Brazil is the world's second fastest growing country in terms of subscriber numbers. However, it does not completely meet consumers' demands for a number of reasons, including the limited catalogue available and the lack of English subtitles. Therefore, many Brazilians are turning to VPNs and proxy servers to get access to the US Netflix video library or geoblocked websites from the US and other countries. In fact, recent market research[3] suggests Brazil is the third-largest VPN market in the world. The country also has the third largest number of unauthorized users on the U.S. Netflix site.

Brazil accounts for a considerable share of the global informal audience. In addition to VPN and proxy use, previous research estimates that over 20 million Brazilians are involved in illegal downloading on a daily basis.[4] Brazil is the largest South American country and as one of the five BRICS nations (along with Russia, India, China and South Africa) it also holds an important position as a major emerging economy.[5] Its media landscape is shaped by local, European, Hispanic and Anglo-American influences – and as an enclave of Portuguese within South America's Spanish-language media ecology, it has a particularly complex and cosmopolitan media landscape. For all these reasons, Brazil warrants attention as a unique site for understanding global media flows, both formal and informal.

This chapter investigates how Brazilian television audiences create an alternative system of TV viewing through geoblocking circumvention practices. My analysis draw on various sources, including articles and editorials from newspapers, magazines and blogs, as well as online reader comments, forums, and other online spaces where these practices are discussed.

---

2   Data source: Alexa, www.alexa.com.
3   Jason Mander, 'GWI Infographic: VPN Users', *Global Web Index*, 24 October 2014, http://www.
     globalwebindex.net/blog/vpn-infographic.
4   IPEA, 'Download de Músicas e Filmes no Brasil: Um Perfil dos Piratas Online [Music and Movies
     Download in Brazil: The Online Pirates Profile]', *Communicados do IPEA* 147, Rio de Janeiro, RJ:
     Institute of Applied Economic Research, http://desafios2.ipea.gov.br/portal/images/stories/PDFs/
     comunicado/120510_comunicadoipea0147.pdf.
5   Jim O'Neill, *The Growth Map: Economic Opportunity in the BRICs and Beyond*, New York: Portfolio/
     Penguin, 2011.

Overview of the Media and Digital Landscape in Brazil

To understand TV streaming in Brazil, it is important to consider the context in which these activities take place. Limited access is the main reason why people download media. As in most nations, Brazil's TV system is shaped by broadcast rights and licensing arrangements that often result in delays or the total unavailability of television shows. Audiences in Brazil who wish to watch American TV shows may have to wait months, or even years, until they can see these shows locally. Furthermore, much of the population is priced out of the market for legal DVDs, which are too expensive for the poorest communities.

Since the 1950s, US TV shows have been popular with Brazilian audiences. In the early 1970s the government started to invest in national television production to minimize the reliance on U.S. imports. Ever since then, Brazilian telenovelas have become increasingly popular as well as nationally and internationally recognized for the quality of their plots and production. Local telenovelas have a wide audience and are mostly offered on free-to-air television.[6] In contrast, U.S. TV shows are primarily aired on cable television.[7]

What is generally understood, in regards to Latin American television programming, is that free-to-air TV caters to the mass audience while cable caters to elites, and the advertisers that target them. In late 2014, there were over 19 million subscribers to cable television in Brazil, which corresponds to 29% of households.[8] Having a cable connection is an essential status symbol for the middle classes. Surprisingly, about 33% of cable subscribers only watch free-to-air television channels: they pay for the service to get a better signal or to not feel 'inferior' to friends and family who have cable television.[9] Cable audiences are also concentrated in the southeast region,[10] the most populated and urbanized area of the country, composed of the states of Rio de Janeiro, Sao Paulo, Minas Gerais and Espirito Santo. While Brazilian free-to-air TV offers relatively good quality content, people are starting to want access to a wider selection of programming. However, not everyone can afford the cost of a cable connection, which means that TV viewing in Brazil is organized along class lines.

Socio-economic inequalities also shape internet access and use in Brazil. Although internet access has grown in the 2000s for a number of reasons – including falling broadband prices,

6   Marcia Rejane Messa, 'A Cultura Desconectada: Sitcoms e Séries Norteamericanas no Contexto Brasileiro [The Disconnected Culture: Sitcoms and North American Series in the Brazilian Context]', *UNIrevista* 1 (2006). Also available from http://www.unirevista.unisinos.br/_pdf/UNIrev_Messa.PDF.
7   'Cable Subscribers Have a Much Higher Commercial Importance than Free-to-Air Audiences, as They Make More Purchases' http://veja.abril.com.br/110401/p_142.html.
8   'Brasil Registra 19,24 Milhões de Assinantes de TV Paga em Agosto [Brazil Records 19,24 Million Cable Subscribers in August]', *Anatel*, 1 October 2014, http://www.anatel.gov.br/Portal/exibirPortalNoticias.do?acao=carregaNoticia&codigo=35223.
9   Ricardo Feltrin, 'Assinante de TV Gasta até R$ 300 por Mês e só vê Globo [Cable Subscribers Spend up to R$ 300 per Month and Only Watches Rede Globo]', *Folha de São Paulo*, 07 March 2014*n CensorshipPortfolio / om Lehn, for Free with Torguard' if they are advancing* http://f5.folha.uol.com.br/colunistas/ricardofeltrin/2014/03/1421563-assinante-de-tv-gasta-ate-r-300-por-mes-e-so-ve-globo.shtml.
10   'Brasil Registra 19,24 Milhões', *Anatel*.

federal government investment in school computers, and free wi-fi in public spaces – internet access is still restricted to a portion of the population. In Brazil, 120 million people (60% of the total population) have access to the internet, and 48% of these users have home connections.[11] Internet access at home is most common in highly populated cities with high concentrations of wealthy people, such as Sao Paulo and Rio de Janeiro, and less common in rural states such as Maranhao and Piaui.[12]

These socio-economic factors help to explain the uneven take-up of video streaming in Brazil. In recent years streaming services have multiplied as telcos and media companies invest in VOD platforms. Figure 1 illustrates some of the services available:

Service	Availability	Price (US$)	No of videos
Netflix	Available to the general public	$6.60 per month	1500+
Now	NET HD subscribers	Free / from $1.30 per title	20,000+
Cine Sky HD	Sky HDTV subscribers	From $3.30 per title	36
Sky Online	Sky subscribers	$5.20 per month or pay per view	2,300+
Vivo Play	Available to the general public	$5.20 per month	5000
GVT on demand	GVT subscribers only	Free / $1 per video	5000
ClaroVideo	Available to the general public	$4.60 per month or pay per view	1200+
HBOGo	HBO/Max on Sky subscribers only	Free for cable subscribers	1500+

11   'Numero de Pessoas com Acesso a Internet no Brasil Supera 120 milhoes [Number of People with Internet Access in Brazil Exceeds 120 Million]', *Nielsen*, 30 July 2014, http://www.nielsen.com/br/pt/press-room/2014/Numero-de-pessoas-com-acesso-a-internet-no-Brasil-supera-120-milhoes.html.
12   Marcelo Cortes Neri, 'Mapa da Inclusao Digital [Map of Digital Inclusion]', report, Centro de Políticas Sociais. Fundacao Getúlio Vargas and Fundação Telefônica, 2012.

Service	Availability	Price (US$)	No of videos
Telecine Play	Telecine subscribers only	Free for cable subscribers	1500+
Muu	Globasat subscribers only	Free for cable subscribers	3000

However, despite the proliferation of legal streaming services, Brazilian internet TV viewing is still substantially informal in nature. Like the vibrant pirate DVD economy, which is still a strong feature of Brazil's urban streetscapes, unauthorized TV streaming and downloading is a mainstream practice.

On the internet, it is possible to find a great number of user-led informal video networks provided by Brazilian audiences. Torrents, still the most popular option in Brazil, can be easily accessed from major trackers like The Pirate Bay as well as numerous local websites, such as Filmesviatorrents.com.br which maintains an organized database of films, television shows and anime. File-hosting websites and cloud storage platforms are also used to share video content, with catalogues organized by title, season and episode number. Generally, they are offered with subtitles in Portuguese. Brazilian internet culture has also produced sophisticated fan-driven translation systems. The *legender* (fansubber) community translates Western television shows and films, mostly from the US and UK, into Brazilian Portuguese.

Streaming unauthorized material from YouTube is another popular option. Users have uploaded countless films and television shows on YouTube, which are available in dubbed versions or with subtitles in Portuguese. Further, global entertainment companies often make available on their websites, or Facebook pages, teasers, promos, trailers and sneak peeks of television shows and films. Often this content is geoblocked. However, after observing the Facebook page of US networks like ABC and NBC, I noticed that within a couple of hours after the videos have been released, it was possible to find them on YouTube with subtitles in Portuguese. The most popular informal video streaming website in Brazil, which has a catalogue of films and television content[13], is MegafilmesHD.net. They claim to have over 23,000 films in their archive. Another informal streaming service is Popcorn Time, which promotes its own (paid) VPN service (VPN.ht) so that audiences can use it anonymously.

It is also important to consider the legal context to these practices. Recent years have seen a number of significant developments in Brazil, most notably the passing in 2014 of Brazil's pioneering *Marco Civil* law [Civil Rights Framework for the Internet]. Like a Bill of Rights for the Brazilian internet, the *Marco Civil* '[e]stablishes principles, guarantees, rights and obligations related to the use of the Internet in Brazil,'[14] introducing a safe harbor system and

---

13   When not considering YouTube and websites with pornographic content.
14   *Draft Bill Proposition*, The National Congress, Brazil, EMI N° 00086 - MJ/MP/MCT/MC, 2011. http://

setting out principles for national internet governance, including net neutrality, freedom of expression, and the right to privacy. The bill is viewed internationally as a significant development for expression and civil rights online. Other BRICS countries have pursued more restrictive internet governance systems as a response to the piracy problem. In contrast, Brazil has taken a dramatically different approach:

> …as soon as Brazil signed Marco Civil into law, it became the largest country to enshrine net neutrality in its legal code, among its other welcome provisions on privacy, intermediary liability and accessibility and openness of the internet…With Marco Civil passed into law, Brazil, in its domestic law, is asserting itself as a potential world leader in internet freedom.[15]

The *Marco Civil* is currently undergoing another revision including a public consultation process. In early 2015, Netflix executives joined the discussion, declaring their support for the bill and reassuring their Brazilian subscribers that they would not experience any issues. However, the *Marco Civil* is yet to address VPNs and geographic circumvention practices.

Enforcement of internet and piracy laws in Brazil remains patchy. When it comes to copyright crime, penalties are rarely enforced because of limited policing capacity. Given Brazil's overcrowded jails, copyright infringement is treated as a minor infraction. The government prefers to invest in copyright education rather than prosecution. The high levels of digital piracy in Brazil, therefore, appear to be a result of (but not limited to) a lack of law enforcement, the high cost of accessing cable television, and restricted access to international video content in general.

Circumventing Geoblocking in Brazil Through VPN and Proxy 'Pirata'

A quick search of Brazilian internet sites will produce hundreds of piracy and circumvention resources, such as VPN and proxy services, step-by step instructions in blogs, video tutorials on YouTube, and numerous advice articles and FAQs. Some of the websites and blogs have illustrated step-by-step guides on 'how to set up a VPN' or 'how to use proxy to camouflage your IP address'. As with user-generated torrents, subbing and streaming services, the VPN 'pirate' network is highly collaborative.

Circumvention tools have many uses in Brazil. Some people use VPN and proxy services to access websites that are blocked in the location where they are accessing internet from, such as libraries, schools and at work. Therefore, they use these services to access websites such as those with video content (e.g. YouTube) or social media, such as Facebook. Proxy services such as Unlocator are often preferred for their superior speeds; these may be more

---

direitorio.fgv.br/sites/direitorio.fgv.br/files/Marco%20Civil%20-%20English%20Version%20sept2011. pdf.

15   Melody Patry, 'Brazil: Towards an Internet 'Bill of Rights', *Index on Censorship*, 12 June 2014, https:// www.indexoncensorship.org/2014/06/brazil-towards-internet-bill-rights/.

suited to streaming than encryption services. In my observation of circumvention communities I also noticed that many Brazilians recommend Hola Unblocker as an alternative to the paid and more complex VPNs. The Hola browser plugin is free to install and use – but as noted in the Introduction to this book, it has been known to sell user bandwidth to third parties for botnet attacks.

There are also audiences that want to access video content from their original sources. For instance, since late 2014, accessing the US Netflix catalogue has been a popular discussion topic in Brazilian internet forums. There are two main motivations for accessing the US Netflix service. First, Netflix Brazil has a limited catalogue: the US version offers many times more content, whereas the local version generally offers a lot of content that has already screened widely in Brazil. Second, Netflix subtitles are only available in Portuguese; there are no English captions available, as in the U.S. Netflix service. This is a source of disappointment for the many Brazilian students who use captions to practice their English language skills. They naturally prefer the U.S. service.

Figure 1. English captions on streaming content are highly valued by some Brazilian internet users, especially language students

Interestingly enough, Brazilian Netflix fans have also produced a Portuguese subtitling workaround for those using the U.S. site. There are many tutorials on how to incorporate subtitles created by amateur subtitlers, such as the Legenders, into the video content available in the U.S. Netflix.

In terms of understanding these practices as piracy, I have frequently observed in forums that the argument 'if I pay for a Netflix subscription in Brazil, I should be able to access the US catalogue' was often used. There is also an 'all or nothing' attitude, with many users stating that 'if Netflix start blocking my VPN I will move to Popcorn Time, downloads, and torrents'. I did notice however, that there were many people in these discussions either defending Netflix Brazil, accepting their policies – to a certain extent – on geoblocking and distribution rights.

I have also noticed a certain willingness to pay for access to content among Netflix VPN pirates, which is quite different from the attitude of audiences that informally download content.[16] Some Netflix subscribers even mentioned that they have minimized or even ceased torrenting since they signed up for the service. Everyone who mentioned the monthly subscription of R$9.90 (about USD6) per month said the price was fair.

Once again, it is important to note that only 60% of the population in Brazil have access to the internet. Among them, over two million people subscribe to the Netflix Brazil service and of this number, only certain users have the tech know-how and English skills to be a Netflix VPN pirate (assuming that they use their Netflix Brazil account details to connect to the US Netflix). This is an elite community – highly educated, middle-class people from the cities. They are the target audience not only for Netflix but for other VOD services.

Paying Pirates or Netflix Audiences?

The popularity of Netflix in Brazil not only reflects the growing interest in VOD but also illustrates a great demand from early adopters who are not satisfied with free-to-air and pay-TV. Yet, for many audiences the limited Netflix Brazil catalogue is the main motivation for using VPNs to access the U.S. service.

Netflix's CEO, Reed Hastings, has mentioned that they plan to end the geoblocking of their services one day, however negotiating intellectual property on a global scale is complex. Geographic circumvention is a competitive informal business model. It can be predatory, it can be collaborative but above all, it can inform industry about unmet demand and market gaps. The many different ways of circumventing geoblocks in Brazil raises questions about the differences between pirates versus audiences. Are they paying VPN pirates or legitimate Netflix audiences?

References

'Brasil Registra 19,24 Milhões de Assinantes de TV Paga em Agosto [Brazil Records 19,24 Million Cable Subscribers in August]', *Anatel*, 1 October 2014, http://www.anatel.gov.br/Portal/exibirPortal-Noticias.do?acao=carregaNoticia&codigo=3522.

Draft Bill Proposition, The National Congress, Brazil, EMI N° 00086 - MJ/MP/MCT/MC, 2011. http://direitorio.fgv.br/sites/direitorio.fgv.br/files/Marco%20Civil%20-%20English%20Version%20sept2011.pdf.

Garcia, Gabriel. 'Netflix Bloqueia Usuários que Burlam Restrição Geográfica [Netflix Block Users who Circumvent Geographic Restriction]', *Abril*, 4 January 2015, http://info.abril.com.br/noticias/internet/2015/01/netflix-bloqueia-usuarios-que-burlam-restricao-geografica.shtml.

Feltrin, Ricardo. 'Assinante de TV Gasta até R$ 300 por Mês e só vê Globo [Cable Subscribers Spend up to R$ 300 per month and only Watches Rede Globo]', *Folha de São Paulo*, 07 March 2014, http://f5.folha.uol.com.br/colunistas/ricardofeltrin/2014/03/1421563-assinante-de-tv-gasta-ate-r-300-por-mes-e-so-ve-globo.shtml.

---

16   This observation emerged from my previous research, which was conducted before Netflix came to Brazil. See Vanessa Mendes Moreira De Sa, *Rethinking Pirate Audiences:An Investigation of TV Audiences' Informal Online Viewing and Distribution Practices in Brazil*, PhD diss., School of Communication Arts, University of Western Sydney, Australia, 2013.

IPEA. 'Download de Músicas e Filmes no Brasil: Um Perfil dos Piratas Online [Music and Movies Download in Brazil: The Online Pirates Profile]', *Communicados do IPEA* 147, Rio de Janeiro, RJ: Institute of Applied Economic Research, http://desafios2.ipea.gov.br/portal/images/stories/PDFs/comunicado/120510_comunicadoipea0147.pdf.

Mander, Jason. 'GWI Infographic: VPN Users', *Global Web Index*, 24 October 2014, http://www.globalwebindex.net/blog/vpn-infographic.

Mendes Moreira De Sa, Vanessa. *Rethinking Pirate Audiences: An Investigation of TV Audiences' Informal Online Viewing and Distribution Practices in Brazil*, PhD diss., School of Communication Arts, University of Western Sydney, Australia, 2013.

Messa, Marcia Rejane. 'A Cultura Desconectada: Sitcoms e Séries Norteamericanas no Contexto Brasileiro [The Disconnected Culture: Sitcoms and North American Series in the Brazilian context]', *UNIrevista* 1 (2006). Also available from http://www.unirevista.unisinos.br/_pdf/UNIrev_Messa.PDF.

Neri, Marcelo Cortes, 'Mapa da Inclusao Digital [Map of Digital Inclusion]', report, Centro de Políticas Sociais. Fundacao Getúlio Vargas and Fundação Telefônica, 2012.

'Numero de Pessoas com Acesso a Internet no Brasil Supera 120 Milhoes [Number of People with Internet Access in Brazil Exceeds 120 million]', *Nielsen,* 30 July 2014, http://www.nielsen.com/br/pt/press-room/2014/Numero-de-pessoas-com-acesso-a-internet-no-Brasil-supera-120-milhoes.html.

O'Neill, Jim. *The Growth Map: Economic Opportunity in the BRICs and Beyond*, New York: Portfolio/Penguin, 2011.

Patry, Melody. 'Brazil: Towards an Internet 'Bill of Rights', *Index on Censorship*, 12 June 2014, https://www.indexoncensorship.org/2014/06/brazil-towards-internet-bill-rights/.

Silva, Rafael. 'Netflix Bloqueia Acesso de Assinantes Usando VPNs [Netflix Blocks Access to VPN Subscribers]', *Tecnoblog*, December 2014, https://tecnoblog.net/172153/netflix-bloqueio-acesso-vpn/.

IRAN: A FRICTION BETWEEN STATE IDEOLOGY AND NETWORK SOCIETY

HADI SOHRABI AND BEHZAD DOWRAN

75 MILLION

Total population

23 MILLION

Estimated number of internet users

69%

Proportion of internet users who use circumvention tools

330,000

Number of Twitter followers for President Rouhani, despite Twitter being banned in Iran

President Rouhani: 'Supporters of internet filtering should explain whether they've successfully restricted access to information? Which important piece of news has filtering been able to black out in recent years?'

The Iranian movie *Bullet Proof* (dir. Mostafa Kiayee, 2012) depicts the rise of audio-visual black markets after the 1979 Islamic revolution. Losing his music store during Islamization, our protagonist Salim starts to sell unauthorized products on the black market. In one scene, Salim leaves his house with a bag full of unauthorized audio cassette tapes. At a street stall, a chubby boy is calling out 'New Cassette!', 'New Cassette!', but he changes his words to 'New Ahangaran!'[1] when an Islamist militiaman is passing. Salim meets his business partner in a public park to deliver the bag, but the Revolutionary Guard officers chase them and arrest his partner; Salim manages to run away. Twenty years later, we see Salim has upgraded his devices to CDs and DVDs instead of audio cassettes. He is also negotiating with a partner to enter into an emerging market: satellite dishes.

The movie portrays the black market keeping pace with technological changes, from audio and video cassettes in the 1980s to DVDs and satellite television in the 2000s. Soon after the 1979 Islamic revolution, the clerical rulers imposed Islamic principles on almost all social

---

1   'New Ahangaran' means, a new eulogy from Sadegh Ahangaran, an iconic eulogist during Iran-Iraq war in the 1980s. His performance encouraged many young Iranians to volunteer in the war.

and political institutions, from marriage, divorce and penal codes to banking and commerce. The state attempted not only to transform social and political structures, but also to control people's moral attitudes. Books, newspapers, magazines, music, and movies were subjected to extensive regulation and censorship. The state-owned television and radio dominated the media landscape in the post-revolutionary era.

The new regime presented its restrictive policies as defending Islam and Iranian national interests against western 'cultural invasion' and 'soft war'. Underlying these representations were the authorities' concerns about the increasing secularization of society and the growing alienation of youth from the state. Unwilling to acknowledge the ineffectiveness of forceful Islamization, the hardliners have accused the western media of subverting Islamic values and threatening the state's political legitimacy.

The black market of CDs and DVDs is still alive. Around Enqelab square in Tehran, many video dealers sell uncensored Hollywood movies. At times the police raid the area and confiscate the DVDs. Nevertheless, the internet and satellite television have largely replaced such markets. Reducing the regime's grip on information flow, new communication technologies have provided Iranians with unprecedented access to global news, information, and images. Feeling gravely threatened, the government has invested vast sums of money, instituted several councils and bodies, and devised many policies, laws and regulations to control and curb cross-border information flow. In what follows, we describe the methods employed by the government to restrict citizens' access to global media content and those employed by citizens to circumvent censorship – from illegal satellite dishes to VPNs, proxies and peer-to-peer networking. In particular, we focus on the internet and satellite television, the technologies that have generated significant political and cultural conflicts in Iran and created video cultures outside official channels.

Satellite Television: a New Video Culture

To understand internet circumvention in Iran, we must take a step back to consider an earlier kind of unauthorised media. Since the 1990s, foreign-based Persian-language satellite channels have mushroomed, posing a serious challenge to the regime's monopoly over broadcast media. The satellite television networks offer all sorts of programs, ranging from news, commentary and politics to music, entertainment and soap operas. The state has banned satellite television 'to protect the country's cultural borders and the foundations of family' against immoral content. The law bans selling, buying, installing, and using satellite television equipment such as dishes and receivers. Nevertheless, the majority of Iranians easily access these channels by installing dishes on rooftops and balconies. The Minister of Culture and Islamic Guidance, Ali Jannati, reported that 71 per cent of people in Tehran watch satellite TV.[2] Although this figure is likely to be inflated, watching satellite TV has no doubt become a widespread practice among city dwellers.

---

2   Setareh Derakhshesh, 'Breaking the Law to go Online in Iran', *New York Times*, 24 June 2014, http://www.nytimes.com/2014/06/25/opinion/breaking-the-law-to-go-online-in-iran.html.

The authorities have used various methods of crackdown. At times, the police raid buildings and confiscate dishes. They have used helicopters to scan rooftops and cranes to seize dishes from balconies. Police have abseiled down the sides of tall buildings in search of dishes. These methods have largely been futile because the dishes have soon reappeared on rooftops. These familiar cat-and-mouse games have been memorably depicted in Iranian movies such as Parisa Bakhtavar's *Tambourine* and Abdolreza Kahani's *Absolute Rest*.

The state has also employed more sophisticated and effective methods such as satellite jamming. Powerful noise signals are sent directly to satellites such as HotBird and Eutelsat, mixing frequencies and jamming their signals. Home viewers then see scrambled images on screen. BBC Persian and Voice of America (VoA) have been the typical targets. Iran has never acknowledged using such methods, but international organizations have claimed that the jamming signals are sent from within Iran. The UN telecommunications body (ITU) and the European Union have called on the Iranian government to stop satellite jamming and electronic interference. It is also widely believed that the Revolutionary Guard runs the jamming system. Not surprisingly, the regime uses this method more actively at times of political upheaval and during elections.

Despite the attempts outlined above, Iranians have integrated satellite television into their daily lives. Political channels such as BBC Persian and Voice of America (VoA) continue to influence public opinion by highlighting and disseminating news, images, videos and information that the state tries to suppress. Persian-language entertainment channels such as Manoto have attracted large audience by running western-style talent shows and competitions. Other channels such as GEM TV and Farsi One have attracted viewers by screening popular movies and soap operas. None of the above mentioned methods have proved effective in discouraging ordinary people from watching satellite TV. At times of political upheaval, the state has been relatively successful in jamming some political channels; at other times, however, satellite channels have managed to reach out to viewers and help create a video culture very different from the ideologically-fuelled one promoted by the state television.

A Halal Internet

Statistics on the number of Iranian internet users are inconsistent. While the Iranian government counts about 40 million internet users out of a population of 75 million, the World Bank estimates the number to be around 23 million.[3] The Iranian Minister of Culture and Islamic Guidance, Ali Jannati, reported that 9.5 million Iranians use Viber and 4 to 5 million use Facebook.[4] Although the Universal Declaration of Human Rights considers everyone entitled 'to seek, receive and impart information and ideas through any media and regardless of frontiers', Iran, which is a signatory, has blocked social media sites such as Facebook and YouTube, political dissidents' blogs and websites, and international news websites.

---

3   Iran's Internet Penetration Management Portal, 2014, Penetration Rate Report, 2014, http://www.
     iriu.ir/matma/; The World Bank, Internet users by country, 2014, http://data.worldbank.org/indicator/
     IT.NET.USER.P2.
4   Mehr News Agency, '9.5 Million Viber users in Iran', 5 Feb 2015, http://www.mehrnews.com/news/.

The London-based advocacy group Small Media reports a threefold strategy employed by the government to control the internet. Firstly, Authorities aim to 'prevent' users from accessing the perceived threatening content through keyword filtering, URL blacklisting, and broadband speed limitations. For example, users who attempt to access YouTube see the following image, which reads: 'Access to the requested website is not possible', and introduces a list of miscellaneous websites. Next, they exploit technology to 'intercept' those who have managed to get around censorship through monitoring, tracking and blocking internet traffic. Lastly, internet activists and developers are arrested and connections are throttled during political turmoils.[5]

Figure 1. Iranian internet users see this government notice when trying to access blocked websites. It reads: 'Access to the requested website is not possible. Please click here to access reports and complaints'

Taking office as President in 2013, Hassan Rouhani criticized internet censorship, raising hopes for reducing internet barriers (to be discussed further below). However, he faced fierce opposition from conservative rivals. In 2014, as soon as the ICT ministry issued 3G and 4G licenses to two mobile-phone operators, a leading cleric called on the government to revoke them because 'dirty pictures and clips' could poison young minds. Comparing these technologies to 'unsanitary and muddy water', and worrying about 'all sorts of polluted films without any filtering', he declared that '3G mobile communication services and higher are against Sharia [Islamic law] and moral and human norms'.[6]

---

5 Kyle Bowen and James Marchant, 'Internet Censorship in Iran: Preventative, Interceptive, and reactive', Small Media report: Revolution decoded, 2014, p.26, http://smallmedia.org.uk/revolutiondecoded/.

6 Thomas Erdbrink, 'Tehran unfetters cell phones, and the pictures start flowing', The New York Times, 2 September 2014, http://www.nytimes.com/2014/09/03/world/asia/iran-speeds-up-cellphone-connections.html.

Perhaps Iran's most ambitious plan for extending its control over the internet has been the launching of a 'walled-off' national internet. The network will connect government minis-tries, universities, banks, healthcare, tax systems, and other state institutions through local servers. Although users will benefit from higher speed and better cyber-security, many are concerned that the government's main motive is to consolidate its control over the internet. In response to such concerns, Iran's ICT minister, Mahmoud Vaezi, claimed that the national internet 'is not in competition with the internet' and that 'if users cannot find the data that they are looking for on the national internet, then they will be able to access the internet to search for it, instead'.[7] Put it simply, the government aims to obtain the capacity of switching off the internet without disrupting public services, banks, and corporations. It is, however, unlikely that the government could completely detach Iran from the global internet; the more likely outcome would be a 'dual-internet structure' like that currently used in some other authoritarian countries.[8]

Work on the national internet project started in 2005, and has progressed slowly since then. In recent years, at least two events caused the conservative authorities to be more deter-mined to carry the project through. In the aftermath of the 2009 presidential election, where millions of Iranians took to the streets to protest against Mahmoud Ahmadinejad's disputed victory, the regime experienced an unprecedented challenge to official media control. During rallies, protesters used their mobile phones to take pictures and video footage of police brutality and violence, posting them on social media. Global news coverage of the regime's brutal crackdown led to the condemnation of the regime by many international human rights organizations and governments. The second alarming event was the Stuxnet attacks on Iranian nuclear facilities in 2010, where the country's prized nuclear arsenal was overtaken by a computer virus, thus highlighting the perceived threat posed by foreign, unauthorised digital technologies to the Iranian state.

Internet Circumvention Tools

Despite government restrictions, users often find ways to get around internet censorship. In a survey conducted by Iran's Ministry of Youth Affairs and Sport, 69 per cent of respondents said they use anti-filtering software.[9] Ironically, users can even buy VPNs through official online payment gateways, such as PardakhtNet! Given how easily available these VPN ser-vices are, it is widely believed that segments of the ruling establishment (including elements within the Revolutionary Guard) facilitate the trade to earn money.[10] In this environment, critics rightly question the effectiveness of numerous laws, policies, and regulations in place to control internet access. Criticizing his conservative opponents, the moderate president Hassan Rouhani asked: 'Supporters of internet filtering should explain whether they've successfully restricted access to information? Which important piece of news has filtering

---

7   Small Media, http://www.smallmedia.org.uk/.
8   Christopher Rhoads and Farnaz Fassihi, 'Iran vows to unplug internet', *Wall Street Journal*, 28 May 2011, http://www.wsj.com/articles/SB10001424052748704889404576277391449002016.
9   Iranian Student News Agency, 69 Per cent of Iranian Youth use Anti-filtering, According to the Findings of a New Survey, 27 April 2015, http://isna.ir/fa/news/.
10   Small Media, http://smallmedia.org.uk/.

been able to black out in recent years?' He continued: 'Filtering has not even stopped people from accessing unethical [pornographic] websites. Widespread online filtering will only increase distrust between the people and the state'[11].

Users take advantage of numerous tools to get around censorship. A Freedom House survey revealed that VPNs, Google (Reader, Translation, Cache), and Your Freedom are the most popular circumvention tools in Iran. The survey listed the most popular tools in Iran as the following: Dynaweb, Freegate, Freenet, Garden GTunnel, Google, Gpass, HotspotShield, JAP, Proxy, Psiphon, Tor, Ultrasurf, Your Freedom, and VPN.[12] Filtershekanha (means 'Filter breakers') is an email list with over 100,000 subscribers through which information about VPNs is distributed among users. Another survey of 423 users, conducted by Small Media, found that Hotspot Shield, Psiphon, and Kerio are favored by users.[13] Other surveys have also reported the widespread use of the web proxy service Hotspot Shield and Psiphon3, a peer-to-peer VPN app for Android and Windows.[14] As of 2013, Psiphon claimed to have 700,000 to 900,000 daily unique users in Iran. This number is now believed to have surpassed one million.[15]

Small Media reports that the terrain of internet circumvention is increasingly shifting to mobile, with the most popular tools having easy-to-use mobile-enabled interfaces now. It also points out that, TOR, despite its strong privacy protection, is not very popular among Iranians partly because it has been constantly attacked by the government. Overall, Iranians seem to care more about ease of access than security. There are also anti-filtering tools that are unique to Iran. For example, Simurgh is 'Iranian stand-alone proxy software' which has been widely used since 2009; due to its small size (1 MB), users with low speed connection can download it easily. It is also free. This software has been recently used by Syrian dissidents.[16]

The Political Context of Circumvention

Despite common perceptions, most Iranians do not go online specifically in search of 'forbidden' political material; rather they wish to go about their everyday lives by accessing social media such as Telegram, Viber, Facebook and the like to communicate with their

11   Saeed Kamali-Dehghan, 'Iran's President Signals Softer Line on Web Censorship and Islamic Dress Code', The Guardian, 3 July 2013, http://www.theguardian.com/world/2013/jul/02/iran-president-hassan-rouhani-progressive-views.

12   Freedom House, 'Country Report for End Users in Iran', 2011, https://freedomhouse.org/sites/default/files/LOtF_Iran.pdf.

13   Small Media, http://www.smallmedia.org.uk/.

14   Patrick Howell O'Neill, 'The Big Money Behind Iran's Internet Censorship', The Daily Dot, 22 Feb 2015, http://www.dailydot.com/politics/iran-censorship-circumvention-tech/.

15   Resa Mohabbat-Kar and Nicolas Hausdorf, 'Internet Freedom, Snapshot of the Case of Iran', Transparency for Iran, 2010, http://transparency-for-iran.org/wp-content/uploads/TFI-Report.pdf, p.45.

16   It was recently announced that a malicious copy of this software has been circulated as 'Simurgh-setup.zip' that compromises all information on the infected computer. See: The Citizen Lab, 'Iranian Anti-Censorship Software "Simurgh" Circulated with Malicious Backdoor', 25 May 2015, https://citizenlab.org/2012/05/iranian-anti-censorship-software-simurgh-circulated-with-malicious-backdoor-2/.

family members and friends. They share photos, music videos, comedies, shows, and educational material within their social circles; they look for entertainment, search for all sorts of information and read news online. A question that naturally arises is: why then are authorities so sensitive about the free internet? The answer has to do with the ideological nature of the Iranian state.

The clerics and conservative rulers censor the internet for the same reason that they have put in place extremely restrictive measures to uphold Islamic principles and moral standards in public spaces. They are concerned that freedom will inevitably give rise to western lifestyles, mixing with the opposite sex and promiscuity. Despite extensive regulation, conservatives are constantly complaining about the growing un-Islamic practices in society. The same concerns lead them to oppose the unfettered internet. In their view, the free internet would weaken their grip over cultural production and consumption. In a country where interactions between young men and women are severely controlled, it is not surprising that the authorities are worried about online communication. The political power of religion in Iran does not allow for a cultural sphere separate from politics.

Finally, it is worth noting an important difference between Iran and other cases discussed in this book. Iranians struggle with filtering as much as internet speed. Authorities have kept the speed extremely slow as a deliberate method to frustrate users and discourage them from downloading photos and videos. Based on nationwide regulations, ISPs are permitted to provide speed connection only up to 128 kbps to home users, which is 50 times slower than the internet speed in the US.[17] Academics and professionals could receive higher speed up to 512 kbps and in special circumstances up to 2 mbps. As mentioned earlier, the government attempt at providing higher speed 3G and 4G licences to mobile operators was strongly opposed by Parliament and influential clerics. Conservatives continue to obstruct any attempt at raising internet speed until the national internet comes into full operation. They call the national internet a 'Halal' internet, an expression that reveals their concerns about the cultural impact of the free internet and the potential rise of a video culture that could jeopardise their cherished values.

Future Trends

The Islamic Republic of Iran has struggled to maintain and strengthen cultural sovereignty within its borders. By establishing numerous cultural, political, and legal institutions, the regime has invested enormously in constructing and imposing Islamic identity on all spheres of social life. The state has set itself the ambitious task not only of restructuring the entire society on the basis of Islamic values, but also of controlling and guiding people's thoughts and morality. The policies, however, have not been executed very effectively and consistently. Constitutionally, Iranians vote in the government through elections, and despite all state restrictions, at times people have defeated the ruling conservatives. President Khatami

---

17   Timothy B. Lee, 'Here's How Iran Censors the Internet', *The Washington Post*, 15 August 2015, https://www.washingtonpost.com/news/the-switch/wp/2013/08/15/heres-how-iran-censors-the-internet/.

(1997-2005) campaigned for social and political freedom and sought constructive engagement with the West, policies that were strongly resisted by hardliners. In 2013, Hassan
Rouhani won the presidential election after campaigning on moderate foreign and domestic
policies. Many hoped that his government would reduce internet barriers and relax ultra-
conservative regulation of culture and politics.

President Rouhani has symbolically and rhetorically opposed state censorship. While Twitter
is blocked in Iran, Rouhani's Twitter account has over 330,000 followers. Zarif, the foreign
minister, actively tweets about Iran's foreign policy issues. Rouhani has called internet filtering
'futile', saying: 'We cannot close the gates of the world to our young generation'.[18] Despite
these positive signs, as far as media censorship is concerned, Rouhani's discretion is limited.
The decision-making bodies are supra-governmental and mostly controlled by the conservatives. The Supreme Council of Cyberspace (SCC), which is the highest state organization
responsible for devising cyber policies, works under the supreme leader's directive. Given
these limitations, a radical and thoroughgoing change would be unlikely to happen. At best,
Rouhani's policies will bring about slow and incremental changes in the coming years.

The friction between state policies and social reality in Iran offers an intriguing case for media
analysts. Technological changes have provided a good opportunity for ordinary citizens to
circumvent barriers and access global media content. On the other hand, the state has
sophisticated its methods and technologies to maintain its dominance over information
flows. Iranian moderate politicians feel the state will ultimately lose this game. The Culture
and Islamic Guidance minister, Ali Jannati, compared the current prohibition of satellite
television and social media to the banning of video cassettes in the 1980s, as portrayed in
the movie Bullet Proof. Calling such policies 'ridiculous', he said: 'Maybe in five years we
will laugh at today's actions'.[19] However, given that the Iranian Islamic state has defined its
identity in opposition to western culture and imperial powers, it will continue to actively resist
pressure from the western-controlled global media in order to maintain the existing media
communication boundaries in the foreseeable future.

References

Bowen, Kyle and James Marchant. 'Internet Censorship in Iran: Preventative, Interceptive, and
reactive, Small Media report: Revolution Decoded, 2014, p.26, http://smallmedia.org.uk/revolution-
decoded/.

Derakhshesh, Setareh. 'Breaking the Law to Go Online in Iran', New York Times, 24 June 2014,
http://www.nytimes.com/2014/06/25/opinion/breaking-the-law-to-go-online-in-iran.html.

Erdbrink, Thomas. 'Tehran Unfetters Cellphones, and the Pictures Start Flowing', The New York
Times, 2 September 2014, http://www.nytimes.com/2014/09/03/world/asia/iran-speeds-up-cell-
phone-connections.html.

---

18   Arash Karami, 'Iran Cleric Explains He's Not Opposed to "Filtered" 3G Phones, Almonitor, 1
      September 2014, http://www.al-monitor.com/pulse/originals/2014/09/iran-3g-phones-filter-
      unsanitary-water.html#.
19   Michael Pizzi, 'Iran Government Minister: Media Bans May Seem "laughable" in 5 years', Aljazeera
      America, 19 Dec 2013, http://america.aljazeera.com/articles/2013/12/19/iranian-ministermediabansm
      ayseemlaughablein5years.html.

Freedom House. 'Country Report for End Users in Iran', 2011, https://freedomhouse.org/sites/default/files/LOtF_Iran.pdf.

Iranian Student News Agency. '69 Per Cent of Iranian Youth Use Anti-Filtering, According to the Findings of a New Survey', 27 April 2015, http://isna.ir/fa/news/93061710204.

Iran's Internet Penetration Management Portal. Penetration Rate Report, 2014, http://www.iriu.ir/matma/;.

Kamali-Dehghan, Saeed. 'Iran's President Signals Softer Line on Web Censorship and Islamic Dress Code', *The Guardian,* 3 July 2013, http://www.theguardian.com/world/2013/jul/02/iran-president-hassan-rouhani-progressive-views.

Karami, Arash. 'Iran Cleric Explains He's Not Opposed to "Filtered" 3G Phones', *Almonitor*, 1 September 2014, http://www.al-monitor.com/pulse/originals/2014/09/iran-3g-phones-filter-unsanitary-water.html.

Lee, Timothy B. 'Here's How Iran Censors the Internet', *The Washington Post*, 15 August 2015, https://www.washingtonpost.com/news/the-switch/wp/2013/08/15/heres-how-iran-censors-the-internet/.

Mehr News Agency. '9.5 Million Viber Users in Iran', 5 Feb 2015, http://www.mehrnews.com/news/.

Mohabbat-Kar Resa and Hausdorf Nicolas. 'Internet Freedom, Snapshot of the Case of Iran', *Transparency for Iran*, 2010, http://transparency-for-iran.org/wp-content/uploads/TFI-Report.pdf.

O'Neill, Patrick Howell. 'The Big Money Behind Iran's Internet Censorship', 22 Feb 2015, http://www.dailydot.com/politics/iran-censorship-circumvention-tech/.

Pizzi, Michael. 'Iran Government Minister: Media Bans May Seem "Laughable" in 5 Years', Aljazeera America, 19 Dec 2013, http://america.aljazeera.com/articles/2013/12/19/iranian-ministermediabans-mayseemlaughablein5years.html.

Rhoads, Christopher and Farnaz Fassihi. 'Iran Vows to Unplug Internet', *Wall Street Journal*, 28 May 2011, http://www.wsj.com/articles/SB10001424052748704889404576277391449002016.

Small Media. http://www.smallmedia.org.uk/.

The Citizen Lab. 'Iranian Anti-Censorship Software "Simurgh" Circulated with Malicious Backdoor', 25 May 2015, https://citizenlab.org/2012/05/iranian-anti-censorship-software-simurgh-circulated-with-malicious-backdoor-2/.

The World Bank. Internet Users by Country, 2014, http://data.worldbank.org/indicator/IT.NET.USER.P2.

CUBA: *VIDEOS TO THE LEFT* – CIRCUMVENTION PRACTICES AND AUDIOVISUAL ECOLOGIES

FIDEL A. RODRIGUEZ

30%

Proportion of Cubans aged 16-54 who have access to the internet

$2

Hourly cost for a 100 Mbit/s fiber connection in CUC/USD

0%

Proportion of internet users who made online purchases in 2014 from Cuban accounts

0%

Proportion of internet users who paid for a video streaming service in 2014 from Cuban accounts

'*Starting today, people in Cuba with internet connections and access to international payment methods will be able to subscribe to Netflix and instantly watch a curated selection of popular movies and TV shows.*' – Netflix press release, 9 February 2015

Havana, January 2015. A young reggaeton singer is detained by the police in a luxurious house on the outskirts of the city. The arrest is quickly reported in foreign news media outlets, with Reuters first breaking the story. These reports describe a pending court case in Florida, involving alleged major fraud of the U.S. Medicare health program. Photos of the singer's extravagant lifestyle are published in the media, where he poses with bundles of cash and firearms.

The singer's arrest is captured by bystanders and neighbors on mobile phones. While there is no coverage of the arrest in the Cuban media, amateur videos soon begin to circulate via unregulated wifi networks that operate across Havana. A few days later, another video appears on YouTube, this time recorded by a motorcyclist who was driving by the scene of the arrest. In the following weeks, a recording of the singer's police interview also starts to circulate across the city, passed around through USB drives. Finally, these materials make their way into commercial pirate distribution, appearing as a folder in *el paquete* ('the package') – a regularly updated compilation of pirated video and music files that is circulated across Cuba through thousands of local redistributors.

The story of Gilbert Man, the stage name of the artist in question, reveals how video circulates informally in Cuba today. Geoblocking is not a major issue for Cubans – slow internet connections make video streaming almost impossible, and access is mostly limited to government offices and institutions – but circumvention is a mainstream, everyday practice. Recent years have seen the emergence, *a la izquierda* ('to the left'), of a surprising ecology of transnational video circulation practices making use of diverse technological workarounds. These processes draw attention to the transformation of media access in the country, in the context of an expanding but still limited internet infrastructure. They also reflect the distinctive media geography of Cuba, which partakes in global flows of digital video content, but in a unique way that combines networked and offline distribution systems.

The term 'to the left' does not refer to a party-political position in Cuban everyday speech. Ironically, it refers to all types of non-formal methods to access goods or services. This phrase has become popular since the 1990s, referring to the economic struggle of ordinary people. It evokes the Cuban style of proxy access to all sites, through all connections.

Skipping Back: Revolution, Videos and Access

Universal access to culture has been a foundational ideal of the Cuban revolutionary project since 1959. As part of the political demands of the new era,[1] cinema production became a priority for the government, and a national institute dedicated to cinema – the Instituto Cubano del Arte y la Industria Cinematográficos – was founded in April 1959. In practice, this vision was undermined by the economic and political ruptures of the Cold War. During the 1960s, Cuban policymakers approved the use of unlicensed cultural materials – including foreign copyrighted materials such as movies and books – as they were seen to be valuable for the cultural development of the nation. However, this universal vision of access coexists with state regulation of culture and media, according to the political programme of the Communist Party. This policy limits access to audiovisual content to officially sanctioned government spaces and facilities.

In response, a massive, extra-legal culture of media circulation has emerged. Officially banned movies are widely available, leading to much public debate about censorship. State-run TV channels screen pirated HBO programming on a daily basis. Despite the increasing cost of living, TVs, DVD players and digital devices for recording and playback can be purchased privately and are no longer distributed by the state. The acquisition and use of this equipment has become an important status symbol for Cuban families.[2]

---

1   Yanet Toirac, *Política cultural: Una propuesta de enfoque comunicológico para su estudio*, PhD diss., Havana University, Cuba, 2009.
2   Anna Cristina Pertierra, *Cuba. The Struggle for Consumption*, Coconut Creek, FL: Caribbean Studies Press, 2011.

Until 2007, the sale of VHS or CD/DVD equipment was illegal. Nonetheless, private video rental outlets proliferated across the country. Despite their illegal status they were generally tolerated by the authorities. For the first time, these practices put private citizens and household businesses in a social environment of audiovisual consumption, and relocated media consumption to private spaces.[3]

In the pre-digital period, a small official VHS movie rental and sales circuit existed in Cuba, but prices were prohibitively expensive for most people. Hotels and shopping centers stocked a small selection of prestige Cuban movies on VHS, with pricing aimed at the tourist market. Another program in the early 2000s established movie rental facilities in some theaters, featuring a catalog of quality titles, but lacking the variety of the private video stores. Aside from a few other small-scale initiatives, these are the only authorized systems of home video distribution organized by the Cuban government. The few video-streaming repositories managed by state institutions include only a small selection of titles, and do not carry the more popular Cuban productions.

In 2013, a landmark reform of economic regulation in Cuba allowed private sale of pirate CDs and DVDs in the streets, and specified the kinds of tax that such enterprises would pay. In the case of Cuban media the regulations permit public screening for noncommercial purposes and with the recognition of the authors. This system of sanctioned small-scale distribution continues today. It is a matter of some controversy, however, because some artists regard the system as tantamount to official sanctioning of piracy At the same time, "the pirate" does not exist as a criminal figure in Cuba.[4]

There have been other changes in Cuban media policy along the way. For example, in 2013 a new ruling led to the mass closure of private 3D cinemas, which had become popular in recent years – however two years later the government announced that some state-owned 3D cinemas would reopen across the country.

Another important practice is the acquisition of cable TV receivers, which are still illegal for Cuban citizens to own. This informal cable TV system in Cuba requires the installation of a modified receiver acquired on the black market, and operated on a sublease basis. Wiring is run through the roof and attached to the telephone wiring in areas near the signal receiver. These channel packages usually include American TV programming aimed at the Cuban community of emigrants in Miami. In 2007 and 2009, various investigations confirmed access to these services as a common cultural practice among families in different neighborhoods of Havana.[5]

---

3   Anna Cristina Pertierra, 'Private pleasures: Watching videos in Post-Soviet Cuba', *International Journal of Cultural Studies* 12.2 (2009): 113-130.
4   Karina Abad, *La piratería en Cuba*, Law School, Guantánamo University, 2013, Cuba, http://caribeña. eumed.net/wp-content/uploads/pirateria-cuba.pdf.
5   Yanet Barrera, *La revuelta del espectador: Estudio exploratorio sobre el consumo mediático alternativo*, MA Thesis, Havana University, Cuba, 2009.

Even when media devices like computers and HDD players are not available through shops, they can be acquired on the black market. Official statistics from 2014 suggest a very small percentage of private ownership of these items,[6] but the real figures are likely higher.

Since the 1980s the government has been involved in community ICT programmes, and these have also been instrumental in the daily experience of media and internet use in Cuba. One initiative, known as the Youth Computing Club, offers free or low-cost access to computers along with training in computer skills. These clubs are joined together in a national network that offers blogs and social networking sites, which also connects to other national internal networks linked to the educational and health sectors. Through membership of these networks, some Cubans are able to get online regularly – one example is the Infomed network of health workers who acquired free access to the internet in September 2015. This opening-up of internet access represents an important increase in the number of home connections. However, access is restricted to 25 hours a month, on a very low-speed connection. While networks such as these are limited by the infrastructure they use and the legal framework governing them, these home internet networks could nonetheless play a major role in the development of a nation-wide content-sharing platform.

Internet Dilemmas

Cuba has been connected to the internet by satellite since 1996, through a special license from the United States Department of Commerce, as an exception to the laws forbidding economic relations with the island. In 2012 – before the first optical fiber cable connection was established with Venezuela – Cuba's connectivity rate was 458 Mbs input/229 Mbs output,[7] comparable to that of an apartment building in the United States. In light of the lack of available bandwidth and infrastructure the government's official internet policy was to prioritise connectivity to government institutions and select user groups.[8] Hence the Cuban internet came to be officially understood as a repository of information, tools for electronic commerce and a means for information dissemination.[9] This approach to internet regulation was also shaped by the conflict with the United States, which has long funded projects involving ICTs as tools of political subversion to undermine the Cuban government.[10]

Personal use of social networking sites at government institutions was usually restricted or limited to low-traffic times. As a result, the practical knowledge of forms of proxy access

---

6   National Statistics Office, *Tecnologías de información y las comunicaciones: Indicadores seleccionados*, 2015, http://www.one.cu/ticis2014.html.

7   Milena Recio, 'La hora de los desconectados. Evaluación del diseño de la política de "acceso social" a Internet en Cuba en un contexto de cambios', *Bimestre Cubana* 116.41 (2014), http://www.bimestrecubana.cult.cu/ojs/index.php/revistabimestre/article/viewArticle/177.

8   Milena Recio, 'La hora de los desconectados'.

9   Elaine Díaz and Firuzeh Sokooh, 'Internet y las TIC en Cuba: Notas para un debate sobre políticas públicas', *Temas* 2013, https://telos.fundaciontelefonica.com/url-direct/pdf-generator?tipoContenido=articuloTelos&idContenido=2014070113270001&idioma=es.

10   Patricia Moloney, 'Promoting Global Internet Freedom: Policy and Technology', Congressional Research Service, 2013, https://www.fas.org/sgp/crs/row/R41837.pdf.

to these sites became a shared secret. Nonetheless, for almost all Cubans the very slow internet speeds made social networking impossible until the wifi zones appeared in 2015 (see below).

In 2012, the state-owned telecommunications company ETECSA implemented the first open internet access service. Costing 4.50CUC per hour (US$5.10), the service was available at workstations in municipal offices, after registration of personal data. The price was extremely high, and even providers considered it excessive.[11] As a result, this initiative received much criticism. However, the Cuban First Vice President said in a national convention on ICTs and cybersecurity in January 2015 that the state was willing to extend open internet access across the country. This was followed by the announcement of a plan to connect all schools in Cuba and improve the internet infrastructure of universities, where limited access was already available. In July, ETECSA started a wireless internet service in 35 public spaces around Cuba at a price of 2CUC per hour.

This rate is still considered high, but has resulted in a substantial increase in use. According to the National Statistics Office, in 2014 there were 3 million internet users, representing 27 percent of the total population.[12] Nonetheless, Cuba still comes in at 160th place on the International Telecommunication Union's ranking of global ICT use and access. These facts, combined with the country's history of informal interchange and non-market cultural consumption, help to explain the diversity and complexity of video circulation practice in present-day Cuba, which interface with global networks but use primarily *offline* distribution methods within Cuba.

Videos Without Time or Space: 'The Package'

In parallel to these structural constraints on internet access, various workarounds have emerged in Cuba. One well-documented phenomenon is USB sharing, which since the mid-2000s has become an efficient system for digital media circulation in Cuba.[13] Over

---

11   Milena Recio, 'La hora de los desconectados'.
12   National Statistics Office, 'Tecnologías de información y las comunicaciones'.
13   This has been documented by a number of researchers. See: Yanet Barrera, Yanet *La revuelta del espectador. Estudio exploratorio sobre el consumo mediático alternativo*, MA Thesis, Havana University, Cuba, 2009; Cecilia Linares et al., *El consumo cultural y sus prácticas en Cuba*, Cuban Institute of Cultural Investigation Juan Marinello, La Habana, Cuba, 2009; Anna Cristina Pertierra, 'If They Show "Prison Break" in the United States on a Wednesday, by Thursday it is Here: Mobile Media Networks in Twenty-First Century in Cuba', *Television and New Media* 13.5 (2012): 399–414; Dayne Castañeda and Daynet Fonseca, *Teleadictos: Conquistando la TV por la izquierda. Aproximación a la construcción de sentidos a partir del consumo mediático informal de programas audiovisuales en el asentamiento precario San Pablo en Santiago de Cuba*, Bachelor Thesis, East University, Cuba, 2014; Cinthya Cabrera, *Rutas USB, Acercamiento a la gestión de contenidos audiovisuales en el formato Paquete que realizan actores no institucionales en redes informales en La Habana*, Bachelor Thesis, Havana University, Cuba, 2015; José Raúl Concepción, *La cultura empaquetada: Análisis del consumo audiovisual informal del Paquete semanal en un grupo de jóvenes capitalinos*, Bachelor Thesis, Havana University, Cuba, 2015; Isabel Echemendía, *Copi@ y Comp@rte una vez a la semana: Acercamiento a los principales rasgos que caracterizan el consumo audiovisual informal del Paquetes Semanal en dos grupos de jóvenes de la capital de Mayabeque*, Bachelor Thesis, Havana University,

time this form of distribution has become standardized in a commercial format known as *el paquete* (the package). These compilations comprise one terabyte of diverse media content – television, movies, software, magazines and music – all updated on a weekly basis. The *paquete* typically includes: the latest episodes of TV shows direct from the United States, Spain, Mexico, Brazil, and Colombia; a selection of new documentaries; Cuban television shows; the latest music videos; and multiple TV programs from Miami. According to one study, 35% of the Havana population (almost 3 million people) are regular consumers of *el paquete* – although a lot of people access it through friends for free.[14] The mysterious origin of the weekly *paquete* is a source of collective obsession in Cuba, because until 2015 there were very few places that had the bandwidth to download such a large amount of data. Nonetheless, different researchers have confirmed that content in the *paquete* comes from has diverse sources, from cable antennas to P2P download sites.[15]

The price of the *paquete* is variable, depending on where you live and what day of the week you buy it.[16] The content selection within each weekly *paquete* is also variable, because distributors are known to add and remove videos as the *paquete* moves through the network, from the original compilers through to the high-level brokers ('first hands', 'big fishes') and ultimately to street-level retail and rental sites. At each level, distributors – mostly part-time or temporary workers who have become involved in the *paquete* business to make some money on the side – may add or remove content to suit local tastes, meaning that the product is rebuilt at each stage. Although some *paquete* distributors have implemented feedback mechanisms to cater to their customers' demand, user involvement in the selection of programming usually happens only during the final stage of street-level distribution.[17]

Figure 1. An example of a paquete

Distribution of the *paquete* is typically carried out discreetly, often through licensed street-side DVD vendors or private photocopying and printing centres. These activities are widely tolerated by officials. Several high-ranking government figures have publicly stated that they

Cuba, 2015; Vanessa Márquez, *El consumo del Paquete semanal en La Habana*, Social Research Center, Instituto Cubano de Radio y Televisión, 2015.

14   It is estimated that around 80% of users access the *paquete* for free, by sharing with friends and family. Vanessa Márquez, *El consumo del paquete*.
15   José Raúl Concepción, *La cultura empaquetada*.
16   Cinthya Cabrera, *Rutas USB*.
17   Cinthya Cabrera, *Rutas USB*.

do not intend to ban this trade. As a result, the *paquete* trade is widespread in the streets as well as on digital networks. For example, in the Cuban online marketplace Revolico.com – a Craigslist-style classifieds site for Cubans which, ironically, is accessible only through proxies – dealers advertise their various offerings and freely offer their mobile phone numbers. Interestingly, the contents of the *paquete* often include scraped data from Revolico.com so that people without internet access can browse its listings.

The social significance of this phenomenon has led to a broad public debate on the topic, involving senior officials in Cuban cultural policy. The level of media coverage is unprecedented for an informal market activity. These discussions have drawn new attention to certain aspects of the Cuban media environment: copyright legislation and its implementation, national internet infrastructure, consumer education, cultural policy, and the status of Cuban audiovisual production. Quality of content and the protection of national culture are particularly popular topics of debate. As a result, in 2015 the aforementioned Youth Computing Club began to distribute (for free) a *paquete*-like compilation created by government-linked cultural organizations, offering a selection of pirated 'quality' content, including movies and TV series.

Figure 2. A private photocopying and printing business in Havana openly advertises pirated videos. Photo: Fidel A. Rodriguez

The spread of *paquete* distribution has also led to the development of an advertising market, including unregistered advertising agencies. Digital publications generated exclusively for the *paquete* have multiplied. These publications cover topics underserved by the official Cuban press, including fashion and celebrity culture. Likewise, the *paquete* has also become a distribution space for locally-developed mobile apps. Even on state television broadcasts, the unique watermarks of certain *paquete* distributors can often be made out, revealing the origin of some of this content.

Informal Wireless Networks

Another popular means of video distribution in Cuba is through urban wifi networks. Concentrated in Havana, but also found in other parts of the country, these illegal networks are organized by communities of video game players. While none of these networks are connected to the internet, they nonetheless have their own forums, social network sites, massive voice chats, streaming stations, and FTP servers for downloading pirated video. It is impossible to determine the number of users with any precision, but the number of users is large and growing. In early 2015, one of the network's main sites had about 20,000 registered profiles. Complex forms of identity management and collective decision-making have evolved to regulate these networks.[18]

In these wifi communities, FTP content sharing is one of the most popular activities. Movies can be transmitted between different users in seconds. The weekly *paquete* is often available for download, thanks to an agreement with (and agreed payment to) the distributors. Some forms of local user-generated content are also available, including machinima, parody videos, flash mobs and remixes. FTP sharing etiquette is informally regulated, and has become a source of controversy within the community. Inappropriate downloading behavior can lead to a user being temporarily 'banned' through IP address blocking.

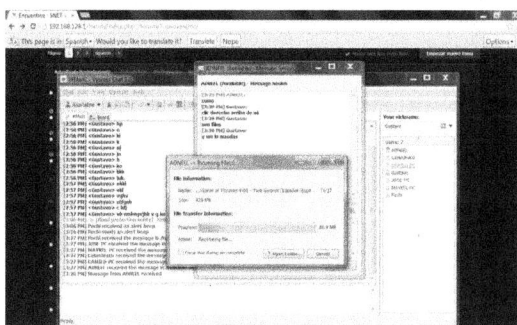

Figure 3. A Game of Thrones file transfer on an informal wireless network

The network is also used to check the scores of European football league matches. While the Cuban TV networks regularly broadcast live Bundesliga matches, along with some other leagues, a number of very popular teams can only be viewed in delayed broadcast. As a workaround, certain users of the wifi networks (those with internet or satellite TV access) upload short videos and game highlights from the broadcast, captured with their cell phones aimed at the TV screen.

Because of its illegal nature, this infrastructure is hidden. To keep a low profile, the community forbids commercial activities on the network. Internet-access sharing is also forbidden, along with political or religious debate. Except for some cases of commercial trading of internet access, the Cuban authorities have tolerated the existence of these networks. It is understood that the police have even offered protection when network hardware has been stolen (a common occurrence). Informal networks such as these are still illegal under Cuban law, but a range of evidence – including leaked documents, public statements by officials, and similar experiments by state authorities – suggest that this kind of network may have a place within official ICT and internet policy in Cuba.

---

18   Félix González, *Usos de los videojuegos en redes inalámbricas informales en La Habana*, Bachelor Thesis, Havana University, Cuba, 2015.

Transnational Ways to See: Video and the Diaspora

With a large community of Cuban immigrants in the United States, Canada, Latin America and Europe, transnational articulation of family ties is one of the most important social dynamics in the daily life of Cubans. Given the high cost of telephone calls and restricted internet access, communicating with family abroad can be a challenge. In 2015, a call to the United States cost about 88 cents a minute. In response, there is a longstanding tradition of asynchronous video exchange with the family through video letters and YouTube video uploads.[19]

It is therefore not surprising that Cubans are experimenting with online chat, using the aforementioned urban wifi networks as a means of access. Aside from Facebook video chat, the most widely used is the Chinese tool IMO for its low bandwidth requirements and high speed. Today, wifi-connected public spaces in Havana are full of people video chatting with family abroad (even though these users would probably prefer a more private environment). Software tools like IMO are usually shared among users through another popular Bluetooth application, Zapya, which is also frequently used for organized file-sharing meet-ups in parks and public spaces. In contrast, Skype is difficult to use in Cuba, as it is blocked to preserve the monopoly of the national telephone company. Those Cubans who do use Skype typically do so through VPN subscriptions maintained by friends and family outside Cuba.

Family ties are also strengthened through transnational consumption of Cuban music and culture. From Youtube to VOD sites, the proliferation of online streaming spaces provides access to Cuban-produced content for audiences outside Cuba. This system of video sharing is a response to the lack of an official streaming service for Cuban television, and the limited understanding of audiences outside the country.

Despite the access challenges, these forms of transnational video culture are increasingly widespread in Cuba. Video streaming is not practiced in the same way as in other countries, but the Cuban digital mediascape is nonetheless full of emergent forms of digital video consumption and communication that make efficient use of limited infrastructure.

Figure 4. A VPN advertisement in Revolico.com

---

19   Carlos Marcos Calzadilla, *Contar la Isla en videos. Un acercamiento a los rasgos que caracterizan el discurso sobre familias transnacionales cubanas a través de videos de usuarios no profesionales en YouTube*, Bachelor Thesis, Havana University. Cuba, 2014.

The Future

The diverse video practices described above are taking place in a context of rapid political and economic transformation in Cuba, particularly with regards to communication. For example, Netflix's announcement in 2015 that it would soon open its services to Cuban customers – even before it was available in major markets like Spain – crystalized some of the new scenarios associated with the normalization of diplomatic relations with the United States. But it also exposed the contradictions of digital culture in Cuba. Even though no Cubans could realistically access Netflix, due to the lack of credit cards and high-speed internet access, they were nonetheless already able to view all the latest *House of Cards* episodes through the multiple circulation methods described above.

Within these transformations, copyright will become increasingly important as a cultural policy issue. Interestingly, copyright enforcement in Cuba seems to have faded as a priority for the United States, as evidenced by the country's disappearance from the Special 301 list of most-infringing nations. At the same time, Cuban producers of media and commodity goods, such as tobacco and rum, have become more interested in actively exploiting their trademarks overseas. In September 2015 the major record label in Cuba, EGREEM, signed an agreement with Sony Music giving them global distribution rights to the entire EGREEM catalogue – the most important in the country. These developments reflect a changing attitude to copyright in Cuba. They may also entail new restrictions in the digital distribution of Cuban content, such as the many unauthorized YouTube uploads of Cuban recording artists which may now be subject to takedown requests by Sony.

While restricted internet access is a fact of life in Cuba, diverse circulatory practices provide effective workarounds for these blockages. The cultural consequences of this informal infrastructure are significant. Looking ahead, we may start to see a different kind of Cuban communication policy emerging, one that transcends a focus on containment and regulation, and instead uses the creative potential of an open, networked culture of circulation. Cuba now has the opportunity to pursue an alternative path of socioeconomic and cultural development, in line with the revolutionary project, but not limited by copyright trade guidelines or government restrictions.

References

Abad, Karina. *La piratería en Cuba*, Law School, Guantánamo University, 2013, Cuba, http://caribeña.eumed.net/wp-content/uploads/pirateria-cuba.pdf.

Barrera, Yanet. *La revuelta del espectador. Estudio exploratorio sobre el consumo mediático alternativo*, MA Thesis, Havana University, Cuba, 2009.

Cabrera, Cinthya. *Rutas USB. Acercamiento a la gestión de contenidos audiovisuales en el formato Paquete que realizan actores no institucionales en redes informales en La Habana,* Bachelor Thesis, Havana University, Cuba, 2015.

Calzadilla, Carlos Marcos. *Contar la Isla en videos. Un acercamiento a los rasgos que caracterizan el discurso sobre familias transnacionales cubanas a través de videos de usuarios no profesionales en YouTube*, Bachelor Thesis, Havana University. Cuba, 2014.

Castañeda, Dayne and Daynet Fonseca, *Teleadictos: conquistando la TV por la izquierda. Aproximación a la construcción de sentidos a partir del consumo mediático informal de programas audiovisuales en el asentamiento precario San Pablo en Santiago de Cuba,* Bachelor Thesis, East University, Cuba. 2014.

Concepción, José Raúl. *La cultura empaquetada: Análisis del consumo audiovisual informal del Paquete semanal en un grupo de jóvenes capitalinos*, Bachelor Thesis, Havana University, Cuba, 2015.

Díaz, Elaine and Firuzeh Sokooh, 'Internet y las TIC en Cuba: Notas Para un Debate Sobre Políticas Públicas, *Temas*, La Habana, 2013, https://telos.fundaciontelefonica.com/url-direct/pdf-generator?tipoContenido=articuloTelos&idContenido=2014070113270001&idioma=es.

Echemendía, Isabel, *Copi@ y Comp@rte una vez a la semana. Acercamiento a los principales rasgos que caracterizan el consumo audiovisual informal del Paquetes Semanal en dos grupos de jóvenes de la capital de Mayabeque*, Bachelor Thesis, Havana University, Cuba, 2015.

González, Félix. *Usos de los videojuegos en redes inalámbricas informales en La Habana*, Bachelor Thesis, Havana University, Cuba, 2015.

International Telecommunication Union. 'Measuring the Information Society Report', Geneva, Switzerland 2014, http://www.itu.int/en/ITU-D/Statistics/Documents/publications/mis2014/MIS2014_without_Annex_4.pdf.

Linares, Cecilia et al. *El consumo cultural y sus prácticas en Cuba*, Cuban Institute of Cultural Investigation Juan Marinello, La Habana, Cuba, 2009.

Márquez, Vanessa. 'El consumo del Paquete Semanal en La Habana', Social Research Center, Instituto Cubano de Radio y Televisión, unpublished version, 2015.

Moloney, Patricia. 'Promoting Global Internet Freedom: Policy and Technology', Congressional Research Service, 2013, https://www.fas.org/sgp/crs/row/R41837.pdf.

National Statistics Office. 'Tecnologías de Información y las Comunicaciones: Indicadores Seleccionados', 2015, http://www.one.cu/ticis2014.html.

Pertierra, Anna Cristina. 'Private Pleasures: Watching Videos in Post-Soviet Cuba', *International Journal of Cultural Studies* 12.2 (2009): 113-130.

_____. *Cuba: The Struggle for Consumption*, Coconut Creek, FL: Caribbean Studies Press, 2011.

_____. 'If They Show "Prison Break" in the United States on a Wednesday, by Thursday It Is Here: Mobile Media Networks in Twenty-First Century in Cuba', *Television and New Media* 13.5 (2012): 399–414.

Recio, Milena. 'La hora de los desconectados. Evaluación del diseño de la política de "acceso social" a Internet en Cuba en un contexto de cambios.' *Bimestre Cubana* 116.4 (2014), http://www.bimestrecubana.cult.cu/ojs/index.php/revistabimestre/article/viewArticle/177.

Toirac, Yanet. *Política cultural: Una propuesta de enfoque comunicológico para su estudio*, PhD diss., Havana University, Cuba, 2009.

THE USA: GEOBLOCKING IN A PRIVILEGED MARKET

EVAN ELKINS

36%

Percentage of American homes that subscribe to Netflix.[1]

20,000

Number of VPN communications the NSA aimed to survey per hour in 2011, according to the Edward Snowden documents.[2]

$39.95

Cost for a yearly subscription to popular VPN service Private Internet Access, in US$.[3]

22.6%

Percentage of North American Pirate Bay users who use a VPN service, according to a 2013 survey [4]

'Every now and then we feel the burn in the States, too' – Lifehacker, blogger Adam Pash, 2010.

The hashtag #NBCFail, which popped up regularly on social media in the summer of 2012, represented yet another chapter in the long story of American audiences' irritation at the often shallow, shoddy character of their national broadcast networks. This time, the target of viewers' ire was NBC's coverage of that year's Summer Olympics in London. Frustrated with tape-delayed events and the network's US-centric commentary, United States viewers naturally sought out the BBC's telecast as an alternative. Savvy viewers who did their research may have stumbled upon the BBC's iPlayer platform. The iPlayer was livestreaming the BBC's coverage of the Olympics, and thus promised live, superior coverage and an escape from NBC's jingoistic slant. Upon navigating to that platform, however, Americans

---

1   Rex Santus, 'Netflix is Now in 36% of Homes Across the United States', *Mashable*, 12 March 2015, http://mashable.com/2015/03/12/nielsen-ratings-2014.

2   Jacob Appelbaum et al., 'Prying Eyes: Inside the NSA's War on Internet Security', *Der Spiegel*, 28 December 2014, http://www.spiegel.de/international/germany/inside-the-nsa-s-war-on-internet-security-a-1010361.html.

3   'Buy Safe and Secure VPN', *Private Internet Access*, https://www.privateinternetaccess.com/pages/buy-vpn.

4   Ernesto, 'Find out Who's Using The Pirate Bay…and Why', *Torrent Freak*, 29 August 2013, https://torrentfreak.com/find-out-whos-using-the-pirate-bay-and-why-130829.

found this message: 'BBC iPlayer TV programmes are available to play in the UK only'.

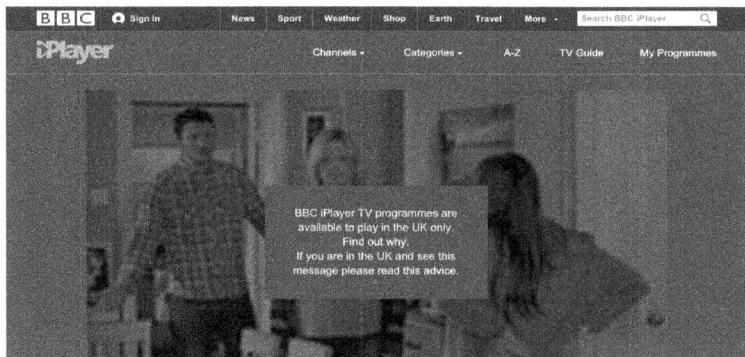

Figure 1. An example of geoblocked content on BBC iPlayer

In these moments, US residents confronted an experience of transnational viewing with which many around the world were already familiar. Viewers living in other countries under-stand geoblocking as a form of power emanating from major media conglomerates, many of which are rooted in Hollywood-based (yet globalized) cultural industries. As many of this book's other chapters make clear, geoblocking is just a part of the everyday viewing experience for people around the globe – albeit an often-frustrating one. Many of these experiences involve attempts at accessing American programming through platforms like Hulu or the American version of Netflix. But given that many of the platforms usually targeted in global complaints about geoblocking are, in fact, available in the US, what does geob-locking look like from *within* the United States? And how and why do people circumvent it?

Geoblocking in the United States is generally invisible – until it isn't. In other words, where-as viewers around the world have grown used to (which is not to say complacent about) geoblocking as a banal occurrence, it's something that many Americans likely only have a faint awareness of, to the extent that they even know it exists. American viewers that do encounter geoblocking are likely to fall within two overlapping audiences: diasporic groups and viewers who consciously seek out media from across borders (for example, cinephiles or fans of British television). This makes it a somewhat difficult phenomenon to grasp onto in the country. Geoblocking circumvention certainly doesn't have the same currency as it does in, say, Australia or the European Union. Put simply, most Americans have likely never experienced geoblocking or, at the very least, do not run into it regularly. Their relative wealth of access makes geoblocking – and its circumvention – less of a nationwide *cause célèbre* and more of a 'niche' or intermittent experience.

Geoblocking and Market Hierarchies

Many platforms that distribute American content use geoblocking, because the US cul-tural industries have been particularly militant with regard to preserving and controlling the distribution paths of intellectual properties. They do so following a business strategy that industry executive and author Jeff Ulin refers to as, naturally enough, 'Ulin's Rule', wherein the distribution value of media content is maximized through the exploitation of four factors: 'time, repeat consumption (platforms), exclusivity, and differential pricing'.[5] These factors are controlled through the development of distinct spatial and temporal distribution windows that geoblocking helps maintain. So, for instance, a film's US theatrical run would represent one window, and subsequent availability of that film on Netflix in Germany a few months later would represent another. In retaining distribution windows and ordering them along geographic borders (whether local, national, regional, continental, etc.), certain territories become more valuable or 'useful' to American media firms as markets, and release dates, prices, and different versions of texts and platforms are set accordingly. At the risk of generalizing what are in fact rather complex decisions about global distribution markets, this strategy enables powerful American media industries to 'rank' (even implicitly) the importance and value of particular markets relative to each other. In the age of DVD, this ranking was made apparent through the numerical region code system, with North America designated as Region 1. These rankings are still present in the practice of geoblocking even if they are less overt.

As this might indicate, if geoblocking can be explained functionally and practically by pointing to long-established industry practices, its cultural impacts are, for many viewers, more damaging and insulting in their valuing of certain territories over others. For instance, one *Wired* wiki article on how to access Pandora via VPN refers to geoblocking as a system of '*xenophobic* restrictions [that] are the result of U.S. and international copyright laws and restrictions.'[6] Although it's not entirely accurate to suggest that geoblocking exists purely because of copyright law (rather, it comes about through a combination of copyright restrictions, the media industries' international distribution and licensing agreements, and platforms not having been introduced to particular territories), the fact that some see it as a xenophobic and discriminatory practice spurred on by predominantly American corporate interests reflects the entanglements between geoblocking, American industrial power, and cultural difference. So, in addition to its more practical functions of shaping the distribution of media content, geoblocking reminds people who live in particular territories of their place within a global hierarchy of media access. If geoblocking is about access, and access is connected to power, then we can begin to think about the cultural and political consequences of geoblocking and, in turn, the reasons it makes people so angry. In addition, inquiring about what platforms are unavailable where (or, if they are technically available, how their costs and content libraries differ from the same platforms in other countries) raises questions about *why* the world is marked by differential access to new media.

If the US and its corporate interests are usually considered major forces shaping the geoblocking of platforms and content around the world, this makes geoblocking a tricky and curious phenomenon to investigate *within* the nation's borders. Many major entertainment platforms that remain geoblocked in territories around the world – Amazon Instant Video,

---

5   Jeff Ulin, *The Business of Media Distribution: Monetizing Film, TV, and Video Content*, Burlington, MA: Focal Press, 2000, p. 5.
6   'Access Pandora from Anywhere in the World', *Wired How-To Wiki*, 13 May 2010, http://howto.wired. com/wiki/Access_Pandora_From_Anywhere_in_the_World. My emphasis.

Hulu, iTunes, HBO Go – were created by US-based corporate entities to serve the American market first and foremost. Hulu in particular can essentially be considered a national broadcasting platform. Although its library has since grown to incorporate film, cable and "international" TV programs, trailers, and news, it was created by two of the major American commercial television networks (NBC and Fox) as a nationally bound exhibitor of broadcast programming. So, while geoblocking is not a part of the national conversation as much as it is in other countries, this doesn't mean that it is nonexistent in the US.

Major Geoblocked Platforms in the United States

The most infamous geoblocked platform in the United States – at least until 2011 – was the Swedish streaming music platform Spotify. Spotify was initially only available in Europe, and during its early years American listeners, critics, and industry figures alike made a lot of noise about the cornucopia of free (or at least cheap) music that remained just out of their grasp. While American consumers are less familiar with the experience of video geoblocking, given the industrial might of Hollywood, a few common scenarios can nonetheless be identified and are described below.

VOD Platforms Developed in or for Another Territory

A commonly repeated axiom holds that the development of VOD platforms has lead to – or at least sustains – an increasingly fragmented media environment. Even a quick look at the vast array of global streaming and OTT services geoblocked outside of their home countries (BBC's iPlayer, Hulu Japan, France's TF1 on-demand platform, to name just a few) bears this out.[7] Whereas, in the age of DVD, the region-code system ensured that viewers had to contend with one relatively centralized system of regional lockout, the issue becomes more complex for viewers contending with a VOD environment marked by many different options, contingent availability, and constantly shifting libraries. While seeking out geographically available platforms can be frustrating for viewers, sometimes when a VOD platform is geoblocked in the United States, it doesn't matter much to American users both because the US offers a comparable service and because geoblocked platforms naturally will not expend promotional energy in a territory where it doesn't exist. For example, LoveFilm, a Netflix-like British VOD service that was incorporated into Amazon Prime Instant Video UK in early 2014, was never particularly missed or lamented in the US. Ask American users if they wish they had access to LoveFilm, and the only ones likely to have heard of it will be British expats or tourists. Put simply, with Netflix, Hulu, and Amazon Prime Instant Video (US) taking up so much space in the market, American viewers needn't bother with LoveFilm. Unlike, say, Spotify, which before its entry into the US market offered something quite literally unavailable (free, unlimited a la carte streaming of a seemingly comprehensive popular music library), LoveFilm was just another VOD service meant for a specific market of UK-based

---

7   Space is far too limited to catalog the scores of VOD platforms available around the world, but
     a comprehensive, if by this point somewhat out-of-date, snapshot of the global streaming film
     landscape can be found in the appendices in Dina Iordanova and Stuart Cunningham (eds), *Digital
     Disruption: Cinema Moves On-Line*, St. Andrews: St. Andrews Film Studies, 2012.

viewers. Save the frustrations of British ex-pats, tourists, or business travelers from the UK looking to access their home platform, geoblocking in this instance shores up a more banal kind of market segmentation.

Local, National, and Regional Television Platforms

As TV networks and channels around the world develop online platforms or distribute their content to VOD services, they face the problem of maintaining spatial control over distribution routes. The putatively global nature of the internet theoretically makes broadcasting's long-held and difficult-to-regulate 'omnidirectionality' (to quote media historian Thomas Streeter) even more pronounced.[8] However, the ability to trace the geo-location of internet-connected devices through IP address filtering actually makes it quite easy for TV networks to control the distribution of television programming through official, commercial or public-service streaming platforms.

Given a healthy contingent of Brit TV fans (and #NBCFail advocates) in the US, the BBC's aforementioned iPlayer is routinely one of the most sought-after geoblocked VOD platforms. An on-demand platform available via the web and some mobile devices, the iPlayer offers BBC television and radio programs for streaming or download primarily to users based in the United Kingdom. Those who pay the UK's television license fee (an annual £145.50 fee for all television-owning households that funds the BBC), have access to both the platform's livestreamed and on-demand programming. So, the iPlayer is unavailable to those who don't or can't pay this fee (such as viewers living in the US). And while this particular geoblocking arrangement reflects the public nature of the BBC, private-sector platforms in the UK like Sky Go are also geoblocked to preserve territorial exclusivity of international distribution deals and to minimize bandwidth costs incurred by out-of-market audiences.

Beyond the US/UK axis, many public and private national or regional television platforms are unavailable in the US for similar reasons (i.e., Americans don't pay taxes and license fees to use the service and/or broadcasters are beholden to territory-based distribution and licensing agreements). France's TF1, Canada's CBC, Qatar's Al-Jazeera (more on them in a bit), Australia's ABC, and many others have developed streaming video services that are geoblocked in the US. This can be a problem for diasporic viewers in particular – including students, tourists and foreign workers in the United States – who might not care as much about accessing HBO Go but may want to access media from their home countries via one of these geoblocked platforms. At the same time, some media industries that envision their audience as fundamentally transnational (e.g., Nollywood, Bollywood, various East Asian and Latin American media companies) distribute their content to VOD platforms that are *not* geoblocked in the US. These include platforms that specialize in various kinds of "international" or non-US content (e.g., the Nollywood streaming service iRokoTV and the Korean TV portal DramaFever) as well as major US-based platforms like Netflix and Hulu. The latter have overtly targeted Latino and Mexican-American diasporic audiences in particular, with Hulu

---

8   Thomas Streeter, *Selling the Air: A Critique of the Policy of Commercial Broadcasting in the United States*, Chicago: University of Chicago Press, 1996, p. 61.

carrying a number of telenovelas through its partnership with American Spanish-language media company Univision. So, while VOD and OTT platforms from throughout Latin America, like Televisa's Veo app, remain geoblocked within the US, these programs may be available through other avenues. Indeed, part of the reason these services are geoblocked in the US is because American cable and streaming companies own the local rights to programs that would otherwise be available through those apps. So, the availability of particular content and platforms can be complicated for diasporic viewers in the US, and it's often contingent on how highly the American media industries value that audience.

YouTube, UGC, and Independent Videos Unavailable in the US

Geoblocking in the US (and elsewhere) is not limited to individual platforms, nor is it necessarily limited to platforms that were developed as extensions of corporate brands. Often, individual videos or channels on digital distribution platforms like YouTube will be geoblocked to certain territories. This has become an issue as the platform has shifted from distributing exclusively user-generated content to partnering with major corporations and multi-channel networks (MCNs). Indeed, YouTube's policy on geoblocking limits the practice to corporate users who have a Content ID account (i.e., those who "own exclusive rights to a substantial body of original material that is frequently uploaded by the YouTube user community").[9] So, individual user accounts don't have the option to geoblock videos, but corporate media and brand accounts do. And while many of these accounts follow the standard practice of serving the United States first and foremost and blocking out other countries, others (again, like the BBC) block US viewers from their content. Other online video platforms, such as Dailymotion, allow developers to geoblock videos in particular countries (including the US) using the platform's API.

Moments of Circumvention: Making Geoblocking Visible

These conditions suggest that geoblocking circumvention is a more specialized practice in the US. This reflects the different standing of region-free DVD in the US relative to much of the rest of the world during the DVD era. While region-free players were common in many nations during the 1990s and 2000s, in the United States they were harder to come by, and mostly found within immigrant and cinephile communities.[10] Although the fragmented nature of the streaming video environment and the secretive nature of circumventing geoblocking make it difficult to precisely calculate who regularly engages in the practice, one can surmise that these same audience segments would be drawn to circumvention practices for many of the same reasons that they sought out region-free DVD players.

But beyond speculating, where can we actually observe the most visible and pronounced

---

9   'How Content ID Works', *YouTube Help*, 2015, https://support.google.com/youtube/answer/2797370?hl=en.

10 A 2001 *Washington Post* piece reporting on DVD region codes suggested that the major consumers of region-free DVD players in the US comprised a 'small market' made up of 'immigrants who want to watch movies from their home countries, language students, and foreign-film enthusiasts.' James C. Luh, 'Breaking Down DVD Borders', *Washington Post*, 1 June 2001.

moments of geoblocking circumvention in the US? As I alluded to, Americans more broadly tend to become aware of geoblocking during moments like the Olympics or the World Cup, when they seek out broadcasts (and announcers) perceived as superior to the US's often poor coverage. Diasporic viewers and ex-pats looking for media from their home countries can also run into geoblocking – British-American viewers attempting to access the iPlayer or Venezuelan-Americans bumping into the geoblocked Venevisión YouTube channel, for instance. As with many of the other examples in this book, these viewers look to proxies and VPNs. Of course, most online guides instructing users on how to use VPNs address, even implicitly, a non-US audience, as these tend to be the viewers who more regularly experience the frustration of geoblocking. Even some of the exceptions to this rule acknowledge that geoblocking is not primarily a US concern. Many of these come from the blog Lifehacker, which regularly instructs its primarily US-based readership on a variety of tips and hacks meant to make life easier. The blog has posted several tutorials on how to use VPNs, with one suggesting, 'Non-U.S. users frequently encounter the annoyance of geoblocked content when trying to access popular sites like Hulu, but every now and then we feel the burn in the States, too.'[11] Regardless, popular VPN services like Private Internet Access, Hide My Ass, and Hola have drawn Americans to their user base who use it to access platforms like the iPlayer.

Still, VPN use in the US is as much about online security and privacy broadly as it is about circumventing geoblocks. VPN use is part of a larger culture of suspicion and caution spurred largely by whistleblower Edward Snowden's massive leak of documents revealing the National Security Agency's (NSA) spying program. One doesn't need to spend too much time on tech sites and forums like Ars Technica, Boing Boing, and Reddit to find questions, suggestions, and debates surrounding the use of VPNs and other privacy and security technologies. Much of this discourse follows a familiar and distinctly American blend of libertarianism, tech-utopianism, and intense valuation of privacy, and from the perspective of American users it touches on geoblocking specifically only intermittently – a state of affairs that contrasts with many of the global case studies provided in the rest of this book. Americans concerned with online surveillance compare and contrast VPNs against other kinds of security and encryption systems (e.g., HTTPS, Tor), and indeed the security status of the VPN has come into question as of late due to the recent revelation from the Snowden docs that the NSA can decrypt VPN communications.

Whether used as a way to circumvent geoblocks or as a more general anti-surveillance maneuver, VPNs have an anti-establishment edge to them. Because users often regard geo-blocking as an oppressive – or at least unfair – system of discrimination, there's a tendency in popular and academic discourse to celebrate its circumvention as a form of rebellion against anti-competitive media industries and unjust copyright regimes. Indeed, in keeping with the close correspondences between the American tech industries and libertarian ide-ology, users often argue that geoblocking violates the free market and oppresses personal

---

11   Adam Pash, 'How to Access the BBC iPlayer (and TV Like Doctor Who) from Outside the U.K.',
        Lifehacker, 29 March 2010, http://lifehacker.com/5504681/how-to-access-the-bbc-iplayer-and-tv-
        like-doctor-who-from-outside-the-uk.

freedoms. But looking at circumvention in the United States, and considering the privilege that Americans generally enjoy, it's worth asking whether US-based users circumventing the geoblocked iPlayer platform, for example, should be considered resistant – particularly in an era when public media is routinely under attack. Indeed, a premise that often shapes popular debates and discussions about geoblocking is that everyone *should* have access to the same content at the same time and the same price, regardless of geographic location – a version of a broader cultural attitude that media scholar Lucas Hilderbrand has called 'access entitlement.'[12] Because American audiences have generally enjoyed the privilege that comes with living in a premier media market, US frustrations about geoblocked platforms reflect assumptions that Americans should be able to access online art and entertainment made available to those living in other parts of the world.

This all indicates that it's important to consider *why* particular platforms are geoblocked and under what conditions, as well as what it means when people try to circumvent geoblocking in these different conditions. There's a tendency to assume that because a particular platform is not available in a territory, the platform owners should be to blame. But the lack of iPlayer and Al Jazeera English in the United States in fact speaks not only to the desires of those agencies to prohibit American viewers from accessing these platforms but also to the power of the American cable companies in shaping what US viewers do and don't have access to. Regarding the iPlayer, the BBC announced that the platform would be made available in the United States, but that was put on hold after threats from cable companies who were worried that the iPlayer would carry shows already aired by US cable network BBC America. So, the cable networks threatened to stop carrying BBC America if BBC Worldwide introduced the iPlayer to the US.[13] Al Jazeera English is unavailable for similar reasons. At the launch of cable channel Al Jazeera America in the United States in 2013, Al Jazeera English geoblocked its livestream and its YouTube news reports in the US at the behest of the American cable and satellite companies (though it eventually dropped the geoblock on the YouTube videos).[14] Essentially, the cable companies wanted to avoid competition from Al Jazeera English.

One consequence of this is that instead of gaining access to the 'original' national version of a platform, US viewers can watch a different adaptation of it. In other words, geoblocking helps sustain a 'glocalized' approach to international expansion wherein products are adapted to local markets. Now, this isn't always and necessarily a bad thing. Presumably, tailoring a product to a local market could make it more appealing to consumers in that market by making it feel closer to their own cultural experience. At the same time, British

---

12   Lucas Hilderbrand, *Inherent Vice: Bootleg Histories of Video and Copyright*, Durham, NC: Duke University Press, 2009, p. 229.
13   Alex Hern, 'BBC iPlayer's US Rollout Blocked by Cable Networks', *New Statesman*, 19 June 2012, http://www.newstatesman.com/blogs/business/2012/06/bbc-iplayers-us-rollout-blocked-cable-networks.
14   Brian Stelter, 'Hiccup for Debut of Al Jazeera America', *New York Times*, 21 August 2013. On dropping the YouTube geoblock, see Janko Roettgers, 'Al Jazeera English Unblocks its YouTube Videos for US-based Viewers', *Gigaom*, 24 September 2013, https://gigaom.com/2013/09/24/al-jazeera-english-unblocks-its-youtube-videos-for-us-based-viewers.

ex-pats and Anglophiles in the US might want access to the national public BBC platform rather than (or in addition to) a commercial BBC America channel that's clogged with James Bond films and *Star Trek: The Next Generation* reruns and that offers commercial-interrupted BBC programming later than its initial UK airdate.[15]

More seriously, though, when viewers in the United States, whether part of a diasporic community or not, want to keep up with news about and from the Middle East, they have turned to Al Jazeera. Many viewers in the US perceive Al Jazeera's coverage as superior to US cable news, and journalist Max Blumenthal captures the cultural significance of the geoblocking of Al Jazeera English in his lament that American viewers will need to use a VPN to find 'an alternative to the mind-numbing, sensationalistic content familiar to CNN, Fox News, and MSNBC.'[16] Here, the circumvention of geoblocking takes on a particular social value in that it enables an escape from the dreck that US news consumers regularly see. Further, for diasporic viewers living in the US, circumventing these geoblocks can help them access news or entertainment from their home territories. Either way, the circumvention of geoblocking can figure as relief from the hegemony of dominant American media.

Conclusion

All this is to say that within a territory that has long operated as a seat of global power, geoblocking reminds viewers of their place within hierarchies of cultural power and privilege in a variety of ways. As a result, the practice of circumvention means something different in different contexts. On one hand, diasporic viewers who are unable to access particular platforms might see this as yet another experience indicating their geo-cultural displacement and their position as viewers not regularly and immediately catered to by the cultural industries. On the other hand, for US-based audiences, circumventing geoblocked platforms can represent a kind of access entitlement presuming that in a digitally connected age, one *should* be able to access everything. When this access is interrupted, as in when #NBCFail led many Americans to engage in geoblocking circumvention, it serves as a reminder that the United States is not a placeless, universal entity in the global media economy and that it can be subject to many of the disconnections and disjunctures that viewers around the world experience more regularly.

References

'Access Pandora from Anywhere in the World', *Wired How-To Wiki*, 13 May 2010, http://howto.wired. com/wiki/Access_Pandora_From_Anywhere_in_the_World.

Appelbaum, Jacob et al., 'Prying Eyes: Inside the NSA's War on Internet Security', *Der Spiegel*, 28 December 2014, http://www.spiegel.de/international/germany/inside-the-nsa-s-war-on-internet-se-

---

15   For more on the issues that attend geoblocking between the US and UK specifically, see Christine Becker, 'Access is Elementary: Crossing Television's Distribution Borders', *FlowTV.org*, 13 January 2014, http://flowtv.org/2014/01/access-is-elementary-crossing-television's-distribution-borders-christine-becker-university-of-notre-dame.

16   Max Blumenthal, 'Exclusive: Al Jazeera's English Online US Broadcast to End with the Launch of Al Jazeera America', *Mondoweiss*, 1 August 2013, http://mondoweiss.net/2013/08/exclusive-al-jazeera-englishs-online-us-broadcast-to-end-with-the-launch-of-al-jazeera-america.

curity-a-1010361.html.

Becker, Christine. 'Access is Elementary: Crossing Television's Distribution Borders', *FlowTV.org*, 13 January 2014, http://flowtv.org/2014/01/access-is-elementary-crossing-television's-distribution-borders-christine-becker-university-of-notre-dame.

Blumenthal, Max. 'Exclusive: Al Jazeera's English Online US Broadcast to End with the Launch of Al Jazeera America', *Mondoweiss*, 1 August 2013, http://mondoweiss.net/2013/08/exclusive-al-jazeera-englishs-online-us-broadcast-to-end-with-the-launch-of-al-jazeera-america.

'Buy Safe and Secure VPN', *Private Internet Access*, https://www.privateinternetaccess.com/pages/buy-vpn.

Ernesto, 'Find out Who's Using The Pirate Bay…and Why', *Torrent Freak*, 29 August 2013, https://torrentfreak.com/find-out-whos-using-the-pirate-bay-and-why-130829.

Hern, Alex. 'BBC iPlayer's US Rollout Blocked by Cable Networks', *New Statesman*, 19 June 2012, http://www.newstatesman.com/blogs/business/2012/06/bbc-iplayers-us-rollout-blocked-cable-networks.

Hilderbrand, Lucas. *Inherent Vice: Bootleg Histories of Video and Copyright*, Durham, NC: Duke University Press, 2009.

'How Content ID Works', *YouTube Help*, 2015, https://support.google.com/youtube/answer/2797370?hl=en.

Luh, James C. 'Breaking Down DVD Borders', *Washington Post*, 1 June 2001.

Pash, Adam. 'How to Access the BBC iPlayer (and TV Like Doctor Who) from Outside the U.K', *Lifehacker*, 29 March 2010, http://lifehacker.com/5504681/how-to-access-the-bbc-iplayer-and-tv-like-doctor-who-from-outside-the-uk.

Roettgers, Janko. 'Al Jazeera English Unblocks its YouTube Videos for US-based Viewers', *Gigaom*, 24 September 2013, https://gigaom.com/2013/09/24/al-jazeera-english-unblocks-its-youtube-videos-for-us-based-viewers.

Santus, Rex, 'Netflix is Now in 36% of Homes Across the United States' *Mashable*, 12 March 2015, http://mashable.com/2015/03/12/nielsen-ratings-2014.

Stelter, Brian. 'Hiccup for Debut of Al Jazeera America', *New York Times*, 21 August 2013.

Streeter, Thomas. *Selling the Air: A Critique of the Policy of Commercial Broadcasting in the United States*, Chicago: University of Chicago Press, 1996.

Ulin, Jeff. *The Business of Media Distribution: Monetizing Film, TV, and Video Content*, Burlington, MA: Focal Press, 2000.

BIOGRAPHIES

Luis Felipe Alvarez León is a Ph.D. Candidate in Geography at the University of California, Los Angeles. His areas of interest are geospatial technologies and the political economic geography of information and communication. He is currently researching the geography of digital information economies.

Cameran Ashraf is an international human rights consultant and co-founder of AccessNow, a global human rights organization selected as finalist for the 2010 Sakharov Prize for Freedom of Thought, Europe's highest human rights honor. He completed his Ph.D. at UCLA on the geopolitics of internet control and cyberwar.

Chris Baumann is a PhD Candidate in the Department of Media Studies at Stockholm University. He is currently busy working on a dissertation about streaming media players. His research interests include media and information technologies in the domestic space, digital distribution, and media access.

Çiğdem Bozdağ is an assistant professor in the New Media department at the Kadir Has University, İstanbul. Her research and teaching interests are digital media, media and socio-cultural change, globalization, inter- and transcultural Communication and ICTs in education.

Roland Burke is a senior lecturer in history at La Trobe University. He is the author of Decolonization and the Evolution of International Human Rights and has published widely on the history of international human rights and internationalism.

Benjamin Burroughs is an assistant professor of emerging media in the Hank Greenspun School of Journalism and Media Studies at the University of Nevada, Las Vegas. His research focuses on streaming media and technology, media industries, and digital media. His work has been published in journals such as New Media and Society, Journal of Broadcasting and Electronic Media, and Games and Culture.

Behzad Dowran is a faculty member in Iranian Research Institute for Information Science & Technology (IranDoc), Tehran. His research and teaching interests are social identity, new ICTs, and media studies.

Evan Elkins is visiting assistant professor of Media, Journalism, and Film at Miami University. He is currently working on a book manuscript about regional restrictions in digital media technologies. He researches various issues surrounding digital media, media industries, globalization, and cultural identity.

Sandra Hanchard completed her PhD at the Swinburne Institute for Social Research, Swinburne University of Technology, on social media information and everyday life in Malaysia. She has an industry background in big data analytics and data visualisation. Sandra is the founder of DataViz My, which facilitates the Data Science Primer course for the Malaysian Global Innovation and Creativity Centre.

Florian Hoof is an assistant professor in the Department of Film and Media Studies at Goethe University Frankfurt. He conducts research on digital network markets, piracy and media sports and has published on the media history of consulting knowledge and managerial decision-making systems.

Juan Llamas-Rodriguez is a PhD Candidate in Film and Media Studies at the University of California, Santa Barbara, working on a dissertation about life in the age of narco-trafficking. His research encompasses the materiality of media distribution, popular cultures of the Mexico-US border, and the precarity of contemporary labor.

Jinying Li is assistant professor of Film Studies at University of Pittsburgh. Her research focuses on the media and visual culture of East Asia. Her essays have been published in Film International, Mechademia, and The International Journal of Communication, and Camera Obscura.

Ramon Lobato is Senior Research Fellow at the Swinburne Institute for Social Research, Swinburne University of Technology, in Melbourne. His research focuses on the global dynamics of media distribution, copyright, and piracy. He is the author of Shadow Economies of Cinema: Mapping Informal Film Distribution and The Informal Media Economy (with Julian Thomas).

James Meese is a lecturer in communication at the University of Technology Sydney. He conducts research on copyright law, mobile media, privacy law and media regulation and has published research in Television and New Media and the International Journal of Communication.

Vanessa Mendes Moreira De Sa completed her Ph.D. at the University of Western Sydney. Her research interests lie in the area of media piracy with a focus on television distribution on the internet. Her work has been published in the International Journal of Communication and in the edited collection Piracy: Leakages From Modernity.

Aneta Podkalicka is a research fellow at the Swinburne Institute for Social Research, Swinburne University of Technology, in Melbourne. Her current work focuses on media and consumption, including thrift-related consumption and sustainable practices. She is currently working on a book on media-based projects for social change with her colleague Ellie Rennie.

Hadi Sohrabi is a lecturer in sociology at Swinburne University of Technology in Melbourne. His research interests include sociology of the internet and ethnic studies. He has published on the politics of the internet in Iran and Muslims in Australia.

Marketa Trimble is the Samuel Lionel Intellectual Property Professor of Law at the William S. Boyd School of Law, University of Nevada, Las Vegas. Her major areas of expertise are public and private international law of intellectual property, including conflict of laws, transnational litigation, and enforcement of intellectual property rights on the Internet.

Fidel A. Rodríguez Fernández is Professor of Hypermedia Communication at Havana University. He researches multimedia discourse on social networks in Cuba, the circulation of digital objects, migration and video games. He is also a journalist and multimedia producer.

Adam Rugg is a PhD candidate in Media Studies at the University of Iowa. His research examines the evolution of sports video distribution and consumption amidst emerging digital media infrastructures. His work has been published in the Journal of Electronic Broadcasting and Media and Popular Communication.